CONTENTS

ILLUSTRATIONS

*Illustrations without references come from the Cabinet
des Estampes, Bibliothèque Nationale, Paris*

MAPS

PART I

This miraculous conquest cast a halo of glory around us. Henceforth people would believe that the air they breathed was redolent of prodigies and marvels. And when these proud thoughts gave way to more moderate sentiments, we told ourselves that the promised end of our labours was there; that at last we were going to stop, since we could no longer surpass ourselves.

GENERAL COUNT PHILIPPE DE SÉGUR

By directing all his efforts against Moscow, Napoleon thought that he was striking at the heart of Russia. So how great his dismay must have been when he saw that the Russians looked on their ancient capital as no more than a vast accumulation of stones, with which Russia's destiny was not bound up in any way! From that time onwards he must have had a presentiment of the tragic outcome of his venture.

COLONEL BUTURLIN

A DAY OF MOURNING

Peace lies at Moscow!
NAPOLEON

MOSCOW, Monday, September 14, 1812. Dry, scorching summer weather. The old Russian capital was bathed in a diffused light that set a myriad facets aquiver on the surface of the river Moskva. A wonderful day, yet the Muscovites, overwhelmed by despair, thought it was a day of eternal mourning for all true Russians. And the town that was about to fall into the hands of the French poured forth its distracted inhabitants on to the roads leading north and east, the roads to Ryazan, Vladimir, Nijni-Novgorod and Yaroslav.

Families had been seen fleeing from Moscow ever since the capture of Smolensk by the French on August 17th, but the departures had followed a slow and hesitant rhythm. There had been a real panic after September 7th, when it was established that the Battle of Borodino was not the Russian victory that had been rather prematurely announced; from that date it seemed obvious that the Generalissimo, Prince Kutusov, could not avoid a decisive battle beneath the very walls of Moscow. Fearing this, many citizens had left in haste, but a great many more remained. Not until this Monday did all the inhabitants who had stayed behind learn from their Governor, Count Rostopchin, that the army would not defend the sacred city against the invader, just as it had not defended Vilna, Vitebsk, Smolensk and Mozhaysk! The Muscovites fled like autumn leaves swept up by the wind.

The Russian army struck camp at three o'clock in the morning. Starting at dawn, it traversed the whole length of the town, heading south-east, towards the bridge over the Yauza, a small tributary of the Moskva, and the Kolomna gate. This march was 'more like a funeral ceremony than a military march past ... Officers and soldiers wept with rage and despair'. They trudged along in gloomy silence, each man wrapped up in his own thoughts. There was to be no battle! They were simply abandoning the field. Apart from the

supreme commander, Kutusov, on whom the country had pinned
all its hopes, no one knew the purpose of this retreat or when it
would end. There was something sinister about these streets, so
recently animated and teeming with people, in which small, melancholy groups now emerged here and there, like flotsam. Some of
them put anxious questions to the passing soldiers and got no reply.
What could they answer when the whole army was asking: 'Where
are they leading us now?'

The population, which could hardly believe the improbable
truth, flocked behind the soldiers 'in vast multitudes'. General
Mayevski, crossing the town with his men, observed that it was no
longer an army on the march, but the migration of a whole people.
The human flood overflowed the road, spreading out over fields
and meadows to a depth of fifteen miles or more. 'A unique and
distressing spectacle: the Moscow road is covered with serried
ranks of all kinds of carriages and pedestrians hastening on and
trying to get ahead of each other ... People driven by fear, their
faces covered with dust and their eyes full of tears.'

Even those who were closest to Kutusov were as ignorant of his
plans as everybody else. His aide-de-camp, the young Prince
Galitzin, heard these enigmatic words from his lips: 'I consider
this retreat to be providential, for it will preserve our army.
Napoleon is like an impetuous torrent, but Moscow will be the
sponge which will absorb him.'

Perpetual retreat?

Without any doubt there was a plan in the head of Mikhail
Ilarionovich Kutusov, that old warrior of the time of Catherine the
Great, who called him *my* Kutusov, that favourite disciple of the
great Suvorov, who said of him, 'Artful, artful! Intelligent, intelligent! No one could deceive him.' On August 10th last, the hero of
the day after his brilliant victory over the Turks,[1] he was rewarded
with the title of Prince and Most Serene Highness. On the 17th,
supported by public opinion, loudly demanded by the nobility of
the two capitals and the army, he was appointed Field-marshal and
Supreme Commander of the three Russian armies. This was
because the constant retreat since the Battle of the Niemen had
been a great blow to the people. In the town and at court there were

---

[1] The Treaty of Bucharest, putting an end to the Russo-Turkish war, was signed
on May 16, 1812.

angry murmurs: 'What did this "backwards march" mean?' The generals responsible, mainly Barclay de Tolly, advanced like crabs, with Napoleon on their heels penetrating ever further into the heart of the country. One glance at a map was enough to horrify anyone. What was the point of these tactics—if they were tactics— and in the name of what were they losing so many prosperous towns and villages? The word 'treason' went from mouth to mouth. Every- one was so shocked by an unparalleled invasion, the like of which had not been seen for a century, that they could not believe that such a thing was possible without treason or at least inexcusable mistakes by those in command. Also it was common knowledge that disagreement was rife among the army leaders. Finally there was a general outcry: Out with Barclay! Down with foreign generals! A single command in the hands of a true Russian! St Petersburg and Moscow, in agreement for once, raised their voices in unison and they were at one in support of Kutusov.

The military clamoured for him even louder than the civilians, for they were at the end of their tether. Since Napoleon's Grand Army had penetrated into Russian territory on June 24th, the armies of the Tsar had done nothing but refuse to give battle. The skirmishes between the Russian rear-guard and the French van- guard were mere trifles, diversions which were often advantageous, but they had nothing to do with real fighting or defending one's fatherland. It looked as if they were fleeing! Impotent fury filled the troops. Officers, non-commissioned officers and men were dis- satisfied with Barclay and very dubious about his military talents. Where were they retreating to? What was the strategic aim of crossing rivers with or without fords, or getting bogged down in the marshes? For what noble victory were they suffering this summer gone mad, with its unbearable dogdays and sudden cloud- bursts that brought no relief? And when thirst became a torture and water-bottles were empty, all they could find to drink was the green, stagnant water in the ditches. Not to mention the shame and despair they felt when faced with the consternation of the inhabi- tants of those towns that were abandoned without a show of defence.

'So you're handing us over to the enemy?'

'What can we do, little father? Those are our orders!'

When they heard that, the unfortunate wretches made their escape, after reducing their homes and their harvests to ashes.

B

To keep up the troops' morale, they were told over and over again, after Vilna, that the armies of Barclay and Bagration* would join up before Smolensk, that this 'strategic retreat' would end in a 'decisive battle'. But Smolensk had been left burning, in enemy hands.

So there was a general outcry and His Majesty Alexander I was put out. Appoint Kutusov? He could not bear that 'old one-eyed satyr'. A puritan himself, he blamed him for his dissolute courtier's way of life. Arrogant, he could not forgive him for having the mental make-up of a strategist and commander, a gift the Tsar of all the Russias lacked. Cosmopolitan, enamoured of the 'West', he felt no affinity with the 'Russian Russians'. A grudge-bearer, he could not forget that Kutusov had been right in opposing him at Austerlitz. But he gave in—indeed he could not do anything else. Dissatisfied, vaguely anxious, mortified, he bowed to the opinion of an extraordinary commission of six members—nominated by him—and entrusted Kutusov with the supreme command.[1]

The new generalissimo, one-eyed like Hannibal, was sixty-seven years old. There was no doubt about his intelligence and even less about his perspicacity. As for guile, he was steeped in it. He knew that nothing would do him more harm in the eyes of the army, which acclaimed, adored and venerated him, than saying to them: 'The way things are, I wonder what I can possibly do with you!' Yet that was what he was thinking. But he actually said, when reviewing his troops after the surrender of Smolensk: 'Does a general retreat with stalwarts like you?' Immediately afterwards they retreated to Gzhatsk. He always had the right words for the occasion, quite prepared to say the exact opposite if events demanded it. In fact, he did not attach tremendous importance to what he said. It was actions that counted with him and the decision taken as a result of those actions. And no one could boast that they had forced a decision on him since the death of Suvorov. If anyone blamed him for some remark, he would reply: 'If I said it, it was because it was necessary *at that moment*.' And he was generally sincere, at that moment. But being extraordinarily quick to grasp

---

[1] Clausewitz, who can scarcely be suspected of special sympathies for the Russians, wrote: 'Of all the generals contemporary with Napoleon, two army leaders were perhaps worthy of being compared with him: Archduke Charles and Wellington; but, nevertheless, the prudent and wily Kutusov was his most dangerous adversary.'

all the aspects of a situation in an instant, he drew an immediate conclusion from them and reversed his policy without wasting time on barren regrets.

When he received the supreme command from the hands of the Tsar, he said to him: 'Sire, I will leave my bones there, rather than permit the enemy to reach the gates of Moscow!'

He really meant it. Arriving before Smolensk, which was evacuated and burnt out, and had surrendered to Napoleon 'for nothing', he cried: 'The keys of Moscow are lost!' And he made his troops retreat. They accepted this new retreat, because it was he, *our* Mikhail Ilarionovich, who had ordered it. However, to prevent Napoleon reaching Moscow, Kutusov was forced to engage in the 'decisive' battle, which his troops had awaited and desired for so long, but which was an 'inevitable evil', in his view. It was Borodino, which Napoleon called the Battle of the Moskva in his 23rd bulletin.

A Pyrrhic victory for the French. Such a glorious defeat for the Russians that for a moment they could believe themselves victors and send the good news to Moscow and St Petersburg! As for Napoleon, he had hoped for something quite different when he had exclaimed in his order of the day: 'Soldiers! Here is the battle you have been longing for. Henceforth victory depends on you; it is necessary; it will bring abundance and ensure us good winter quarters and a prompt return to the fatherland.'

Nothing had been decided. Napoleon himself remarked resentfully: 'This bloody battle has only served to win us terrain.'

The losses on both sides were enormous, almost unbelievable. Witnesses estimated that the most deadly battle in history had just been fought. The Russians left the field of carnage after such a heroic and obstinate resistance that Napoleon said they 'deserved to win'. He was forced to admit that it was neither an Austerlitz nor a Friedland, that this mutual slaughter was useless when the results were weighed up, and that now he had to start all over again, but in worse conditions.

Like the Russians, the French Emperor remained convinced that Field-marshal Kutusov would not hand over Moscow without a battle: 'I don't admit it for a moment. Either they will defend themselves or they will negotiate.'

He envisaged the possibility of negotiations, as he had done after Smolensk. And why not? he asked. 'We have crossed swords,

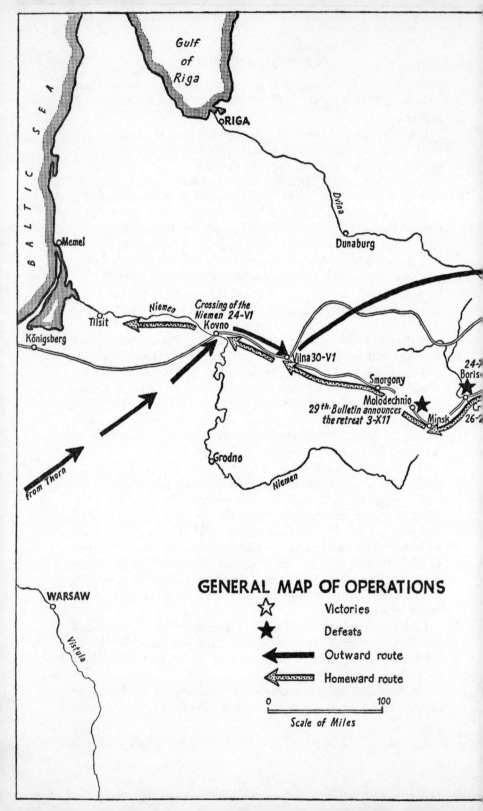

GENERAL MAP OF OPERATIONS

☆   Victories

★   Defeats

◀   Outward route

◁   Homeward route

0   100

Scale of Miles

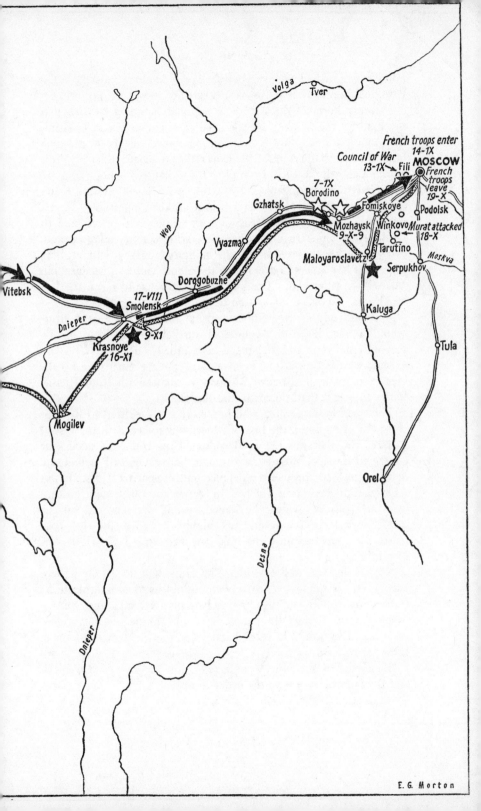

Volga

Tver

French troops enter
14-1X

Council of War
13-1X → Fili

MOSCOW
French
troops
leave
19-X

7-1X
Borodino

Fomiskoye

Podolsk

Gzhatsk

Mozhaysk
9-X-9

Winkovo
Murat attacked
18-X

Vyazma

Tarutino

Moskva

Maloyaroslavetz

Serpukhov

Wop

Dorogobuzhe

Kaluga

Vitebsk

17-V111
Smolensk

Tula

Dnieper

9-X1

Krasnoye
16-X1

Mogilev

Orel

Desna

Dnieper

E. G. Morton

honour is satisfied in everybody's eyes.' What a mistake! The
Russians' honour was by no means satisfied; on the contrary, they
felt deeply humiliated. And their humiliation clung to them like
the mud on the roads. The one-eyed commander felt it so keenly
that, in a letter to Count Rostopchin, he swore that 'he would bury
himself beneath the ruins of Moscow rather than surrender it'. From
September 7th to 13th he trailed his exhausted troops and his
wounded from halting-place to halting-place along terrible roads,
which even the farmers' carts found almost impassable. It was
undulating country, criss-crossed with ravines and intersected by
small rivers and streams with rotten bridges that collapsed suddenly beneath the weight of the military convoys and artillery
wagons. They accepted everything to defend Moscow, because 'our
Mikhail' had decreed: 'The loss of Moscow would mean the loss
of Russia.' He had even written to the Tsar to that effect.

And suddenly on September 13th, at four o'clock in the afternoon, on emerging from a council of war held in the village of Fili,
the supreme commander changed his mind. He declared: 'To save
Russia, we need an army; to save the army we must give up the
idea of defending Moscow. Moscow is not the whole of Russia.
Better to lose it than the army and Russia.'

This was the same man who had so recently written to Rostopchin: 'In my opinion the loss of Moscow is linked with the loss of
Russia.' But that was before Borodino. How could the enemy be
contained outside Moscow at this late hour? General Bennigsen,
in all seriousness, proposed a defence on the Sparrow Hills.[1] It was
a Utopian dream and he knew it. In fact, it was a handsome gesture
or a fine phrase, which, he hoped, would be reported 'to the
proper quarter'. Bennigsen was highly regarded by the Tsar
(Alexander was certainly the only one who found good qualities
in him!).

No, no defence was possible. The army was 'in a hole'; there
was no way of deploying; there were no means of communication;
the enemy would establish themselves on its flanks and control
every way out. Could the people or would the people not understand that that would be total disaster! So the Field-marshal spoke
these terrible words:

'By virtue of the power conferred upon me by the Sovereign
and the fatherland, I give the order to retreat.'

[1] Today the Lenin Hills, south-west of Moscow.

He had realized that by surrendering Moscow, he would save Russia. When and where? Heaven only knew.

His troops, who retreated through the old, sacrificed capital in two columns, had an obscure feeling that they ought to obey him blindly and follow wherever he led them. They agreed to go on trusting him. As for the members of his general staff, they thought he was mad or senile, although they reserved the right to claim the privilege later of having been the first to propose the abandonment of Moscow, if that measure turned out to have been an astute one. All his generals were bad chess players, who could not anticipate a single move. The Tsar was not favoured with great captains and he was always wildly enthusiastic about the most mediocre men 'whose worth is that of a coin whose only quality is its antiquity, but which is no longer in circulation'. He hated the only leader of genius he was lucky enough still to have—even more so now that he had been forced on him against his convictions and against his will.

Meanwhile, the Russian vanguard, commanded by General Miloradovich, reached the Kremlin. There he found two battalions of the Moscow garrison, commanded by General Brozdin, who came, with a band at their head, to swell the retreating troops. That was the limit!

Beside himself with rage, Miloradovich yelled: 'Who was the scoundrel who ordered you to play music?'

Brozdin replied respectfully: 'According to the code of Peter the Great, Your Excellency, a garrison abandons a fortress to the sound of music.'

Miloradovich was on the verge of apoplexy: 'Does the code of Peter the Great envisage the surrender of Moscow. Stop that row at once!'

His Most Serene Highness Prince Kutusov traversed Moscow stealthily, taking the side roads, piloted by Prince Galitzin, a true Muscovite, to whom he said: 'Show me a roundabout route, so that I don't meet anybody.' Nevertheless, they could not help crossing the bridge over the Yauza and it was there, in the middle of the morning, that the old warrior had an extremely disagreeable encounter: Count Rostopchin, Governor of Moscow, on horseback in a military frock-coat, whip in hand, was watching the passage of the troops and hustling on the flow of civilians who were holding up the march of the army. The civilians cast threatening looks at him. Was he not responsible for their distress, for their desperate flight at the eleventh hour? Instead of organizing an orderly evacuation, he had preferred to bluster, affecting a complacent optimism. More than one refugee would have liked to throw in his face the posters with which he had plastered Moscow for weeks. They consisted of curses and threats aimed at Napoleon. The most recent one seemed particularly ridiculous at this hour of distress:

'You will not be able to poke your ugly nose in here! Not only will you never see the tower of Ivan the Great, but you will not even glimpse the Mount of the Salutation in your dreams! About turn and be off home with you!'

Kutusov and Rostopchin did not greet each other. The Governor challenged the Field-marshal, who turned away without a word.[1] After passing through the gate, he dismounted and climbed into a barouche. He sank back into it, facing the capital he was sacrificing and sick at heart.

Rostopchin remained on the bridge. Those who passed in front of him at that fatal hour never forgot the memory of an impassive face 'on which it was impossible to distinguish any emotion'.

Impassive and perhaps a trifle mocking. Count Fyodor Vassilie-vitch Rostopchin had more than one trick up his sleeve.

Near the gate, just as he was spurring his horse to take the road to Ryazan, he turned to his eldest son, Serge, who, at the age of sixteen, had just fought bravely at Borodino:

'Salute Moscow for the last time,' he said. 'In an hour it will be in flames.'[2]

[1] This version, in view of its sources, is the most reliable. But Rostopchin, who as long as he lived continued to show the malice he bore Kutusov by denigrating him in a thousand and one ways, describes the scene differently: 'I found Prince Kutusov and his escort near the bridge over the Yauza. I bowed to him and did not feel inclined to speak to him at length, but he, wishing me "Good morning" (which could be taken sarcastically), said: "I can assure you that I shall not withdraw from Moscow without joining battle." I made no reply, for the only reply to one stupid remark is another one.' (Fragment from Count Rostopchin's memoirs of 1812, copied by his daughter, Mrs Narychkin, together with other passages. The complete text was seized on the governor's death and deposited in the secret Chancellery of Nicholas I.)

[2] Cf. Conclusion: *Who burnt Moscow?*

THE GOVERNOR

*This Rostopchin will be looked upon as a villain or
a Roman; we must see how this action is judged.*

STENDHAL
Journal : Moscow 1812

Two men destined to deal Napoleon a mortal blow had just crossed
paths on the bridge over the Yauza.

Kutusov and Rostopchin detested and distrusted each other. The
Prince was intelligent, the Count narrow-minded. One was wily,
the other sly. In spite of his age, the Field-marshal still had a keen
mind and clear ideas; the much younger Governor was hot-headed
and had woolly ideas. But both were profoundly, 'primitively'
Russian and patriotic. They also shared the unswerving antipathy
felt for them by their omnipotent master, the Tsar of all the
Russias.

Fyodor Vassilievitch Rostopchin was getting on for fifty.[1] He
had been in favour under Catherine the Great, who called him
'Fyo the mad', then Chamberlain and Minister under Paul I. Put
in the background at the beginning of the new reign, he remained
in his town, like the old Muscovite he was, living out of the public
view, but watching everything with a keen and frequently mocking
eye. And then suddenly, last May, he had become Governor of the
former capital, instead of 'good papa' Gudovitch, who was well
liked by his subjects because he did not show too much interest in
them. The Muscovites have always boasted of being different from
other people and they did not like anyone interfering in their
affairs.

Rostopchin was more astonished than anyone at his return to
favour, although he knew perfectly well that he owed it to friendship of the Grand-duchess Catherine Pavlovna, Princess of Oldenburg, younger sister of the Tsar. A sister who was perhaps loved
too tenderly, a confidante, Egeria and mentor all in one, she was
the centre of a coterie that had never accepted the alliance formed

[1] Born March 23, 1765.

after Tilsit. Moreover, it was round the principality of Oldenburg that the quarrel between the two emperors had grown more bitter. So Catherine had several reasons for detesting Napoleon. In the spring of 1812 she had realized, like every serious thinking person, that the stakes were down and war inevitable, and felt the urgent need to put tested patriots in charge of the big towns, especially Moscow. 'Tell Rostopchin,' she wrote to Prince Obolensky, 'that he must inflame the Muscovite nobility. All he needs to do is to show the danger the fatherland is in and the national significance of this war.' (She was one of the very first to have grasped the 'national significance of this war', although she was only twenty-four years old.)

The Tsar was by no means eager to appoint Rostopchin,[1] whom he could not stand, and put up a childish argument in opposition to his sister's requests. The Count, as a civilian official, could not hold a post requiring him to wear a military uniform. Catherine demolished that objection with the remark: 'That's the tailor's job!'

In fact, the uniform did not suit Rostopchin at all, but he did not care. He was beside himself with joy and set out to conquer the Muscovite 'upper crust', whose good opinion was indispensable to him if he was to do an effective job. The good-will of what he called 'the upper spheres' would, he thought, be his trump card, so he became intensely active, paying visits to everyone. Of an impatient, nervous, sanguine nature, he also had something of the conjurer's gift for throwing dust in people's eyes. He liked to repeat to his intimate friends that his most valuable assistants were stupidity, baseness and vanity. As for doing what his protectress had especially commissioned him to do—showing the danger the fatherland was in—he did not remember that for a long time. On the contrary, in the salons where he set himself out to please and make people appreciate his judgment and wit, he assumed an oracular tone when he cried in a loud and brassy voice: 'Napoleon? We won't even let him cross the frontier!'

That was in the month of May 1812. The Tsar had been with the armies since April. There he devoted his time to the 'paradeomania' inherited from the father he detested and to strategic studies

---

[1] Alexander detested everyone who had been devoted to his father, Paul I, and who suspected him of having approved the latter's assassination on March 11, 1801; Rostopchin was among them. (Cf. Conclusion.)

of which he understood nothing. In Moscow, the season was brilliant—the most brilliant people had known for a long time. And suddenly on June 27th, *The Moscow News*, in its fiftieth number, informed its readers of Napoleon's entry into Russian territory.

The oracle of the salons was caught out but refused to be abashed, in spite of the news. Now he went about saying firmly: 'War? Yes, it's war all right. That doesn't mean that Napoleon will reach Moscow.'

And he prophesied 'an easy victory through perseverance and courage'. Considering himself to be the right man in the right place, he endeavoured to be omniscient and ubiquitous. He knew his duty better than anybody. It was summed up under two heads: keeping up the people's morale and hunting down subversion.

As regards morale, he had great difficulty in fighting the steadily increasing unrest. Beginning with No. 54, *The Moscow News* had been publishing a daily report of the military operations. Instead of the rout of the Grand Army announced by the governor, the news consisted solely of the withdrawal of the Russians and the lightning advance of the French! So Rostopchin decided to 'work on the minds of the people, to arouse them and prepare them for any sacrifice for the salvation of the fatherland'.

First of all, he recruited 'agents', whose task was to mix with the crowd in the streets and public places, 'in order to spread certain rumours, maintain patriotic enthusiasm or diminish the disagreeable impression made by bad news'. At the same time, he had posters from his own pen printed, put on the walls or distributed to people's homes. Their contents were deliberately trivial. The Count thought that he was speaking the language of the lower classes and addressing the man in the street on an equal footing. A personage of his own invention, 'Karniushka Tchikirin', apostrophized Napoleon and his army, holding them up to ridicule. These posters, according to eminent thinkers, were 'eyewash for the illiterate', 'a knockabout turn at a fair'. In any case, they made no impression on anybody.

As for hunting down subversion, the Count devoted himself to it with great zeal. He had always been the sworn enemy of Martinists, Illuminati, Freemasons, Jacobins and revolutionaries, 'between whom he could see little difference' and whom he consigned to the bottomless pit. He was an out-and-out xenophobe and especially a

Francophobe—Gallophobe (as he used to say), although it did not stop him talking French at home, never Russian. In this he resembled everybody in fashionable Moscow society.

For Moscow, reliquary of the past, which enshrined antiquated traditions, stubborn prejudices and ancient customs within its gilded walls, Moscow, so Russian, stagnating gently in its indolence, an obsolete town attached to an outworn world, loved France passionately.

People spoke only French in the salons; worse still, they could hardly write three lines in their native language correctly! They had their children brought up by tutors and governesses who had come from Paris—or claimed to have done so. The majority of them, poorly educated, were emigrés and the children of emigrés, or people who had come to fabulous Russia in search of the daily bread they could not earn at home.

Trade in luxury goods was also a French preserve. The fashionable world would not have been what it was without 'the French shops' of the Bridge of the Marshals—the *Kuznetski Most*—a broad thoroughfare north of the Kremlin, the rendezvous of elegant women and dandies. Smart little shops with typically Parisian signs or large stores looking more impressive, installed on the ground floor of some noble palace, offered their tempting wares—liqueurs and delicate lingerie, fashion books and albums, perfumes, groceries, leather goods, wines, lace and hats. Among the most popular shops was that of Mme Rose Aubert-Chalmé, a lady destined to figure in a ridiculous episode with Napoleon. Meanwhile she sold spices, lace and beaver bonnets.

The theatre was also French. A company of actors had settled permanently and artistes as famous as Mlle George came to give performances and even stay in Moscow for a time. In short, there was a whole French colony, a veritable little enclave in the town, with its parish centred on the Church of Saint-Louis-des-Français and its priest, the Abbé Surrugues.*

The Abbé was a frequent visitor to the Rostopchin home, *persona grata* with both the Count and the Countess. The latter, attracted by the Roman Catholic religion, was preparing her conversion in great secrecy; as for the governor, he had found in the person of the priest a fervent ally against 'the troublemakers'. So there was nothing surprising about the Count's making an exception when he wrote to the Tsar begging him to expel all the French from Moscow:

'They are harmful to Russia ... and are only waiting for the arrival of Napoleon to proclaim freedom. Rid Russia of them, Sire, and keep only the ecclesiastics.'

According to the Count, all the French were spies in disguise or 'preachers of Illuminism'. The worse things got, the more his 'Gallophobia' grew, until the day when he had his French chef, Arnold Tournay, whipped in the public square and then—a much more serious matter—deported forty French men and women to Nijni-Novgorod in deplorable conditions.[1] Lastly, he ordered the imprisonment of a certain Mouton, accused, together with a young Russian called Verestchagin, of translating proclamations by Napoleon and distributing them around the town.

In addition to these vitally important occupations and pre-occupations, Rostopchin had another most absorbing task—supervising the mysterious labours of a German called Leppich.

Leppich, alias Schmit, had arrived in Moscow on June 8, 1812, recommended to the governor by the Russian Minister in Stuttgart, himself influenced by the Würtemberg Minister for Foreign Affairs, Count Ferdinand von Zeppelin. The German offered Russia an invention rejected with disdain by Napoleon in 1811. It was an air-craft, 'worked by turning wings and steered by a rudder', which would carry cases full of explosives to be 'rained down from high in the heavens' in sufficient quantities to exterminate whole army corps, and, of course, the great French general staff, including Napoleon.

The Count was tremendously enthusiastic about the invention. He wrote to the Tsar 'that it could change the art of war'. For once he was right ... provided that Leppich succeeded. He actually promised to have 'the great machine' ready for August 27th. Supplied with lavish subsidies by His Majesty, the inventor was installed five miles from Moscow on Prince Repnin's estate of Voronovo. He was given everything he asked for: a hundred work-men, silk, steel and vitriol. On August 3rd, the governor felt it was his duty to inform his subjects as follows:

[1] For the affair of the deportation of the forty French subjects which does not directly concern our theme, see the appendices.

'I have been commissioned by the Sovereign to have a large spherical balloon made in which fifty men will be able to fly where they want, with and against the wind. You are going to learn the result and rejoice over it. If the weather is fine, a small balloon will make a trial and fly over the town tomorrow or the next day. I am warning you about it so that when you see it you will not think it comes from the Villain; on the contrary, it is devised for his misfortune and downfall.'

Leppich spent nearly 75,000 roubles a month, but Rostopchin kept on asking for more on his behalf, writing to Alexander that he must be given 'as much as a million if he should succeed'. It does not seem to have crossed the governor's mind for an instant that he might have come across a charlatan, Besides, was it so? It was a possibility, but not a certainty. At all events, he believed that this miraculous invention formed an important factor in the coming victory and that its moral effect would be immense, since the Muscovites had always been hungry for marvels.

Although the 'workshops' and 'laboratories' themselves were a 'forbidden zone', and the mansion was surrounded by walls and the gate was locked, the people had the right to walk their ten miles there and back on Sundays to look at the isolated estate and go home satisfied, convinced that they had seen with their own eyes the instrument destined to smash the infamous invader to smithereens.

But at the end of August Rostopchin had to sing a different tune and write to the Tsar: 'With a broken heart, it is my duty to inform Your Majesty of Leppich's failure. It seems obvious that we must give up any hope of success. Leppich is a charlatan and madman.' He, his workmen and his materials were sent off to Nijni-Novgorod, where he vanished without a trace. As for his balloon, the French troops who occupied the Rostopchin estate after the burning of Moscow discovered the following items: a half-burnt-out nacelle; a large piece of wood shaped like a sphere, which undoubtedly served as a mould, 180 large flasks of vitriol, 70 barrels and 6 vats 'constructed in a most peculiar way'. That was the official inventory 'of objects found at the castle of Voronzovo relating to the aerostatic balloon, or infernal machine, which the Russian government had had made, ostensibly for burning up the French army and its depots, by a man called Schmit, undoubtedly an Englishman, but styling himself a German national.'

The Tsar at Moscow

The news remained bad throughout July and during the first fortnight of August. Napoleon advanced as if he was strolling in the park at Fontainebleau and the generals—Barclay de Tolly, Bennigsen and Bagration—beat a retreat but never fought. Nevertheless, Moscow continued its indolent existence. People went out strolling and visited the French shops; they went on giving balls—even if these meetings seemed less gay than the winter before. Moscow had traditionally invented popular songs about everything and the Muscovites hummed this satirical refrain:

> 'Long live the military profession
> That gives us all we wish for,
> Retreats in time of war,
> Parades in time of peace.'

The Muscovites would have been glad to display their patriotism and their loyalty to their sovereign, but since Peter the Great had made a proud granite city rise from the marshes of the north, the Divus had built his temple elsewhere. Moscow had been forced 'to bow its head to St Petersburg like a Dowager Empress to a new Tsarina.'[1] It had become 'a retired capital'. The show was at St Petersburg, the spectators at Moscow. But if the young Tsar deigned to come, he would find that all these aristocrats, preserved as if in amber in the memories of a glory which had tarnished with their decorated uniforms and their gold braid, were still fit to serve him! And the people would go through fire for their Little Father, their *Batiushka Gossudar*.

These demonstrative people were given the opportunity to show themselves off on July 25, 1812.

Alexander had left Vilna on June 30th, leaving it to Napoleon. From there he had reached the camp of Drissa, the brain child of the German engineer Pfühl, in whom he trusted blindly. But Pfühl loved theory and despised practice. To all clear-thinking strategists the camp was a trap and it had to be evacuated. From then on violent controversies sprang up inside the general staff, so that the Tsar, who was anxious to please everyone, while doing just what *he* pleased, did not know what course to choose. In the end he was given to understand with infinite tact that he 'was persisting in following a profession which was completely foreign to him', and

[1] Pushkin: *The Bronze Horseman*.

he was advised to go to Moscow 'to cheer up people's spirits there'.

'Ancient Moscow rushes to meet its Sovereign,' wrote a deeply moved witness. And a romantic young woman, who found the Sovereign 'so melancholy and so handsome', related in her Journal that the crowd massed in the courts of the Kremlin and its vicinity 'undulated beneath the moon like the sea in summer'.

Three days later Alexander electrified the Assembly of the Nobility and the Guild of Merchants with a speech 'stamped with nobility and grandeur', and everyone felt 'ready to sacrifice a part of his wealth to save the rest'. For a tremendous financial effort was needed to organize militia troops. The money was offered at once, without stinting. Some noblemen undertook to equip whole regiments. It was a magnificent display of generosity, devotion and self-denial. It was with good reason that the Russians said: 'Everything is done with exaggeration at Moscow. Moscow has never been noted for its restraint. When someone's in love there, it's to distraction; when he hates, it's to the death; when he gives, it's in millions!'

Alexander showed that he was very moved. To stiffen his morale, Rostopchin declared pompously, but with some truth:

'Sire, even though unfortunate circumstances force you to adopt the course of withdrawing before a momentarily victorious enemy, the Russian empire will always remain formidable at Moscow, terrifying at Kazan and invincible at Tobolsk!'

On the night of July 30th the Tsar pinned his diamond 'cipher' on the shoulder of the governor and conferred full powers on him, but without giving him any directive.[1] And Rostopchin announced: 'I have been given the mission of using improvisation to solve this problem: *Napoleon and Moscow!*'

He immediately drafted a new poster, in which he combined a threat to Napoleon with flattery of Alexander, whom he compared to Peter the Great: 'Charles of Sweden was more robust than thou, Emperor of the French, and of royal blood, but he went to fight under the walls of Poltava and never came back!'

At last Moscow had emerged from its age-old lethargy. The miracle had been performed by the Tsar. The whole population

---

[1] 'The cipher' was a diamond brooch forming the initials of the Tsar or Tsarina. It was the highest distinction—an immense honour bestowed on a courtier, a lady of the Court or a minister.

2. Overwhelmed by the loss of Moscow, 'illuminated' by its burning, stimulated by his sister Catherine, Tsar Alexander I wrote to her: 'I would rather cease to be what I am than come to terms . . .'

3. . . . while Napoleon waited day after day for him to make peace proposals. 'I have waged war on Your Majesty without animosity.'

had been conquered by his charm, which no one had ever been able to define, but which everyone had felt—individually or collectively —including Napoleon. Alexander had only had to proclaim the fatherland in danger and call the people to arms, for the city, which he had disdained until then, to offer him within a few days a corps of militia 80,000 strong, armed from head to foot. He could return to St Petersburg satisfied.

Henceforth 'at the promenade', no one was interested in the women of fashion. People only had eyes for the young men and the middle-aged who had joined the army again, all clad in superb new uniforms. They heard the noise of boots and the clanking of sabres, which, owing to the inexperience of their owners, got caught in the ladies' furbelows! The recruiting of the Saltikov and Dmitryev-Mamonov regiments took place in tents of purple silk ornamented with golden tassels. Stirring music was played while the volunteers signed a register bound in flaming red velvet, encrusted with the imperial arms. Many people's patriotism took the naivest and most ridiculous forms, as described later by Pushkin, that '*enfant terrible* of Russia':

'The dandies stopped showing off. In fact, they were really frightened. In society, the enemies of the French language and the Bridge of the Marshals carried the day. Mr so-and-so emptied his snuffbox of French snuff; another burnt a dozen French booklets; yet another gave up Château Lafite and took to eating cabbage soup. They all vowed never to speak French again, they all preached the patriotic war, at the same time as they were preparing to go to their far-off estates.'

In all great upheavals there are always people whose bewilderment makes them ineffective, but Moscow as a whole was now animated by a fine patriotic fervour. The news of the fall of Smolensk on August 18th was a terrible blow to the city.

The enemy had drawn dangerously close. They had seized one of the most important positions without anyone having done anything to stop them. It was yet another victory for Napoleon, won virtually without firing a shot. Nevertheless, from his point of view it was another disappointment. The large-scale battle, for which he had been preparing since the end of June, had not been fought. Worse still, he was entering a town completely destroyed by the fire

c

the Russians had lit before they retreated once again. In spite of
writing to Marie Louise: 'My affairs are going well', he was looking
for a way of letting the Tsar know that 'he wanted nothing so much
as to conclude a peace'. And both Murat the rash and Daru the wise
begged him not to continue this senseless, dangerous pursuit.

But Moscow was unaware of this. The enemy was approaching
apace! That was all they could think about. The news was cried in
the streets. People ran backwards and forwards to each other's
houses. Prudent merchants left with their stocks. A young lady,
Mrs Khomutova, wrote in her Memoirs:

'Misfortune weighed on everyone like a stone; danger united
everybody. The streets emptied hourly. Flight! that was the *leitmotiv* of conversation. Carry off one's property, bury it, wall it up!'
The houses were littered with trunks, the streets congested with
carts, heavy carriages and light barouches. But what to take? One
householder did not want to abandon his collection of snuffboxes,
another his miniatures, another his cellar and yet another his books.
Prince Gagarin sent his pictures to the country and Rostopchin
informed the Tsar that he was putting 'all the national possessions
and treasures' in safety.

Nevertheless, the governor preserved his optimism and verve.
To satisfy the mystics who came, Bible in hand, to prove that
Napoleon was none other than Apollyon, 'the angel of the bottomless pit', according to the ninth chapter of *Revelation*, he ordered a
twenty-four-hour procession. He reviewed the militia and had them
blessed by the Metropolitan, Platon. In the salons he boasted:

'Do me the honour to believe that as long as I am Governor I
shall never hand the keys over to Napoleon.'

'And if you are forced to?'

'Me? Force me?'

'But, my dear Count, Vienna, Berlin, Madrid ...'

'Moscow will *not* imitate them and will remain alone in its way
of reacting.'

In a different way, he repeated the same thing to the people,
whom he would have found just as hard to convince as the salon
frequenters and clubmen, had not the appointment of Prince
Kutusov given everyone hope again.

However, after Borodino all was confusion and disorder, increased tenfold by the arrival of vast numbers of wounded. There
were not enough beds, bandages and nurses; the population did

their best to alleviate the misery with make-shift measures. On September 8th camp-fires were suddenly spotted some twenty-five miles away. Russians? French? Undoubtedly the latter on the heels of former, as usual! However, Rostopchin did not order, or even recommend, the people to evacuate. Let everyone do as he thought best! Why panic for nothing?

But on September 9th Napoleon took Mozhaysk and this time the governor sounded the alarm bell:

'In order to join-up as quickly as possible with the troops that are marching to meet him, H.H. Prince Kutusov has left Mozhaysk to occupy a fortified position that the enemy is unlikely to reach for some time. The Prince is going to be sent 48 cannons and ammunition. He says that he will defend Moscow to the last drop of his blood and that he is even ready to fight in the streets of this town. The tribunals have been closed, but do not let that worry you, my friends. We have to put our affairs in order. We do not need tribunals to conduct the trial of the Villain; nevertheless, if it seemed necessary, I would alert the young men of the town and the countryside, and in two or three days I would give the signal. Then arm yourselves well with axes and pikes, or, better still, take pitch-forks—the Frenchman weighs no more than a sheaf. Tomorrow I shall visit the wounded in the Hospital of Saint Catherine. I will have a mass said there and have the water blessed for their prompt recovery. As for me, I am well; I had a bad eye, but now I see very well with both eyes.'

Here, in spite of the usual absurdities, the language was sincere; the poster that followed this proclamation later even had a certain epic note. It was the only one from which all facetiousness was banned:

'Arm yourselves as best you can. Come on foot or on horseback. Bring only three days' supply of bread with you. Mass together on the three mountains and I shall be with you. Together we shall exterminate the Villain. Glory to those who resist. Eternal memory to those who fall. Woe at the Last Judgment to those who evade their duty!'

This order was to be postponed almost immediately, to the bitter disappointment of a fanatical crowd, who for once had taken one the governor's posters seriously and hurriedly flocked to the Sparrow Hills.

Meanwhile, the enthusiasm of Rostopchin, convinced he was effectively helping the generalissimo to defend Moscow, had become infectious. Excited ladies swarmed at the home of Fyodor Vassilievitch, burning to form a battalion of Amazons. Better still, the actors of the Russian theatre proposed to dress up as Roman senators and receive the French troops at the gate, where they would deliver a noble harangue!

When the Count was summoned to the village of Fili on September 13th, he had no doubt that it was in order to establish the plan for the defence of Moscow with Kutusov. So he hurriedly composed a new poster:

August 31st–September 12th.

'I leave tomorrow to visit H.H. Prince Kutusov to take, jointly with him, the measures to exterminate our enemies.

'We shall send these visitors packing and we shall make them give up the ghost!

'I shall return for dinner and we shall all lend a hand to make mincemeat of these traitors!'

At Fili he learnt that 'his' town was to be abandoned outright. He returned, pale and drawn. His perpetual smile had disappeared. He sent away the Countess and six of their children,[1] keeping only the eldest with him. On the evening of the 13th, when he received a visit from Prince Eugene of Würtemberg, Kutusov's aide-de-camp and a close relation of the Tsar through his mother, née Princess of Würtemberg, he addressed the following astonishing words to him:

'If I were consulted, I would not hesitate to say "Burn the capital rather than deliver it to the enemy". That is Rostopchin's opinion. But of course the governor whose mission it is to see to the safety of the town cannot give such advice.'

'For my part,' retorted the Prince, flabbergasted, 'I am not Russian and there is only one Russian who is entitled to give this advice.'

Returning to the headquarters of his division, he turned over in his head the words he had just heard. Later, Major-general von

---

[1] Sophia, the future Countess de Ségur (born in 1799), was the fourth of the seven Rostopchin children.

Betzke heard him mutter: 'It's incredible! It would be a colossal deed, and yet it would be the heroic remedy in this terrible crisis!' Enigmatic words on which von Betzke made no comment, though he understood them later and repeated them to Clausewitz.*

The same day, at Fili, Rostopchin had made a similar remark to the Field-marshal, to which the old man had only lent a distracted ear: 'If you leave Moscow without a battle, you will see it in flames after your passage.' Later, a lady from the 'high society' that the Governor valued so much affirmed that he had outlined the measures he would take 'to unleash the scourge' to an astounded audience. 'He expressed himself,' the lady wrote, 'coolly and calmly, as if he had been talking about a firework display lit thanks to him!'[1]

On September 13th Rostopchin wrote a despondent letter to the Tsar: 'The Commander-in-chief's resolution decides the fate of Your Empire, which will foam with rage when it learns that the City which contains the grandeur of Russia and in which rest the ashes of your ancestors[2] is to be handed over to the enemy.' But he also said: 'I vouch for it with my life, Sire, that Bonaparte will find Moscow as deserted as Smolensk. Everything has been taken away. Moscow will be a desert in his hands—*if fire does not consume it*—and may become his tomb.'

Already, on August 24th, the governor had sent word to his great friend, General Bagration: 'I cannot imagine the enemy entering Moscow . . . But it would be a good idea to let Napoleon know that he will find only the site where once the capital stood . . . He will see nothing but burning timber and ashes.' Undoubtedly he was thinking of Smolensk, burnt by its inhabitants, and besides he believed that the abandonment of Moscow was impossible. But why should not Moscow do the same as Smolensk, if ever the necessity arose?

On the night of September 13th Count Rostopchin had summoned the chief of police Ivachkin to his mansion of the Lubianka and ordered him to have all the fire-engines covered with matting and put on the road to Ryazan. Those which there was not time to remove were to be destroyed on the spot. The fire-brigade and most of the municipal police would leave at dawn. They were given

---

[1] Baroness du Montet: *Souvenirs*, p. 140.
[2] Up to Peter the Great, the Romanoffs had been buried in the Cathedral of the Archangels at Moscow. Afterwards, the Cathedral of Saints Peter and Paul at St Petersburg was used.

a rallying point. Two squadrons of dragoons were to escort them. Before leaving, police officers were to close all the taverns, break the barrels of vodka and spirits, and burn the fire-brigade's lighters moored alongside the quays. At the same time, he ordered the doors of the prisons to be opened early next morning. He certainly did not premeditate at this moment making the prisoner Verestchagin his scapegoat, but the crime was to be committed a few hours later.

On September 14th, between nine and ten o'clock, when the Count was getting ready to leave the town and his coach and horses awaited him at the foot of the steps, he saw that a large crowd had gathered near his residence. 'The furious populace (which had been standing there since before daylight) rushed towards the governor's palace, shouting that they had been deceived,' an eye-witness tells us. Rostopchin appeared on the first floor and was met with 'angry exclamations'. That was the moment when a diabolical idea occurred to the hard-pressed Governor. He ordered his aide-de-camp, Obreskov, to bring the prisoners Verestchagin and Mouton to him. The Russian, son of well-to-do merchants, had been arrested and imprisoned the preceding July for having circulated the alleged translation of two apocryphal proclamations by Napoleon that had appeared in the foreign press.[1] It was a serious crime, because since the invasion it had been forbidden to read or refer to foreign newspapers. The Frenchman was accused of aiding and abetting.

When Obreskov had brought the two prisoners to the foot of the steps, the Governor went down. A month later, when the Minister of Justice summoned him to explain his abominable action, he gave a written account of what he did afterwards:

---

[1] These fictitious proclamations were entitled: 'Letter from the French Emperor to the King of Prussia' and 'Discourse by Napoleon to the Princes of the Confederation of the Rhine'. The police officer, Brokker, Rostopchin's henchman, judged that these texts could not but demoralise the population, since they contained such phrases as: 'I declare today that within six months the two northern capitals will see the conquerors of Europe inside their walls.' Verestchagin had put forward a stupid defence, claiming that he had found the newspapers in the street, 'near the French shops'. Besides, he declared, he had translated and distributed the texts 'for patriotic purposes', to warn his fellow-citizens of what threatened them. He denied having invented the texts—which he probably had done. This defence was more artful, for if he confessed that he was their author, his crime became more serious. The affair was apparently connected with Rostopchin's hatred of the Postmaster, Kliutcharev. Indeed, an attempt was made to make the latter confess that he had supplied Verestchagin with the newspapers containing these 'subversive documents'. As for Mouton, he was accused of having helped with the 'translation'.

'As for Verestchagin, just before the villains entered Moscow, I delivered this traitor and State criminal to the people, who, seeing in him the spokesman of Napoleon and the forerunner of all their misfortunes, assuaged their vindictiveness on him.'[1]

As a matter of fact, after claiming that Verestchagin was a traitor and indeed 'the only man in the whole population of Moscow to want to betray his fatherland', after telling the unfortunate youth that the Senate had condemned him to death, he ordered the dragoons of his personal guard to sabre him. The soldiers hesitated and struck the wretched young man a few feeble blows, but the crowd rushed on him and tore him to pieces. Then, turning to Mouton, the Governor said with a magnanimous gesture: 'I am sparing your life. Go to your own people and tell them that the wretch I have just punished was the only Russian to betray his fatherland!'

After which, Rostopchin re-entered his mansion and left it again by a back door with his son Serge and Obreskov. He had horses brought up, leaving his barouche behind. A little later he was on the bridge over the Yauza, where his encounter with Kutusov took place. He would not be long in rejoining him at the first halting-place on the road to Ryazan.[2] But before that he met General Barclay de Tolly again; the General, surrounded by his staff, had stayed behind to let his army corps march past and had seen the passage of the fire-engines, accompanied by a military escort. Seeing the Governor of Moscow arrive, the General asked him: 'Why have you taken them away?'

'I have good reasons for it,' retorted Rostopchin haughtily. He had placed his stakes. He had made his arrangements so that his town should not fall into the enemy's hands intact. To him, it was not a question of a strategic calculation, but of something quite different. If Moscow could not perish like a warrior, defending himself with arms in hand, it should succumb as an expiatory victim, immolated for the salvation of the fatherland, for the destruction of the 'ungodly'. The responsibility of his undertaking did not scare him in the least. He would shoulder it alone. Had not the Tsar given him full powers? Since he was forced to leave

---

[1] Letter discovered by the Soviet historian Eugene Tarle in the State Library, Manuscript Department, Voyenski Archives, No. N/5.

[2] Before that, he stopped at his property of Voronovo, to which he set fire. (Cf. p. 74 and Appendices.)

himself, he made arrangements for the task to be performed by
police officers, who were left behind, some of them disguised as
beggars or workmen, by habitual criminals, who were promised an
amnesty in exchange for a 'great patriotic exploit, and by seminarists,
convinced that they were serving a holy cause for the fatherland
and the Church, since Napoleon was Antichrist. He had had all
these people supplied with the necessary materials, including the
'Congreve rockets', stocked by the hundred on the Repnin estate in
Leppich's time. Each of these future incendiarists received a small
round metal plaque, the size of a crown, which would enable them
to recognize each other. They were to act as soon as the enemy
arrived in the town.

Leppich's brilliant invention, on which Count Fyodor Vassilievitch Rostopchin had so naively based his hopes, had failed. It had
been essential for him to discover another one, produced by his
fertile imagination, and also, it must be admitted, inspired by his
sincere patriotism. He alone had worked on it in order to produce
successfully what Count Philippe de Ségur was to call 'the great
infernal machine, the sudden nocturnal explosion of which would
devour the Emperor and his army.'

3

A DAY OF GLORY

*... It was as if Moscow, like a European princess
on the borders of her empire, adorned with all the
riches of Asia, had been brought there for her
marriage to Napoleon.*

CHATEAUBRIAND
Mémoires d'Outre-Tombe

AT two o'clock in the afternoon of September 14th, Napoleon's
Grand Army scaled the low range known as the Sparrow Hills
that guarded the venerable city. The hills seemed like the climax
of the arduous and death-dealing route they had covered in eleven
weeks. From the River Niemen to the River Moskva it had been a
mad, incomprehensible race that had consumed both men and
horses. Time and again they had believed that they were on the
eve of a decisive battle! Time and again the Emperor had exclaimed:
'Now I have them!'

At Vitebsk and Gzhatsk it was the same story as at Smolensk and
Vyazma; the Russian camp, which had been just ahead the evening
before and had seemed to be waiting for them, had disappeared at
dawn like a mirage. They hurried in pursuit, suffering from heat,
humidity, dust and hunger. The number of horses that died of
exhaustion passed the bounds of imagination; sometimes 5,000 had
been lost over a distance of thirty leagues! The number of sick
soldiers left by the wayside was terrifying. 3,000 were abandoned
at Vilna! This was not surprising, since, 'overwhelmed by the fires
of a devouring sun', they were reduced to drinking stinking brackish
water, with nothing to eat but a niggardly ration of biscuits. As they
advanced they found themselves without bread, fresh meat or wine.
They looted left and right, whenever they found a house which its
owners had not burnt before fleeing or which the Cossacks had not
already stripped of all its foodstuffs.

But they kept on marching just the same, because they had
confidence in Napoleon, because they all still had the conviction
they had had for fourteen years; it was still and always would be:

> ... The grand nation accustomed to conquer
> and the grand general leading the grand army.

From the top of the *Mount of Salutation*,[1] where only forty-eight
hours before the Russian vanguard had been all afire with the hope
of defending Moscow, the French troops now gazed at the 'forty
times forty churches' that shimmered gold, silver and blue beneath
a magnificent sky. When Captain Gervais cried: 'This is the end
of our troubles!' he was expressing the hopes and feelings of them all.

Satisfaction showed on their bronzed faces, which were covered
with a thick layer of dust streaked with sweat, and everyone was
wondering if what he saw was really true. Then a great clamour
arose; the clapping of thousands of hands and an immense cheer
were heard. Like sailors who shout: 'Land! Land!' at the end of a
long, arduous voyage, thousands of mouths yelled: 'Moscow!
Moscow!'

And there, descending from his berlin, was the Emperor. The
Eagle was placed on the mountain. A few days previously, at
Mozhaysk, which he had reached just after Kutusov had left, he
had announced:

'Peace lies at Moscow. The Battle of the Moskva will open my
brother Alexander's eyes and the capture of Moscow will open the
eyes of his Senate!'

He immediately sent a letter to all the bishops in France:

'*From our imperial camp at Mozhaysk, September 10, 1812.*
'The Rt Rev. the Bishop of ...

'The passage of the Niemen, the Dvina and the Borysthenes
(*Dnieper*), the Battles of Mogilev, the Drissa, Polotsk and Smolensk,
and lastly the Battle of the Moskva, are so many motives for offering
solemn thanks to the God of the armies. Therefore it is our intention that on receipt of the present letter you act in concert with the
proper quarters: bring my people together in the churches to recite
prayers in conformity with the usage and rites of the Church in
such circumstances. As this letter has no other purpose, I pray
God to keep you in his holy care.

NAPOLEON.

Mozhaysk! 'One vast hospital,' observed General Gourgaud,* to

---

[1] *Poklonnaya Gora*: Mount 'of Salutation' or 'of Greeting', so called because every
Russian traveller, on seeing the holy city from this height, saluted it by prostrating and
crossing himself.

his consternation. 'Sanitary conditions are catastrophic . . .' To be sure the same distress had prevailed among the Russians, but they have taken away all their wounded and 'had not left a scrap behind them'.

But that had not stopped the Emperor from staying three days in this town three-quarters destroyed by the enemy—a foreshadowing of another imminent and much more tragic piece of destruction. But who could have foreseen such a calamity?

Napoleon had set off again from Mozhaysk in his carriage at noon on September 12th. He had not ridden on horseback since the great battle.

Now, on September 14th, he gazed proudly at the spectacle below him and exclaimed with visible emotion:

'So there it is, this famous town! It is high time!'

His voice had become clear and youthful again—the voice of his triumphs. It had lost that raucous note, inaudible at times, caused by a stubborn cold caught on the eve of Borodino. His face also seemed transformed, rid of that puckered, livid mask which reflected worry and illness. For ten days the doctors Yvan and Métivier had been unable to arrest a dysuria from which he had been suffering.

He turned to General de Caulaincourt,* Duke of Vicenza, his Master of the Horse, and pointing to the domes and the crenellated mass of the Kremlin, and the sparkling water, cried: 'Are they abandoning all that, Caulaincourt? It isn't possible!'

But since it was true, since against all reason, the unforeseeable had happened, it was obviously because the Tsar wanted to negotiate.

The Emperor's general staff surrounded and congratulated him, and he thanked them with a hint of mockery in his eyes and in his voice. All these plumed marshals, these generals with their chevrons, had wanted him to stop when they had only reached Vitebsk! Why, they had asked, move still further from France, bases and reinforcements? 'Peace will flee ahead of us like battle,' one of them said. 'The enemy will quickly bring itself up to strength on its home territory, whereas we . . .,' said another. They were unanimously of the opinion that it was madness to stretch the lines of communication so far. Napoleon guessed that even on this day, at this superb hour, many of them would like to savour their triumph for two or three days, for the glory, and then fall back on Vitebsk. But they did not understand the situation at all. Peace lay at Moscow!

Around him were grouped the chief of staff of the army, Berthier, Prince of Neuchâtel and Wagram;* Joachim Murat, King of Naples; Eugène de Beauharnais, Viceroy of Italy; Duroc, Marshal of the Palace;* Marshal Mortier, Duke of Treviso;* and Marshal Davout, Prince of Eckmühl, as well as Generals Caulaincourt, Lauriston* and Gourgaud. Their faces looked cheerful under the Emperor's searching look. Come then! Grievances were forgotten—for the moment.

There had been enough idling; it was time to get down to work. The machinery had to be installed without delay. Eugène, with the 4th Corps, would set up his headquarters in the north, at the St Petersburg gate, and make advanced reconnaissances of all the northern roads. Prince Poniatowski, with his Poles of the 5th Corps, 'will watch the suburbs in the south and deploy as far as the road to Kolomna'. The Prince of Eckmühl, with the 1st Corps, would place himself behind Eugène and 'occupy all the region of the west'. Marshal Lefèvre, Duke of Danzig, would take possession of the Kremlin with the Old Guard, and the King of Naples, with the vanguard of the cavalry and the First Infantry Division (the Dufour division) would first enter the town to assemble a deputation of notables to present themselves to the Emperor. Then he would have the mission of pursuing Kutusov step by step, 'pushing him as far as possible along the road to Ryazan, once he was well away from the gate'. The purpose of this pursuit was not defined very clearly. It was mainly a matter of following the enemy's movements in order to learn what his intentions were, for the plans of the one-eyed commander were as much a mystery to the French as they were to the Russians.

At three o'clock in the afternoon, beneath a blazing sun, the Russian rearguard, hindered in its march by refugees, caught in a bottleneck at the Kolomna gate, had not finished leaving the town. Then General Miloradovich suddenly learnt that the King of Naples and his lieutenant, General Sebastiani, had come down from the Mount of Salutation with the French vanguard and were preparing to enter Moscow by the Dorogomylov gate, in the south-west. This was bad news. The last Russian units, commanded by General Kaptsevich would be cut off from the main body of the army that was retreating. Two cavalry corps, twelve pieces of artillery and ten regiments of Cossacks would be lost! After the losses of men and material between Vilna and Smolensk, and the enormous losses at Borodino, this would be an additional catastrophe. Quick, let there be a parley!

Miloradovich immediately sent an emissary to Murat, who had been constantly on the heels of the French rearguard ever since Mozhaysk, 'driving it onto the fleeing army', but confining himself to harmless skirmishes. And here he was, entangled with the Russian units at the entrance to the town, as a result of the unforeseen disorder. The situation amused him and he took advantage of it to show off in front of the Cossacks, many of whom knew him from Tilsit, where he had paraded complacently and made a deep impression. In the eyes of those horsemen he was an almost legendary figure with his big white plume, his grey linen tunic trimmed with sable, his extravagantly curly hair, black as jet, his trimmings, frogs and loops forming brilliant arabesques and picturesque interlaced designs.

There he was, swaggering in front of the men he condescendingly called 'those warriors who are still barbarians'. He gave them the jewels he had on him, his watch and General Gourgaud's, 'a very pretty jewel received from an illustrious hand', in short, everything he could collect from his entourage in a few minutes. He was playing the first act of the comedy he constantly put on for the Russians, one that turned into tragi-comedy in less than a fortnight and then into a tragedy pregnant with consequences for the Grand Army as a whole. But who had ever been able to put a stop to the follies of Joachim Murat, King of Naples? What bitter lesson would ever teach him wisdom?

He was asked for a truce. How could he refuse it after all his frivolous behaviour? All the more since Miloradovich had warned him in friendly fashion that if the French attacked him inside the town, he would defend himself 'to the last extremity', even if he had to die beneath the ruins of Moscow. In itself, this prospect did not scare Murat, but even he had had enough of campaigning. Like everyone else, he longed for the pleasant existence of the conqueror, to which he had become only too accustomed. Moreover, Napoleon would be furious if battles and destruction interfered with the enjoyment of this day and spoiled the triumphal entry that was planned. So Murat hastened to send a letter to the Emperor, who agreed to grant the enemy a truce during which they would not be harried and no engagements would be sought. The majority of the French vanguard would stay in the suburbs about five miles from the Dorogomylov gate and every individual belonging to the Russian army, as well as the military effects that the French might still find in the town would have a free passage until 7 a.m. on Tuesday, September 15th.

This meant that, with 'the two armies disentangling themselves', the Russian rear-guard would be able to pass intact; and that, once the stragglers had caught up with the others, once everybody had left Moscow in a southwesterly direction on the road to Kolomna and Ryazan, Field-marshal Kutusov could sensibly grant his harassed troops a twelve-hour halt-cum-bivouac in the environs of the village of Pankovo, some ten miles from the town. At the same time the halt enabled the refugees to move ahead, relieving the congestion on the roads and putting an end to their interference with the army's movements.

——Perhaps the truce granted by Napoleon was his first mistake.

At five o'clock, the Emperor came down from the Sparrow Hills in a carriage and stopped just outside the Dorogomylov gate. He got out, then called for a horse. He rode along the right-hand side of the road, followed by a small suite, as far as 'the extreme tip of his vanguard'. An officer tells us that 'a tall Polish Jew, in national costume,' approached him and 'gave explanations which seemed to refer to certain places in the town'. Napoleon looked in the direction of Moscow, then inspected the entrenchments that the Russians had constructed recently. He reached the houses that flanked the gate. At that moment the vanguard began to march past him to make their entrance into the town, since he had decided that the Russian rearguard was far enough ahead for there to be no more risk of 'entanglement'.

The troops passed unhurriedly through the suburb of Dorogomylov and forded the River Moskva, because the bridge had been demolished by the retreating army. Napoleon gave orders for it to be restored immediately. The Marquis de Chambray, who was near him, saw him beaming with pleasure, for His Majesty 'has no doubt that the occupation of Moscow will be followed by a peace meeting his wishes'. However, he did not enter the town, because his staff thought it preferable first to carry out reconnaissance missions and clearing up operations, if necessary. But it was not fear of snipers that held Napoleon back. He was waiting for someone to approach him, bringing him, symbolically or otherwise, the keys of the city. He was waiting for the 'notables' whom Murat was supposed to send him.

Finally he tired of waiting and sent General Durosnel,* on whom he conferred in advance the post of Governor of Moscow, to explore the town with an elite body of gendarmes, establish order if necessary and 'take possession of the public establishments'. He specifically instructed him 'to speed up the departure of the deputation of authorities' that the King of Naples must surely have assembled.

'It will,' he added, 'be the best guarantee we can give the inhabitants of our peaceful intentions.'

In the town, Durosnel came across a Frenchman called François Xavier Villiers, reader in French at the University and master of a boys' boarding school. This man had been imprudent enough to address the general in his native tongue. He immediately found himself attached to him as interpreter and, whether he liked it or not, the first person to 'collaborate with the occupying power'. He was one of those French emigrés with years of residence in Russia, many of them naturalized Russians, whose sympathies were with the Tsar rather than the Emperor.

Durosnel made Villiers take him to 'the Regency of the Government', the Municipal Council, the Police Headquarters and the Governor's Palace. There was no one anywhere! Murat himself had found neither magistrates nor 'authorities'.

The Emperor grew more impatient every minute. To while away the time, he dictated to Caulaincourt a letter to the High Chancellor Cambacérès at Paris and another to Maret, Duke of Bassano,* at Vilna, telling them both of his arrival in Moscow. He sent more scouts into the town and then began to pace up and down outside the gate. The sun began to set.

Next he sent his aide-de-camp, General Gourgaud, for information, after which he forded the river, walked 'to the end of the street on the other side', returned to speed up the repair work on the bridge 'so that the munitions could cross' and finally, unable to restrain himself any longer, he ordered Count Daru, Quartermaster-general, to go to see what was happening.

'Fetch me those boyars!' he said.

Boyars! That archaic word would have made a Russian smile.

There had not been any boyars since Peter the Great. As for the 'notables', there had not been any since that morning. Moscow was empty. Napoleon had sought a distant princess and found a dead beauty!

And indeed it was an aura of death which enveloped the columns that were entering Moscow and spreading out through its streets. A few inhabitants were watching behind their closed shutters; here and there someone hailed a passing officer and forewarned him of 'a vast trap' into which the French army was going to fall. That only increased the general feeling of insecurity. The majority of the houses appeared to be deserted. Not a wisp of smoke came from the chimneys. 'Not a sound arose from this vast and populous city,' a soldier noted. It seemed to him as if 'two hundred thousand inhabitants had been struck dumb and paralysed by some enchantment'. Everything looked strange and frightening. One 'feels chilled with fear, not seeing a living soul'; another 'listens with a secret shudder to the horses' hooves which alone break the silence'. Anatole de Montesquiou admitted that the further he advanced the more he was overawed 'by the astonishing consternation emanating from the silence and the desolation'. An officer wrote to his family: 'Never did conquerors make a less triumphal entry, nor one accompanied by more sinister portents.' Who could have expected it? They had never met anything like it before. And each soldier secretly recalled with nostalgia the acclamations of Berlin, Dresden and Milan. Naively, Sergeant Bourgogne was astonished when he did not even 'see a single lady to listen to our band playing the tune of *La Victoire est à nous* (Victory is ours)!'

Napoleon, who was getting more and more irritable at the gate, watched night falling slowly. The only people he had been able to talk to were the officers sent back by Murat, Durosnel and Daru to tell him that no deputation would appear, because there was nobody to form one. He exclaimed:

'Moscow deserted? It's incredible!'

Incredible it was, but reports kept on arriving to confirm it. Nevertheless, the Emperor clung on obstinately, hoping against hope.

A little later, a zealous Polish officer brought him a small, frightened group of French Muscovites—teachers (like Villiers) and tradespeople. They confirmed the complete abandonment of the town by the authorities, Rostopchin, the Governor, having been the last to leave. The majority of the inhabitants had fled. There

4.

(*a*) Murat, 'a legendary figure with his great white plume'.

(*b*) Caulaincourt, who said of the Emperor: 'No one will make him change his mind.'

(*c*) Ségur, who said: 'This miraculous conquest cast a halo of glory around us.'

(*d*) Mortier to whom Napoleon gave the order: 'Above all, no looting!'

5. (*a*) Rostopchin, 'watching everything with a keen and frequently mocking eye'.

(*b*) Barclay de Tolly. 'Officers, non-commissioned officers and men were dissatisfied with Barclay.'

c

d

(*c*) Kutusov: 'What matters, is to save the fatherland.'

(*d*) Bennigsen. Kutusov asked: 'Was your position at Friedland such a good one, then?'

were 5,000 left, maybe 10,000.[1] They, 'the Franco–Russians', as they were called there, had not left because they did not know where to go. Everyone had distrusted them during the last few days. People called them spies. The great families had not risked taking their governesses and tutors with them.

'In other words, there are only Frenchmen left in Moscow?'

'And people from the very lowest class. There are criminals, too, for the Governor had the prisons thrown open yesterday. There's something alarming in the air.'

'What sort of thing?'

'We don't know. Tonight there were mysterious knocks on the doors of some houses and the people were advised to leave because there was going to be a fire in the town. Perhaps Leppich has made his infernal machine.'

But Napoleon was not interested in that. What he had just learnt had annoyed him intensely. He muttered:

'Ah, the Russians don't yet know what effect the capture of their capital will have on them!'

Next he received information that shots had rung out just as a detachment of the cavalry of the Guard had arrived in front of the Kremlin. Some snipers, barricaded inside the citadel, had made a last desperate gesture to try to defend their town. The cavalry had had to break in the doors with cannon fire and kill the defenders, one of whom had tried to stab General Gourgaud. The Kremlin had been occupied without further incident. The Emperor was assured that 'It isn't a palace, but a harmless citadel, built on a height and bordered by the Moskva'. His entourage respectfully advised him not to take possession of it until the following day.

He agreed to this suggestion. His face, noted the Duke of Vicenza, 'bears the marks of his disappointment most strikingly'. He decided to spend the night in a wooden house at the entrance to the suburb of Dorogomylov, on the right-hand side—'about a thousand paces from the main road to Smolensk and three hundred yards from the gate, in what appears to be a deserted inn',[2] as one witness put it.

---

[1] Apparently no one has ever been able to establish the exact figure. According to Russian documents, it was between 10,000 and 15,000.

[2] Witnesses' memories differ on this subject. Caulaincourt says it was a 'wretched tavern built of wood', Bausset that it was a 'fine house constructed of wood'; Baron Fain, Napoleon's secretary, speaks of a 'large inn'; an anonymous text mentions a 'house under construction'. The Chevalier d'Ysarn, an old Moscow resident, speaks of the 'house of a caterer'. The house could still be seen in the last century.

D

Between seven and eight o'clock in the evening the troops of the Old and the Young Guard took possession of the Kremlin, the beautiful palaces around it, the big barracks and the superb arsenal. The ancient citadel of the Tsars amazed the French. 'One thing is certain,' declared Captain Gervais, 'the Château of Vincennes is a mere shepherd's hut compared to the Kremlin.' His enthusiasm made him exaggerate slightly. M. de Bausset, Prefect of the Imperial Palace,[1] was personally disappointed with the living-quarters proper. The Tsar's apartments consisted of three salons, a bedroom and a large state hall. This last was divided in two by a large beam supported by two marble columns; it was 'decorated with gilding blackened with age'. The bedroom was a vast rectangular chamber with windows opening onto the Moskva. A simple partition separated it from a small vestibule. In the left-hand corner, near a fire-place, was a small roll-top desk 'placed so as to cut the corner'. This piece of furniture, says the Mameluke Ali-Saint-Denis, had three green silk screens: 'one was drawn to the right, the second to the left and the third upwards; all three joined up behind'— undoubtedly to protect it from the heat of the fire. In the left-hand corner of each of these rooms was an icon of the Madonna and Child. M. de Bausset* estimated that these appointments were 'squalid for a sovereign as powerful as the autocrat of all the Russias'. This showed that he, too, did not know much about Moscow. It was a long time since the autocrats of all the Russias had resided in this palace-cum-citadel. Peter the Great had changed the tradition; his father, Tsar Alexis Mikhailovich, had been the last one to live there permanently.

Night had fallen. The inhabitants, cloistered in their houses, had hardly noticed that the French were occupying the district, so closely had their entry followed the departure of the Russian troops. Only some unfamiliar bugle calls or an order issued in a foreign tongue had attracted attention. Five hundred yards from the main streets where the cavalry of the Guard were riding past, people had no idea what had happened.

The Rostopchin mansion was occupied by a detachment commanded by Sergeant Bourgogne. Through the windows of the big

---

[1] Louis de Bausset-Roquefort was sent by Marie Louise to take Napoleon the portrait of the King of Rome. Bausset left Paris at the end of July, but did not reach the Emperor until September 6th, on the eve of the Battle of the Moskva (cf. further on).

salon, the sergeant suddenly saw thick smoke in the evening sky,
then swirls of flame, but was unable to tell where they came from.
At the same moment, Mme Fusil, an actress attached to the French
company in Moscow, who was living temporarily with a group of
fellow-countrymen in a wing of the Gagarin palace situated in an
outlying suburb, heard loud knocking at the door. At once she was
seized by the fear which had haunted the French in Moscow for
several weeks now: 'The moujiks are coming to massacre us!'
Cautiously the actress and one of her women friends looked through
the shutter. It was a Frenchman whom they knew; he seemed to be
distraught.

'Good heavens, sir, have they been massacring people in your
street?'

'No, it's caught fire. I've come to seek refuge with you.'

Just then a passing horseman reigned in his mount and asked in
French:

'Whereabouts is the fire? Is it in these parts?'

Louise Fusil was dumbfounded. Too many things were happening all at once. Stupidly she asked the soldier:

'Are you French, sir?'

'Yes, madame.'

'So the French are here?'

'They entered the suburbs yesterday at three o'clock.'

'All of them?'

'Yes, all of them.'

He looked as if he took her for a madwoman. He put spurs to
his horse. Then she climbed onto the roof of the house and saw,
like a meteor in the sky, 'a strange object resembling a flaming
sword'.

Meanwhile, small blazes broke out simultaneously in several
places, especially in the north-east and north-west of the town.
The fire attacked a few shops in the Grand Bazaar—the Gostinny
Dvor—and in the street of the salted-fish market—the Solianka.
Nearby stood the Foundlings' Home, which had not been com-
pletely evacuated and still housed five hundred young children.
The director of this institution, Major-general and Councillor of
State Ivan Akinfievitch Tutolmin, asked the French whom he saw
busy mastering the fire for protection. A courier was sent to the
Emperor to inform him that the Home was under the exalted
patronage of the Dowager Empress Maria Fedorovna.* Napoleon

immediately ordered a 'safeguarding picket' to be posted there. It was nine at night.

The fire that was catching here and there did not seem to worry the Emperor in the least. He, too, had seen the gleams and thought that the soldiers, visiting houses torch in hand, had been careless. He sent word to General Durosnel to restore order and dispatched Marshal Mortier, Duke of Treviso, into the town, impressing on him:

'Above all, no looting! You will answer for it to me with your head. Defend Moscow against all comers.'

In the Kremlin, by ten o'clock at night, M. de Bausset and the Count de Ségur,* who were responsible for preparing Napoleon's apartments, felt overcome with fatigue. They chose a salon that seemed more comfortable than the others to rest in, although it had neither shutters nor curtains, and flopped into armchairs. They fell asleep at once. Between midnight and one in the morning, M. de Bausset was awakened by some 'bright but rather distant flashes of light'. Flames could be seen on the quays, on the other side of the Yauza. A fire started beneath the actual walls of the Kremlin, between the St Nicholas Gate and the Gate of the Saviour. Flames rose from the Stock Exchange, others from the Bazaar. There was a loud explosion, then another. Fresh flames sprang up.

A division of Würtemberg cuirassiers of the Grand Army was camped a little way outside Moscow on a small height to the right of the road to Vladimir. They also noticed the explosion. De Roos, a medical officer, thought that it had 'such terrible force' that he concluded that an ammunition dump 'of very great size' had blown up. 'I cannot say whether it is in the middle of the town or on its outskirts, for it is easy to make a mistake at night.' Immediately afterwards people saw a fire that broke out and seemed to spread. 'The flames illuminated us and all the country around . . . A sea of flame spread over the colossus of the town. The noise became louder and the number of refugees who passed in front of our camp also increased.' According to him, it was midnight at that moment.

At the Dorogomylov gate they had also heard the conflagration break out. At two o'clock in the morning the Emperor was informed that the fire was catching hold everywhere.

The Russian army was bivouacking some ten miles from the town that was bursting into flame. Hearing the detonations and seeing the conflagration, General Ermolov suddenly remembered the words that Rostopchin had addressed to Kutusov at Fili: 'If you leave Moscow without fighting, you will see it in flames after your passage!' And he exclaimed:

'Moscow is hiding the shame of its profanation in its ruins and ashes! Those are our own hands that are spreading the flames. In the voluntary destruction of Moscow the enemy can see the proclamation of its downfall.'

But the harassed, discouraged soldiers who watched the cloudless September sky glowing red, as if with a blazing sunset or the red streaks of dawn, shook their fists and blamed the French for this 'abominable crime'. Then they crossed themselves and some of them exclaimed:

'You're beautiful, our little mother Moscow—*matuchka Moskva* —our holy city crowned with gold!'

The old Field-marshal was sitting outside a peasant's hut, sprawling in his chair and scowling. Unlike Ermolov, he counted on profiting by the conviction of his troops. Let them believe that the fire had been lit by the enemy! That would stimulate them and overcome their dejection. With his one eye he gazed into space and suddenly, banging his fist furiously on his white helmet, he growled:

'It's a terrible shame, but I'll have his head!'

He did not underestimate the adversary to whom he had been forced to make a present of Moscow. He had learnt to appraise him on the field of battle where they had met face to face.

But he knew that he would win.

PART II

———◆———

In truth the issue hung on a very small matter! For I had set out to fight men under arms and not raging nature; I defeated armies, but I could not conquer the flames . . .

NAPOLEON
Mémorial de Sainte-Hélène

Moscow will be reborn from its ashes and the urge for vengeance will be the source of our glory and our grandeur. The gleams from the burning of Moscow . . . will sooner or later light up for us the road to Paris . . .

ALEXANDER TURGENEV
to Prince Viazemsky

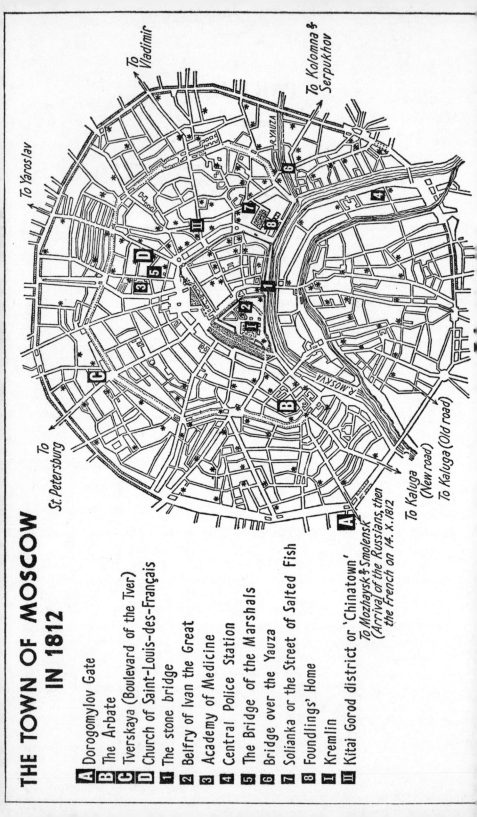

THE TOWN OF MOSCOW IN 1812

A Dorogomylov Gate
B The Arbate
C Tverskaya (Boulevard of the Tver)
D Church of Saint-Louis-des-Français
1 The stone bridge
2 Belfry of Ivan the Great
3 Academy of Medicine
4 Central Police Station
5 The Bridge of the Marshals
6 Bridge over the Yauza
7 Solianka or the Street of Salted Fish
8 Foundlings' Home
I Kremlin
II Kitai Gorod district or 'Chinatown'

To Yaroslav

To St. Petersburg

To Vladimir

To Kolomna & Serpukhov

R. YAUZA

R. MOSKVA

To Kaluga (New road)

To Kaluga (Old road)

To Mozhaysk & Smolensk
(Arrival of the Russians, then
the French on 14.X.1812)

THE CONFLAGRATION

We only lit a candle for you,
But it was a brilliant candle.
We lit for you, O our dear children,
We lit a candle for you : Moscow, our mother.

Popular Russian song about 1812

DURING the night of September 14th the fire broke out in many parts of the town. It was put out in one place, only to start up in another. The inhabitants did nothing to extinguish it. They believed that the French had started the fire and would kill them if they intervened. As for the French, they did not feel like slaving away to save the homes of these inhospitable people.

There was great confusion during these night hours. Explosions were heard. Sentries posted outside noble homes reserved for Napoleon's general staff shouted 'Fire' and panicked. Troops were patrolling every district. They got lost in the maze of narrow alleys and everywhere they saw reddish smoke preceded by small explosions coming from stone palaces and wooden houses alike. Here and there painted and varnished metal roofs collapsed with a roar; and to crown the disorder, terrifying men with beards, carrying torches, emerged from carriage gateways or blind alleys. Strange as it may seem, it took a long time before anyone realized that these people were incendiaries. Then the soldiers tried to arrest them. They were chased and captured or executed on the spot. They died without protest—resigned. 'It is God's will!' Four Moscow policemen were caught in the act of setting fire to a house.

Already the Grand Bazaar had caught fire in the Kitai Gorod or 'Chinatown', the main shopping centre. The troops sent to cut off the fire in this sector immediately realized the extent of the danger, for there were 6,000 or 7,000 shops there. An enormous quantity of goods might easily be lost without gain to anyone. So in less than an hour, while mastering the fire, the soldiers 'saved' furs, carpets, clothes, wines and liqueurs, quantities of hams and large fish, as well as eastern weapons. However, the whole operation was still carried out under strict control. Everything that was taken from the shops was laid out in endless lots. They were guarded by sentries chosen from different regiments, who were posted along a colonnade facing the shops. The common people of Moscow tried to break through the cordon to seize their share of the booty, an effort that brought them thumps and blows from gun butts.

So order reigned for the time being, but animosity grew in the ranks of the soldiers. They were convinced now that the Russians themselves were setting fire to the town and from then on every 'native'—man or woman—was a potential criminal, a dangerous miscreant. The fires, which multiplied with stupefying rapidity and spread with great fury, were no longer regarded as accidents by anyone. The blaze no longer had 'direction nor limits'. Everyone was dismayed not only by 'the new convulsions of the conflagration', but also by the relentlessness of the people who were responsible for it.

However, by dint of hard work under the energetic drive of Marshal Mortier, the disaster seemed to be conquered in the actual town by the early hours. At 6 a.m. the Emperor left his temporary quarters and made his entry into Moscow. A depressing entry, without fanfares, 'in utter silence and without any kind of display'. He rode his favourite hourse, L'Emir. There was not a single inhabitant along his route. He saw a cheerless town beneath a morning sky that gave promise of a sunny day. The victor's face was drawn. The citadel of the Tsars appeared before him in all its bizarre splendour—a mixture of Byzantine, Eastern and Italian Renaissance art. The Red Square, the Red Steps and the Palace impressed Napoleon and his escort. Someone was surprised at finding 'the design of the old palace of the Doges at Venice' in the great staircase and the imposing façade. Until then it had all been spared by the flames; so, with a great resurgence of hope, the Emperor cried:

'So at last I'm in Moscow and in the Kremlin!'

As soon as he had entered, he started to explore, with curiosity and obvious satisfaction. His apartment pleased him, with its view right down to the Moskva and onto the quays that adorn its banks, while beyond stretched an immense horizon of houses, domes and palaces. He ordered that the portrait of the King of Rome painted by Gérard, which M. de Bausset had brought from Paris on the

eve of the Battle of the Moskva, should be hung in his bedroom.[1]
He stopped to look at it for a moment, his features relaxed. But a
thousand urgent tasks called for his attention and he was busy
giving orders about the organization of the town and the care of the
French and Russian soldiers wounded at Smolensk and the Moskva.
He also tried to get information which would help him unravel
what had happened in Moscow during the past few days. He was
soon told about Leppich–Schmit and his balloon. The rockets
and inflammable material that were to have rained down on the
French army had been carefully preserved and used by the incendiaries to light the fires of the previous night.

The flames flared up again at dawn in places, among them on the
quays of the Yauza, but they were checked at once and Murat and
his staff were able to instal themselves in the Balachov mansion in
Yauza Street, before setting off again on the Ryazan road in pursuit
of Kutusov, in accordance with the Emperor's orders.

Marshal Mortier was henceforth Governor of the province and
Count Durosnel, Governor of the town and Town Major.[2] It was
in this capacity that he drafted a proclamation addressed to the
people of Moscow. Actually it was an order:

'Now that the army of H.M. the Emperor and King has taken
possession of the town of Moscow, its inhabitants are ordered:

'1 To make a report to General Count Durosnel, Town Major,
of all the Russians who may be in their homes, whether wounded
or in good health;

'2 To make a declaration within twenty-four hours of the objects

---

[1] Napoleon wrote the Empress two letters about portraits of the King of Rome.
The second one deals with the portrait painted by Baron Gérard and exhibited outside
the imperial tent on the eve of Borodino. (*Unpublished letters from Napoleon to Marie
Louise.*)

'My dear, I have received a beautiful portrait of the little king which Isabey sent me
as a present by an "auditeur". I found it a very good likeness and very beautiful.
Kiss him twice for me. I'm in very good health; my affairs are going well. The heat is
excessive. Adio, mio ben. Keep well and don't worry about your

NAP.

Smolensk, August 22nd.' (Letter No. 76.)

'My dear love, I am very tired. Bausset has handed me the portait of the king. It's
a masterpiece. Many thanks for your thoughtfulness. The picture is as beautiful as
you are. I will write to you in more detail tomorrow. I am ti(red). Adio, mio ben

NAP.

Borodino, 6 7bre.' (Letter No. 87.)

[2] Lesseps soon succeeded him in this office.

belonging to the crown which they may have misappropriated or of which they have knowledge;

'3 To reveal the wheat, flour and spirits that may be in their homes or in the storehouses of the Russian government;

'4 They shall declare and bring to the office of the Town Major, Count Durosnel, all the pikes or other offensive arms, whether firearms or side-arms, which they may have in their homes.

'Moreover, the peaceful inhabitants of Moscow need have no fear about the maintenance of their properties and the safety of their persons, if they conform religiously to the provisions of the present proclamation.'

But this proclamation, like those that followed it, remained a dead letter for the Muscovites who stayed in their town.

Meanwhile, flames were rising along the Pokrova, a very long street that ran through a vast district in the east and continued beyond the gate. The Trubetzkoy mansion was burning. Simultaneously, the houses on the Arbate, only the day before one of the most animated boulevards of Moscow, to the west of the Kremlin, were in flames. Then it was the turn of the thoroughfare that led to the Dorogomylov gate—the route followed by the French troops to make their entry, the evening before. A spectator described the 'black whirlwinds of smoke which rose in the wind'. Starting from the eastern districts, they had spread over the town, 'leaving the nauseating smell of sulphur and bitumen everywhere'. He observed that the fire pursued them rapidly, 'growing with everything it devoured and flowing in a bed of fire, from one end of the town to the other'. And we have another witness who saw 'the trails of fire follow their dreadful course; other furnaces roar up: new torrents flow from them and, driven by the wind, fill in the gaps that the previous streams of fire had not managed to reach'. Finally, Baron Fain, the Emperor's secretary, exclaimed: 'It is as if the earth has opened to supply all these fires that are breaking out!'

The reserves of wheat on the banks of the Moskva blazed up— a bonfire whose sparks spread, falling on a stock of grenades and blowing them up. The carriage market was burning—but Napoleon's troops had already chosen everything they fancied from it. A northwest wind that had sprung up urged on the devastation throughout the day. The Bazaar caught fire again. Within a few minutes the stores of oil and tallow became 'an inextinguishable furnace'.

Since dawn, the soldiers had given up looking for the elusive fire-engines. Incendiaries who had been arrested had unanimously revealed that they had been evacuated by order.

As for the population left behind, it was only beginning to understand that it was the Russians, not the enemy, who were lighting the fires. Then the people, dazed by so many successive and unintelligible misfortunes, placed an icon in front of their houses and left them, taking away what they could. But some of them set fire to their homes before leaving, murmuring: 'It is God's will!'

At nightfall the fire caught hold in a suburb, while apparently there was a lull elsewhere. The Emperor, who was very tired, had retired early and everyone was thinking of going to bed. All was calm and silent in the palace. Everyone was sleeping deeply.

About 10 p.m. Mameluke Ali woke up. He rubbed his eyes and saw 'the whole room brightly lit'. Running to the window, he discovered that the town was ablaze, 'at least the southern and western parts of it'. His account is vivid: 'Imagine a town, I would say as big as Paris, consigned to the flames, and being on the towers of Notre Dame, watching the spectacle during the night'. At the same moment the Duke of Vicenza's man-servant woke his master to tell him the news. Caulaincourt observed that the conflagration threw off such a bright light that it was possible to read at the back of the room. However, as the Kremlin did not seem to be threatened, he decided to let the Emperor go on sleeping. He was worried about his health and his mood. He woke up Duroc, Duke of Frioul, Grand Marshal of the Palace, had the Guard called out and sent an aide to Marshal Mortier's quarters for information.

As soon as he was dressed, Caulaincourt mounted his horse and rode into the town. The wind was blowing from the north and driving the flames towards the centre with extraordinary violence; 'it bellows and seethes like the waves of a tempest. The horizon is a mass of blazing fumes'. Two districts, at least, were on fire. Towards midnight, a third was affected, then yet another. At four in the morning it was an inferno. They could no longer delay waking His Majesty. Constant, his head man-servant, was sent to his bedroom.

During this time looting had begun again around the rekindled Bazaar. Russians and French vied with each other in breaking down the doors and bursting into the cellars of threatened shops. They stole sugar, tea, coffee, leather goods, furs and cloth from the

Orient. They pierced the barrels of vodka (which, naturally, had not all been successfully destroyed before the evacuation of the town). The looting, wrote the Abbé Surrugues, in the eyes of the soldiers, 'frustrated of the hope with which they had deluded themselves', was a reprisal, a sort of compensation for their fatigue and the battles they had fought. Had they not been given solemn promises that at Moscow they would find 'the end of their sufferings and the unlimited satisfaction of all their needs'?

To the Russians, at this hour, looting was both a vital necessity and a moral satisfaction. So Governor Rostopchin had snapped his fingers at the Muscovites? So the rich had fled? All right, the wretched people who had been abandoned would help themselves freely, disputing their booty with the foreign troops! People were still at the elementary, crude stage of looting. They robbed for robbing's sake, so that their neighbour should not have what they had. Soon, with necessity dictating the law, barter, trading and 'fraternisation', to make the pillage more profitable, were the order of the day, but so also, in this mad atmosphere, were violence, excess and demoralization.

When the Emperor was awake and saw the size of the disaster, he became furiously angry, cursing 'the troops' lack of discipline' and 'the abandoned state in which the inhabitants leave their houses'. He blamed the Young Guard and Marshal Mortier. As he had done at Gzhatsk and Vyazma, he repeated several times:

I cannot believe that these people are burning their homes to stop us spending the night in them!'

But he no longer said it jokingly. He looked very preoccupied. Information flowed in and each time it confirmed that the fire-engines had been taken away or destroyed. Members of the Moscow police, hardened criminals, peasants 'and even ecclesiastics' had in every district been surprised by the soldiers in the act of setting fire to combustible material placed in the houses in readiness to burn them down. In one form or another, the reports teemed with confessions:

'The order was given by the Governor to the police, Sire, to set fire to the whole town during the night. Patrols are at work in all nine urban districts.'

Napoleon found it hard to believe such a thing, but successive reports emanating from widely differing sources and places left him in very little doubt. He went from one window to another, watching the spectacle that unfolded at the foot of the ancient citadel where he was still safe for the time being, although 'surpassed in determination'. He saw his fine victory 'vanishing in the whirlwinds of smoke and flames'.

He paced up and down nervously, then sat down again brusquely. His movements were abrupt. No sooner had he sat down, than he stood up and rushed to a window to gaze once more at the fascinating, ghastly sight, the blinding flashes everywhere, the columns of smoke and the immense infernos.

It was the same conflagration that the young, care-free Henri Beyle-Stendhal, attached to the Quartermaster-general, Count Daru, watched from the suburbs of Moscow. 'The most beautiful fire in the world, forming an immense pyramid, which, like the prayers of the faithful, had its base on the ground and its summit in the heavens,' he related in his *Journal*. Above it all hung the moon. It was impressive, to be sure, but most of all it was terrifying.

Napoleon seemed to be overwhelmed by it. He uttered exclamations, sighed and then said in a strangled voice:

'What an appalling sight! All those palaces! What extraordinary determination! What men!'

The wind had become a real equinoctial gale. Towards dawn, its howls swamped the crash of collapsing houses. At daybreak, when Napoleon was getting ready to leave the Kremlin on foot to try to get a closer view of the disaster, two Russians were brought to him, caught red-handed in the act of incendiarism. They told a tale that the French already knew by heart. The interpreter translated it word for word:

'We were ordered to set fire to everything. The houses were pointed out. Everything was prepared. Our officers distributed us in detachments in every corner of the town.'

The signal agreed on was a rocket. That explains the mystery of the 'ball of fire' that the Abbé Surrugues had seen exploding above the Yauza on the night of September 14th and the 'flaming sword' seen by Mme Fusil about the same time. The organizer-in-chief was the Governor, Rostopchin; his second in command the chief of police, Ivachkin. There were other 'chiefs', whose names the prisoners wanted to keep secret, but when they revealed them the French were disappointed; the name of Voronenko, for example, divisional commissioner of police, meant nothing to them, and in any case his subordinates simply could not or would not say how and where he could be found. Some incendiaries were guarded closely, while their fate was being decided. The Emperor ordered that military commissions should be formed in each district 'to pass summary judgment on, shoot or hang incendiaries caught red-handed'.

At nine o'clock in the morning a hurricane was blowing over Moscow. It could almost be believed that a curse hung over the town, for during each of the great fires that had devastated it—the fires of 1547 under Ivan the Terrible and 1626 under Mikhail I Romanoff—a tempest, suddenly unleashed, had fed and multiplied the disaster. The fire, which since nightfall had darted about devouring everything, became increasingly voracious, 'carried to ten distant places in the space of an hour', so it seemed to the stunned spectators. The whole Bazaar was ablaze and this time help was impossible. Wherever they went to search in the houses which were still intact, the French safety teams removed Congreve rockets placed in chimneys or similar places. They discovered bon-fires ready laid, 'incendiary preparations', tow soaked with tar, sulphur and bitumen. Large quantities of these combustibles were even found in the stove-pipes of the Rostopchin palace, in which General Laborde and Jeanneau, a medical officer, had just installed themselves. They were so stupefied by this discovery that they went to find M. de Bausset so that he could see the evidence with his own eyes. It was obvious that the Governor had counted on expelling his French successor in somewhat cavalier fashion!

Flames! Flames! Flames! The fire gained ground steadily. It smouldered here, crawled there, licked the cornices, snatched at doors and got its teeth into trees in the gardens, and they in turn set fire to the houses. Wooden hovels collapsed with a crack at the foot of brick houses that resisted the flames little better, for after three days only 578 remained out of 2,750. The fire slithered from south-west to north-east like a monstrous serpent. It was so fast that many people in the Emperor's entourage, such as M. de Bausset and M. de Turenne, who had carefully chosen a residence to their liking, found themselves forced to move three times during the morning of September 16th.

While the devastating scourge ran along the rampart that enclosed the White Town—the Byelogorod—and approached the Red Gate

6. On the afternoon of September 13th, at the end of a council of war held in the village of Fili, Kutusov had taken a weighty decision: 'By virtue of the power conferred on me . . . I give the order to retreat.' (*A copy of Kivchenko by Ptchelin, National Historical Museum.*)

7.

(*a*) Napoleon stopped at the gates of the town, awaiting until nightfall the 'notables' who could not fail to bring him the keys of the city: 'Where are the boyars?'

(*b*) On the next day, September 15th, the Emperor entered Moscow by the Dorogomylov gate: 'A depressing entry, without fanfares, in utter silence.'

a

b

of the Kremlin, the window-panes sheltering Napoleon trembled and grew hot; sweepers stationed on the roof of the palace constantly swept away the 'flakes of fire' that fell on it. Napoleon, who could still see the river and the quays extending between him and the disaster, now felt as if he was in a fortress preparing for a siege, for the houses surrounding the Kremlin began to blaze. The wind swept up enormous brands that fell down like a shower of fire. Some of them reached the metal roof of the arsenal of the Kremlin and the kitchens. An energetic team of soldiers averted misfortune by means of brooms and buckets, sweeping the brands away and cooling down the roof.

At noon, the stables and one of the towers of the arsenal caught fire. Suddenly, to everyone's horror, sparks fell into the courtyard on to masses of tow that had been used for packing Russian ammunition cases. At the time there were 400 French cases in the yard and in addition some 100,000 pounds of gunpowder had been deposited there. Disaster was imminent. At any minute the Emperor and his suite, together with the Tsarist citadel, would be blown to smithereens! They ran to warn Napoleon of the danger. He appeared at once, for he knew that 'his presence made everything possible for the Guard'. But the gunners who were struggling desperately to check the danger lost their heads when they saw the Emperor expose himself instead of fleeing, and blundered about inefficiently. General de la Lariboisière* begged him to go. Meanwhile an alarming rumour spread: the Kremlin was mined! Russian incendiaries had confirmed it. To crown it all, 'the equinoctial gale, working with the Russians', redoubled in violence. Murat, Eugène de Beauharnais and Berthier arrived on the scene. There was a chorus of supplications and exhortations. They urged the Emperor to leave 'this place of desolation' where he was besieged. He refused emphatically. The more dangerous it was, the more bent he was on staying there. The tow lay tightly packed all over the ground. Sparks rained down. Napoleon and his staff were about twenty yards from the door of the arsenal.

'Sire, I beseech you!'

'No!'

Next it was Bessières* and Gourgaud who came to tell him that the Kremlin seemed to be surrounded on every side.

'Go up to a terrace with the Prince of Neuchâtel and see if it is true,' ordered the Emperor.

E

Gourgaud and Berthier obeyed, but 'the impetuousness, the violence of the wind and the rarefaction of the air caused by the fierceness of the blaze produced a terrible storm of wind', and it was a miracle that they were not carried off by a gust of the equinoctial gale that was still blowing from the west. The impatient Emperor joined them. What he saw could leave him no illusions about the extent of the disaster. He muttered:

'With their own hands! They're Scythians!'

Then Berthier hit upon an argument.

'Sire,' he said, 'if the enemy attacked the army corps that are outside Moscow, Your Majesty would no longer have any means of communication with them.'

Nevertheless, he still vacillated, wanting to be present while his soldiers continued the heroic struggle to save the stables in the courtyard that housed the Emperor's horses and the parade turnouts of the Tsars. On this spot they were under an arch of smoke. Everyone made superhuman efforts to stop the devastating torrent —hoping against hope. The air was afire. People breathed fire. The sappers were struggling to preserve the stone bridge south of the Kremlin and the Emperor made his way to them, with the Generals of the Guard and his aides-de-camp. He joined in the work himself and stayed in the midst of this hail of fire in which a man could not stand still for more than a minute. The Duke of Vicenza noticed this detail: the fur frizzled on the helmets the grenadiers were wearing.

The windows of the Kremlin shattered. There was nothing to breathe but smoke and ashes. The Emperor kept thinking about what the Prince of Neuchâtel had said to him up there on the terrace and suddenly, early in the afternoon, he gave the order to depart.

Later, no one could say exactly who had proposed withdrawing to the castle of Petrovskoye, about two and a half miles from the town to the north-west, behind the quarters of the Viceroy, on the road to St Petersburg. Both Caulaincourt and others were to claim that they had taken this initiative. Built in 1775 for Catherine the Great by Matthew Kazakov, the castle had served solely as a resting place for Paul I and Alexander I when they arrived from the new capital to be solemnly crowned in the old one.[1]

[1] Today it houses the Air Force Academy and has only retained its central, main building.

In the existing uproar, in the midst of the crackle of the flames, the sound of breaking glass, orders shouted at the top of officers' voices and the general confusion, no one had tried to find out if the refuge was habitable. The only thing everyone worried about was getting the Emperor away and finding a way out of the blazing city unharmed.

Their departure from the citadel ringed with flames was something of a gamble. Napoleon sent one of his aides-de-camp, M. de Mortemart, to reconnoitre a passage. When the officer returned to say that there was a clear way through, the Emperor called for his horses. Then, having given orders that a battalion of the Guard should remain behind in occupation of the Kremlin, he took Berthier's arm and calmly descended the great staircase that had once been the scene of the horrible massacre of the Strelitzes, during the reign of Ivan the Terrible. But although he was able to leave by the main door without hindrance, followed by his escort, as he had entered, reach the quay and mount Taurus on the stone bridge (saved by the sappers), he was soon prevented from continuing on his way, assaulted by a gust of wind that hurled a mass of scorching smoke in his face.

It was about four o'clock in the afternoon. The wind had changed again and begun to blow from the south-west; it grew stronger on the quays of the Moskva and the Yauza and acquired such force that at the same moment the Abbé Surrugues thought he could see 'an immense volcano whose crater vomits torrents of flames and smoke'. Another eye-witness saw 'the impetuous wind compress the flames at ground level and then sweep them away into a fine point, like the tongue of flame produced by the blow-pipe of a workman soldering metal'. They all noticed that the ground was so hot that they could not touch it and that it burnt their feet through the soles of their boots. Molten iron and copper ran along the streets.

The frightful cataclysm had made people lose all control. French and Russians were desperately grabbing everything they could lay hands on and the imperial procession could see frantic chases and brawls over precious objects. Sometimes these chases and fights ended brutally in death: pursuers and pursued were caught by the flames or crushed by a falling wall.

In the midst of this inferno, the Emperor had the greatest difficulty in clearing a way. A Russian policeman appeared from heaven knows where. He was promised his life if he would act as guide.

It was a reasonable solution, 'since they were forced to act as at sea, where coastal pilots are taken aboard to avoid the reefs in unknown and dangerous waters'. But the pilot could no longer orientate himself in the streets transformed by destruction. The landmarks —churches and palaces—had disappeared.

The little group was deafened by the wind and blinded by the ashes that flew about and stuck to their skin. The intense heat excited the horses and it was very difficult to keep them to a walking pace. Anatole de Montesquiou recounts that they entered an immense and superb district, the whole of which was burning. There was one avenue that looked safe, but it was an illusion. Obstacles immediately arose; beams tumbled down and roofs caved in. 'Although this street was wide, the flames formed an arch above our heads.' 'We walked,' wrote Philippe de Ségur, 'on an earth of fire, beneath a sky of fire, between two walls of fire. A penetrating heat scorched our eyes, although we had to keep them open and fixed on the danger. A consuming air, sparkling ashes and random flames scorched our short, dry, gasping respiration that was already almost suffocated by the smoke. Our hands burnt when we tried to save our faces and brush away the brands that covered and penetrated our clothes at every moment.' And Montesquiou confirms this: 'We were forced to protect our cheeks, our hands, our eyes with our handkerchiefs, hats and the skirts of our coats.'[1]

The Emperor never stopped grumbling:

'This is going too far! It is a war of extermination, horrible tactics. It is without precedent in the history of civilization. Burning their own towns!'

On their way they came across make-shift gallows from which hung the bodies of incendiaries caught in the act, as a sign attached

---

[1] The accounts of these two eye-witnesses, Montesquieu and Ségur, have been challenged by others who were also on the spot, especially General Gourgaud. (*Napoléon et la Grande Armée en Russie*.) He writes: 'For some time we followed the river bank and entered districts whose wooden buildings were entirely consumed. Although we accompanied Napoleon during the whole of this journey, we did not see the awful horrors that M. de Ségur describes. It is true that we crossed Moscow on ashes. Perhaps we did not take the most direct route, but it is not true that the Emperor ran any danger during this journey.' Although it is obvious that Ségur always amplifies his descriptions and enjoys painting everything in a dramatic light, Montesquiou is more restrained and checking rarely proves him inaccurate or exaggerated. As for Gourgaud, he has a marked penchant for understatement, but we must not forget that he wrote his book for the specific purpose of invalidating, criticising and mocking everything that Ségur had recounted.

to them explained. Other incendiaries had been shot. Their bodies, riddled with bullets, and also with notices fixed to them, lay strewn among the dead horses along the Tver boulevard that led to the north-west gate.

They were advancing too slowly to satisfy anyone and yet time was pressing. And then just at the worst possible moment, the Russian stopped! Obviously he no longer had any idea which way to go and he was terrified. And no wonder! At the same time, the Chevalier d'Ysarn, a Frenchman settled in Moscow since the Revolution, was looking for a refuge and 'saw nothing but flames everywhere. The whole atmosphere above the town,' he wrote to a friend, 'was an ocean of fire that vomited burning brands.' He exclaimed: 'No! Never will the heavens in their wrath show men a more horrible sight: flames everywhere, looters fleeing behind victims and no one knowing where to escape to!'

Napoleon's entourage was unnerved. If their wretched guide dawdled like this, they would be burnt alive in no time! But he seemed to be resigned to this with perfect fatalism: 'God wills it!' At this critical moment, a band of French looters, their arms loaded with booty, and apparently heedless of the flames, caught sight of their Emperor, ran up and offered to lead him to the gate and the Viceroy's camp. They rapidly helped him pass into a sector where there was absolutely no danger, because not a stone had been left standing since noon. At that moment, Napoleon and his escort met Marshal Davout, Prince of Eckmühl, whose headquarters were in a monastery near the Smolensk gate. 'Although suffering from wounds received at the Moskva, he was having himself carried back to the Kremlin to snatch Napoleon from it or perish there with him.' He threw himself into the Emperor's arms 'in rapture'. Napoleon welcomed him, but with the imperturbable calm that was his at critical moments and that he alone of his family had inherited from Madame Mère.

There was one last danger. Before reaching the gate, they met a long convoy of artillery coming up from Mozhaysk, with boxes of ammunition and gunpowder. And this convoy had to make its way along a boulevard that had just caught fire. Passing through the fire, the convoy might easily be blown up and with it the Emperor of France and his suite. After escaping from the danger of the arsenal, Napoleon was now threatened with a new one. But the catastrophe was avoided and that was the last danger they met before their arrival at Petrovskoye at nightfall. They had taken nearly four hours to extricate themselves from the conflagration.

The castle of Petrovskoye loomed up in the darkness. It was an unusual building, surrounded by high brick walls flanked with towers, which the Marquis de Castellane described as 'in a Greek style', as were the columns along the façade. He found that the building as a whole had a 'truly romantic' appearance. Others saw only a 'bizarre-looking eastern construction'. There was some truth in this impression, too. Built to commemorate the victory of Catherine II over the Turks, its architecture was eclectic and freakish. At all events, it had not been looked after and its aura was gloomy rather than romantic. There were no outbuildings; the grounds were overrun. The interior was even gloomier. There was no furniture, not even a chair to sit on. They had to make do with camp beds from Eugène's bivouac, improvised tables and stools. The Emperor was pensive. He spoke to no one and only came out for half an hour to examine the outside of his temporary quarters.

Meanwhile, far from dying down, the fire broke loose furiously in the town. The executed incendiaries could no longer serve as a warning to their accomplices, for there was nothing left for them to do. The wind had carried out their task, 'outstripping all their hands with its infernal breath'. But many of them had been imprisoned and in conformity with orders received, a start was made on judging them on that afternoon of the 16th, during which Napoleon made for the St Petersburg gate at the risk of his life.

The court martial, presided over by General Michel, Commandant of the 1st Regiment of Grenadiers of the Guard, was installed in the Dolgorukov palace. At the first sitting, it condemned to death ten out of twenty-six accused, and sixteen to prison, for oddly enough it estimated that the latter were not 'sufficiently convinced of their crimes'. Among these men were farriers, stone cutters, house painters, policemen, a sexton and a lieutenant of the Moscow regiment. Most of them were assumed identities.

That night a west wind began to blow. It was as impetuous as the day wind and carried clouds of fire to the Red Gate of the Kremlin, the wood market, the old and the new Basmannaya, and the Butchers' Street—the Miassnitzkaya—situated to the east of the Kremlin, and also to the old Foreigners' suburb—the Niemetskaya Sloboda. Now that the east was suffering a general conflagration, it looked as if a sea of fire was flooding the whole town. 'The undulations of the flames agitated by the force of the wind,' noted the Abbé Surrugues (who darted about everywhere, consoling and helping people), 'were an exact imitation of the waves raised by a tempest.' The conflagration was so enormous, so incredible, that many felt it was 'supernatural'. The inhabitants of the Foreigners' suburb, who had been safe until then, fled to seek refuge in the cemeteries. They wandered about there like spectres or people raised from the dead at the Last Judgment, their livid faces lit up by the reflection of the fires nearby. As for the 'Franco–Russians' and the Russians of the Bridge of the Marshals, they could only envisage one safe place: the peripheral camps of the Grand Army.

A certain Marakuyev, a merchant, was on the road that night, not far from Moscow. He noticed in the direction of the great city 'a strong gleam not resembling an ordinary gleam in any way'. On the horizon, the air looked like 'a column heated white-hot that rose quivering from the earth to the sky'. Was Moscow burning? Was it possible? Moscow after Smolensk! He felt that his 'soul was paralysed with pity and terror'.

A strange thing was that, except for the Emperor, the refugees at Petrovskoye felt morbidly attracted to the burning city! Montesquieu confessed: 'After supper we wanted to have another look at this fiery spectacle that was doing us so much harm and to which, in spite of this, we kept returning.' And many of them went back to the immediate outskirts of Moscow. It was pitch dark and the sight was terrifying and grandiose, almost sublime, so closely did it resemble the Apocalypse. The scene changed shape and colour from one minute to another. The fire 'seemed to devour both earth and sky. Great whirlwinds of the densest black arose after the collapse of the largest buildings, making long, broad transverse gashes in and above the flames; one saw volcanoes whose immeasurable eruptions had no limits but the skies'. A vision worthy of a painter or a writer that would have inspired their genius to fantastic and infernal evocations. He ended: 'Often the flames were drawn aside like curtains and displayed to us not only palaces, but also the amphitheatres of palaces, which, at the moment of being devoured, appeared to us thus in a fairylike splendour to bid the world a last goodbye . . .'

The Emperor, who had stayed in bed without sleeping, came out of the palace in the grey dawn and looked at Moscow. The entire city looked like one vast whirlwind of fire 'that rose in a swirling spiral to the sky and coloured it brilliantly'. He saw a 'blazing outline', more than a mile long that resembled a volcano 'with several craters'. (Always the impression of volcanic eruption, that something which reminded people of Pompeii.) Napoleon contemplated this disaster for a very long time in gloomy silence. Some bystanders thought they heard him mutter: 'This betokens great misfortunes for us!' Then, accompanying his words with an expansive sweep of his arms, he cried:

'What an appalling spectacle this blazing town makes! I am losing the reward I had promised my brave army!'

He thought he had foreseen everything: the bloody battle, a long stay in Moscow, a hard winter, perhaps a few minor reverses; but never had his fertile brain even dreamt of this happening—the old capital of Russia destroyed by the Russians themselves. The operational base on which his plans and schemes depended had just been taken from him. This other Eden that he had been promising his army for two months had gone up in smoke. How could they stay there? How could they live like conquerors among the ashes? The memory of other conquered capitals, where it had been so pleasant to linger, was too fresh for the army to accept a stay in Moscow. Like Rostopchin, Napoleon could say, on this ghastly morning: 'Moscow is not Milan, or Vienna or Berlin; it will *not* imitate them and will remain alone in its reactions!'

However, the forces of war at the Emperor's disposal were by no means exhausted. He had left 260,000 men behind him. It was only a question of facing up to this disaster and forming his plans for the morrow. And already he was thinking that the road to the new capital was there, before his eyes, and that it was tempting.

5

ST PETERSBURG AND MOSCOW

The burning of Moscow has illuminated my soul.

ALEXANDER I
to Baroness von Krüdener

ST PETERSBURG was horror-stricken when it learnt of the capture
of Moscow. Already it had visions of Napoleon and his legions at
the gates of the town!

Rostopchin had informed the Tsar by letter dated September
13th of the abandonment of Moscow, news which Kutusov did not
confirm in a letter to his sovereign until the 16th, i.e., three days
later. In his report, the Field-marshal explained the tragic decision
that he had taken at the council of war at Fili, owing to the weaken-
ing of his army after the blood-bath of Borodino. He concluded:
'I venture to point out to Your Majesty, with the expression of all
my devotion, that the enemy's entry into Moscow does not mean
the conquest of Russia.' A sentence which demonstrated once again
the old man's skill in adapting his convictions to the circumstances.
Nevertheless, these words were deeply felt and sincere, even though
they contradicted others spoken or written a few weeks previously.
Henceforth this opinion prevailed and he did not change it again.
Soon events proved him right.

The surrender of the city, which many called 'the heart of
Russia', overwhelmed Alexander, who knew that the whole country
shared his grief. So now his task was to reassure the Russian people
and inspire them with the courage to resist. But he also had to pay
heed to European opinion and think of Sweden and Turkey in
particular. Napoleon, resorting to the policy of Louis XV at the
beginning of the Seven Years' War and during the reign of
Catherine II, had counted on those two countries to strike the
Russian Empire simultaneously in the north and in the south, but
the Turks had signed peace with the Tsar four months before and
the Swedes had opted for Russia. He had to make it absolutely clear
to these allies that Russia was by no means beaten and moreover
that she was determined to conquer.

Consequently the Tsar was anxious to publish Kutusov's report. In a message dated the 17th he had ordered Kutusov to send news of his movements every other day. He accompanied the report by a manifesto, in which nothing was concealed:

'The enemy entered Moscow on September 15th. The dismay that was shown on every face will be understood; but far be it from us to exhibit pusillanimous dejection. Let us rather swear to redouble our perseverance and our courage; let us hope that by fighting for a just cause we shall hurl back on the enemy all the misfortunes he wants to heap on us.'

After this introduction, the sovereign commented on the reasons for the surrender, reasons which he adopted officially, although in reality he was furiously angry with the 'one-eyed satyr'. He concluded, as if he firmly believed it:

'Thus the fleeting triumph of the French Emperor will lead to his inevitable destruction.'

Then he painted a gloomy picture of the enemy's situation:

'We know how painful it is for a Russian to see the devastator of his country in possession of the former capital of the empire. But only the ramparts have fallen into his hands. Abandoned by its inhabitants, deprived of its treasures, it offers a tomb rather than resting-place to the cruel aggressor who would like to erect a new throne there on the ruins of our empire.

'This vainglorious devastator of kingdoms hoped, by taking Moscow, to become the arbiter of our destinies and dictate peace to us. His expectations have been disappointed: he finds in Moscow neither means of domination nor even the means of subsistence.'

At that moment, the last assertion was pure propaganda, because Alexander was not informed of the fire until September 20th.[1] Moscow, as the cruel aggressor would have found it had there been no fire, would certainly have been empty, but in no way devoid of means of subsistence for the Grand Army. The Tsar also anticipated

---

[1] We are not entitled to exclude the hypothesis that he could have been informed of it sooner. But to the best of our knowledge there is no formal proof that he was. The allusion to the 'tomb' seems to be a reference to Rostopchin's letter of September 13: (p. 39) '. . . Moscow will be a desert in his hands . . . and may become his tomb.' (Cf. also Conclusion, p. 186 ff.)

a little—although he showed himself a good prophet in his anticipation—in describing his army as ready to close in upon Napoleon:

'Our forces, which are increasing daily, surround Moscow; they occupy all the roads and will destroy all the detachments that the enemy sends looking for provisions.

'Is there a man in the Russian empire so cowardly as to despair, when all classes of the State are breathing vengeance, when the enemy, deprived of resources and seeing his forces diminish daily, finds himself in the midst of a powerful nation, surrounded by our armies, one of which threatens him from in front, while the other three are intercepting his relief troops and cutting off his retreat? Can this situation alarm a true Russian?'

This meant that he was relying on the two armies of the West, united under the command of Kutusov since Smolensk,[1] the so-called reserve army commanded by the Cavalry General, Tormassov, and the army of the South, or 'Moldavian army', under Admiral Tschitschagov, which had been available since the ratification of the treaty with the Sublime Porte. In conclusion he also made a long statement about the valour of the Russian troops and the dangerous situation of the enemy armies. With a certain grandiloquence, he made this deduction from them:

'The evils of the human race have reached their climax; we need only look around us to see the calamities of war and the cruelties of ambition in all their horror; but we brave them to maintain our liberty and in the interests of humanity. We feel that ours is a righteous action and immortal honour will be the reward of a nation, which, by enduring the evils of a cruel war, by resisting with constancy and courage the man who spreads it everywhere, will obtain a lasting peace, not only for itself, but also for the unfortunate nations that the tyrant has forced to fight in support of his personal quarrel. It is noble, it is worthy of a great people, to return good for evil . . .'

This momentous proclamation, which the sad and dismayed Alexander undoubtedly wanted to believe in with all his heart, was brought to a pious close by an invocation to the Almighty:

[1] At the beginning of hostilities, the first Russian army of the West was commanded by the Infantry General and Minister of War, Barclay de Tolly, the second by the Infantry General, Prince Bagration, who fell at Moskva.

'Almighty God! Is not the cause for which we fight a just one? Cast a merciful eye on Thy Holy Church! Preserve the courage and constancy of this people! May it triumph over its and Thy adversary. May it be in Thy hands the instrument of his destruction and, by delivering itself, redeem the liberty and independence of nations and kings!'

In other words: a national war, a holy war and a war for the happiness of Europe 'enslaved by the tyrant'.

This proclamation bore fruit abroad. Sweden remained true to its alliance with Russia. The Sultan, who had equivocated when he learnt of the fall of Moscow, was impressed by the manifesto. He held as many as three Divans and finally decided to respect the recently ratified treaty. England rejoiced. The 'unfortunate nations that the tyrant has forced to fight'—Austria and Prussia—were thrilled with hope. And yet in the Winter Palace, in the ministries and in private houses, there was talk of evacuation. Apparently in higher spheres they regarded the manifesto simply as a necessary panacea. Had not the Sovereign himself set an example by having some of his treasures put aboard Russian vessels at Archangel and Åbo. It was arranged that this cargo would make for Great Britain at the first signal. So after that it was not surprising that the evacuation from St Petersburg of the cadet corps (the Military Academy) and the Institute for Noble Young Ladies was envisaged; people even wanted to remove the equestrian statue of Peter the Great, the work of Falconet, the glory and talisman of the capital, from its stone plinth to the safety of Archangel. Joseph de Maistre, Minister of Sardinia in Russia, who did not believe that the country could resist and was convinced that Napoleon was going to take St Petersburg, uttered a theatrical cry: 'There is no more Russia! Behind us there is nothing left but Spitzbergen!'

The Dowager Empress felt a strong urge to flee, but on thinking it over decided that her place was with her son; however, she provided the court with 'a spectacle of the most violent perturbation'. The Grand-duchess Catherine Pavlovna's confinement was imminent, so she was sent off to Yaroslav, in spite of her protests. Only the Tsar's wife, the Empress Elizabeth Alexeyevna, remained fearless and believed from the bottom of her heart in the truth of what her beloved husband had published in his manifesto. This German princess had no hesitation in writing to her family: 'So here we are with this horde of barbarians quartered among the ruins of our beautiful capital, but Napoleon will only succeed in exciting the wrath of the nation!'

She was right, of course, and it was also increasingly obvious that Alexander's statement that 'our forces are increasing daily' was coming true. For the partisan movement, born rather experimentally on the day after Borodino, was becoming bigger and more important. Kutusov had agreed to detach his best officers to advise and command these units formed spontaneously by the peasants, who were joined by officials and squireens. Cossacks and hussars were also seconded to them. The *franc-tireurs* were grouped in detachments under the command of the pioneer of this movement, Lieutenant-colonel Denis Davidov, of Captain Dorokhov,[1] who had two thousand men under him, of the brothers Figner, of Commandant Sesslavin, not to mention untrained but remarkable leaders such as the peasant Tschetvertakov. Highly mobile, daring and full of initiative, they were ready to conduct minor operations in the most arduous and unforeseen conditions. Thanks to their genius for being everywhere at once and their relentlessness, they rapidly encircled Moscow like a ring, like a 'moving, fortified wall'; they transformed villages into funeral pyres or fortresses, pursued and wiped out French detachments. Scouring the lines of communications, emerging from sunken roads, copses and woods, sending spearheads right into the army corps' positions, harassing the vanguard, treading on the heels of the rearguard, they literally became the 'hydra with a hundred heads' of which Napoleon spoke later, 'this scourge of God' that the Grand Army feared perhaps even more than fire and frost.

While St Petersburg was in a flurry and the Emperor was champing at the bit at Petrovskoye, at Moscow the conflagration was as terrifying as ever.

The army's Surgeon General, Baron Dominique Larrey, lived through every minute of it on the night of September 15th and said later: 'it would be difficult, under any imaginable circumstances, to find a more horrible sight than that which pained our eyes.' The weather was dry. The wind, always violent, changed incessantly, veering mainly fron north to east, then backing from east to north.

---

[1] The model for Dolokhov in *War and Peace*.

Dense, brilliantly coloured columns of flame rose up everywhere, covering the whole horizon and spreading 'a dazzling light and burning heat' far and wide. 'Hurled in every direction and swept along by the force of the wind,' the flames were accompanied by a 'dreadful whistling and by tremendous explosions caused by the combustion of the explosives, saltpetre, oils, resins and spirits with which the majority of the houses and shops were filled'. Baron Larrey and his assistants (far too few to look after so many sick and wounded) spent some terrible moments because of the panic which reigned in the hospitals during the day of the 16th. A great number of their patients, seeing the flames springing up on all sides and having no faith in the efficiency of the safety pickets, jumped out of the windows; they were crushed on the pavement or died of haemorrhages, because their wounds reopened. Such was the chaos that it was impossible to count the number of victims, but it was believed that about a thousand perished in this way!

On the morning of September 17th, Larrey was in a house situated at the top of what he called 'the free district', i.e. the Bridge of the Marshals. The fire had begun to attack the bottom of this thoroughfare and the French shops were in danger. Their owners, who lived in the vicinity, ran to seek shelter in the Church of Saint-Louis-des-Français, where the Abbé Surrugues was saying mass. He exhorted them to keep calm, then blessed them, after which he went to the scene of the fire, showered with falling sparks and bits of flaming wood, and found that a detachment of grenadiers was already hard at work, armed with buckets, and wetting the roofs of the most exposed houses. It was not long before the French district was saved, and with it the General Post Office and the bank. Since the wind fortunately did not blow in that direction again, the Bridge of the Marshals remained miraculously intact. Napoleon and his army would disappear, Moscow would be reborn from its ashes, the Muscovites would resume their delightful daily round and the French shops would flower again with the spring.

But elsewhere everything was crackling and cracking. The actress Louise Fusil, still sheltering with a group of French friends in the Gagarin palace, which was untouched so far, decided to go to ask Marshal Mortier for a safety picket. It was a risky venture. She had to make hundreds of detours. She saw looters everywhere. People were queueing outside the door of the governor's house. Discouraged, Mme Fusil decided to return to the palace, but the boulevard by which she had come was already in flames. She took another route and came to the Grand Theatre which, being built of wood—Moscow did not yet possess a fine 'modern' auditorium—was one immense bonfire. Turning off into an alley, she was struck in the face by a gust of wind which drove the flames with such force that 'they joined up with the flames on the other side and formed a dome of fire'. A young officer in the Horse Guards gallantly offered to escort the lone woman, perhaps still quite pretty, who seemed to him to be heading recklessly for destruction. She accepted gladly and on the way, in spite of the terrifying surroundings through which they were walking, listened to him 'chatting very nicely' about fashions and the theatre! But the smoke enveloped them, making them gasp and getting into their eyes and up their noses. The actress was in a great hurry to get back to her haven. Imagine her horror, when she finally reached the street, on seeing the Gagarin palace, where two hours before 'there had not been the sign of a spark', completely in the grip of the flames! The occupants had taken refuge in a nearby pavilion. The young cavalry officer advised Mme Fusil and her companions to go to Petrovskoye as fast as possible. Then he rode off in that direction at a headlong gallop.

The little group of victims piled the few objects they had been able to save onto a cart and tried to reach the North-West gate. It was too late. They could not find one street where they could pass. There were gleams of fire, blazing buildings and smoking ruins on all sides. The corpses of executed incendiaries and victims of the fire lay about at all the crossroads. The licentious soldiery was drunk and out of control. There were chases and brawls. The only thing to do was seek some place of refuge, but it was no easy matter. Louise Fusil wrote: 'This town, which I had seen looking so rich and brilliant only a short time before, was nothing but a heap of ashes and ruins through which we wandered like ghosts who come to haunt their former homes. We went from street to street, from house to house: everything bore the marks of devastation . . .'

These exhausted, demoralized wanderers ended by camping in a deserted house that had been stripped bare by looters.

During this time, a fellow-countryman of Mme Fusil, the Chevalier d'Ysarn, who had first sheltered in the cellar of his house when it caught fire, finally left, mounted on a cart drawn by two horses 'saved from the shipwreck'. When they reached the Pokrovka, an avenue leading to the East gate, the Chevalier and one of his friends, M. de Trassène, were stopped by an insuperable obstacle. Light cavalrymen blocked their way and unharnessed one of the two horses, after which they flung themselves on the two 'Franco-Russians', removed their boots and took their watches and money. They protested that they were French and received a coarse retort, like a blow in the face:

'I don't give a damn if you're French! What the hell are you doing here? Only worthless Frenchmen are not fighting with us. You're bloody emigrés!'

However they gave them boots, which were too small and down at heel, and let them go, saying that they were very lucky to keep their coats. Disgusted, they turned back, their 'costume showing they were sufferers from the fire and their wretched boots acting as a suitable passport'. Further on they had another encounter. This time it was a general on horseback whom d'Ysarn (rightly or wrongly) took for General Sebastiani in person. The latter spoke to him:

'Do you speak French, Monsieur?'

'Yes, Monsieur.'

'What on earth are your Russians doing? Has anyone ever seen a capital set on fire like this?'

'I do not know who burnt it, but the results are deadly enough for us.'

'It was your Cossacks, to all appearances!'

(The General took the Chevalier for a real Russian, which was very lucky for him!)

'And where do you see any Cossacks now?' asked d'Ysarn, in exasperation.

'They're at the gates of the town, of course! That's not waging war!'

'They are measures of despair,' retorted the Chevalier, and he was bold enough to add: 'Measures which will bury us all.'

He continued on his way, less afraid of the fire than of the soldiers who were 'rummaging, breaking in doors and windows, forcing cellars and storehouses', while the unfortunate victims of the fire were undressed and had their shoes removed in the street. Many were raped. Muscovites 'hidden in the most secret places were robbed without daring to protest' by the first man to discover

them. They were lucky not to be assassinated! This all went on to
the ghastly background noise: the fall of sheets of metal and pine-
wood beams, the collapse of whole façades and the cries of people
and animals, a deafening din unbroken for forty-eight hours and
all the more impressive because it followed immediately on the heels
of the unusual silence of the great abandoned town. And all the
time there was this nightmare that the Marquis de Chambray—
among so many, many others—could never forget: 'During the
day whirlwinds of smoke that rise up on all sides, forming a thick
cloud that obscures the light of the sun; and at night, flames mixed
with these whirlwinds, which cast an eerie light far and wide . . .'
So far, in fact, that at the castle of Petrovskoye, 'the light of the
fire was so bright that we did not need illumination to read by'—
always provided that there had been any books.

They had no books and not much desire to read, but they had
maps and the Emperor pored over them, trying to establish a plan
of action for the immediate future. In his present situation marching
on St Petersburg seemed the best solution to him. The road to the
north was free, covered by a single army corps under the command
of General Count von Wittgenstein, against whom the 4th Corps
under the Viceroy would drive as a spearhead, manœuvring in such
a way as to surprise the Russians in the rear. Joining the 9th Corps
of Marshal Victor, Duke of Belluno, and the 10th Corps of Marshal
MacDonald, Duke of Tarento, all the forces would then be
assembled on the Lower Duna before October 15th, supported by
Smolensk on one side and Riga on the other. Then the Russian
government would beg for mercy. This project, carefully thought
out on the morning of September 17th, met with the approval of
no one except Eugène de Beauharnais. The others urged the need
for a well-earned rest and care for the wounded. Rest? Was it
possible to rest in this town which had been consumed?

'Don't believe for one moment,' said the Emperor, 'that the men
who burnt Moscow are likely to come and make peace a few days
later!'

It was the first and last time that he uttered this lucid opinion.
During the rest of the Russian campaign, he proved just as prompt
to uphold contradictory opinions as his opponent, Field-marshal
Kutusov. From this time on it was Napoleon's entourage who
asserted vehemently that the Russians would not make peace, while

F

Napoleon himself, in the face of all logic and probability, held the opposite opinion to his first conviction—which had been right.

Meanwhile, to kill the time that weighed on his hands, he wanted to be enlightened about the mentality of the Russian people and looked for a suitable tutor.

Who was it suggested to the Emperor that he should consult Marie-Rose Chalmé, owner of a flourishing milliner's shop on the Bridge of the Marshals, wife of Jean-Nicholas Aubert, native, like herself, of Château-Salins, and manager of a big Moscow hotel? She was about thirty; she was beautiful, charming, 'respectable and respected', highly valued by her aristocratic Russian clients and popular in the French colony at Moscow. But that certainly did not make her an expert in political and economic questions! However, she was the person Napoleon sent for at dawn on the 17th from a camp of the 4th Corps where she had taken refuge.

Because she had left Moscow with what she had on her back, hastening away with her children, she could not make her toilette to present herself at Petrovskoye. But neither could she evade the invitation. So she was very simply dressed and seated in a miserable droshky when she arrived at the gate of the castle, where Marshal Mortier, Duke of Treviso, welcomed her in person, gave her his hand and led her into a large, luxuriously decorated, but empty hall, where the Emperor was waiting in a window recess. He said to her:

'You are very unhappy, *madame*, so I understand?'

They at once began a conversation about which some mystery remains. A little later, Marie-Rose Chalmé confided to the Chevalier d'Ysarn (who always took great care not to compromise himself with the occupying forces) that Napoleon had asked her what she thought of 'the idea of giving the peasants their freedom'. The lady assured him that she had replied: 'I think, Your Majesty, that one-third would perhaps appreciate the boon and that the other two-thirds would have no idea what you were trying to do for them.'

We know nothing else except that an hour later the lady was dismissed and taken back to the military camp with the same ceremony as at her arrival. No light has ever been cast on the real reason for her visit—or rather on the reason for Napoleon's summoning her. Had Marie-Rose boasted to the Viceroy's lieutenants that she had some valuable information? Was she, as many Russians thought afterwards, a spy who had been in the service of the imperial government for a long time? It has also been suggested that it might have been an amorous adventure, but a contingency of that sort in such a place seems most unlikely. In short, we know nothing definite about this interview. What is known, on the other hand, is that the *fatal honour* of having talked to the French Emperor turned Mme Aubert-Chalmé into a pitiful victim. Compromised in the eyes of both the Russians and the 'Franco–Russians' who had stayed well away from the conquerors, both of them fearing reprisals and ostracism, the unfortunate woman followed the Grand Army on its retreat, taking her children, from whom she was separated while on the road. Her husband stayed in Moscow with a clear conscience and was not bothered by the Russian authorities when they returned to resume their duties. He died there in 1826 at the age of fifty-four. But his poor wife died prematurely at Vilna, carried off by a swift illness which people said was typhus.

Throughout the day of Thursday, September 17th, the Emperor was in a taciturn mood. He frequently went outside to watch Moscow glowing and smoking. Couriers arrived continuously to tell him what was happening in the town and describe the looting 'which the fire had made only too legitimate'. Napoleon thought that he would need eight full days to reconstruct his army, to 'gather up the remains from Moscow and drag his soldiers from their great quarry'.

During the night of the 17th, towards three in the morning, heavy rain began to fall, which largely reduced the fire—without extinguishing it—and put the finishing touches to the distress of the homeless. In the morning everything seemed to be over in the heart of the town, but houses were still burning in the suburbs. Here and there new fires broke out, and soldiers discovered more incendiaries, who did not belong to Rostopchin's working parties; they were inhabitants, reduced to despair, who were finishing off the work of destruction. The soldiers who found them shot them on the spot. They lay where they fell, alongside the corpses which were strewn on all sides—the charred bodies of men, horses and dogs.

The Emperor did not want to remain inactive at Petrovskoye any longer. There was every kind of work to be done in the Kremlin. So, as soon as he woke on the 18th, he ordered an immediate return.

Already he had changed his mind and now he declared that the Tsar was going to ask for mercy after the disaster. What good fortune for France and Europe: 'The peace of Moscow will end my warlike expeditions. It will be the end of risks, the beginning of security. A new horizon, new work to be done!'

He was reverting to an idea that he had been nursing for a long time—the same system everywhere; a European legal code, a European court of appeal; one monetary system, the same weights, the same measures, the same laws. Soon he saw Europe 'forming on single people'. 'Everyone, wherever he travels, will always find himself in the common fatherland,' he said. (At St Helena he developed at length for his companions the plan for a *European association* that he had worked upon at Moscow.)

His entourage no longer knew what to think of his projects. Had he not said himself, only yesterday, that the Russians were not the people to make peace after having sacrificed their venerable capital? They respectfully reminded him of this. He retorted testily: 'We shall see what the Russians will do. If they refuse to negotiate, we shall have to make the best of it.'

He returned to Moscow on the morning of Friday, September 18th.[1]

[1] The dates September 19th and 20th, reported by many writers, are wrong, as is proved by letters and decrees from the Kremlin dated the 18th. Another proof, based on an irrefutable fact: it was on the 18th, the actual day of his return, that Napoleon received the Russian Councillor of State, Ivan Tutolmin, in the Kremlin (cf. next chapter, p. 99).

THE EMPEROR'S RETURN

*The thirty-four days' stay in Moscow is an enigma
that nothing can explain : it was the result either
of incredible blindness or of the prestige surrounding a conqueror who triumphed over the whole of
Europe.*

LANGERON
General in the Russian army in 1812, *Mémoires*

BEFORE reaching the gate, Napoleon and his suite traversed the
Viceroy's camps, which were a fantastic sight. 'In the middle of the
fields,' wrote Ségur, 'in thick, cold mud, were vast fires fed with
mahogany furniture, window frames and gilded doors.' Army men
of all ranks—for the officers had looted like the soldiers, carrying
off from their billets everything they fancied—army men splashed
with mud, blackened with smoke, harassed, besotted and many of
them very drunk, lolled in Louis XV easy chairs or on silk sofas.
At their feet was an incongruous mass, the fruits of intensive looting: cashmire shawls, pieces of brocade, 'the rarest furs from
Siberia, cloth of gold from Persia', miniatures, curios and clocks.
Among these soldiers of the Grand Army, that 'Babel on the march'
(as Major Marion wrote to Major Thiébault the very same day), in
the midst of all these French, Prussians, Bavarians, Saxons,
Würtembergers, Swiss and Poles, apparently heedless of their
appearance and their discipline, wandered Russian civilians and
Franco–Muscovites, watching jealously over the few familiar, useless objects they had saved from the fire. The refugees felt in
comparative safety here, since the troops either paid little attention
to them or tolerated them good-naturedly.

Nobody, military or civilian, had much to eat and they were
cooking 'a black hotch-potch and half-grilled horse-flesh running
blood' in silver utensils on fires stoked with the valuable furniture
of Russian aristocrats. 'A curious admixture of abundance and
want, of wealth and filth, of luxury and misery!' exclaimed a
witness.

Over the short distance that separated the camps from the town, the imperial procession met more large groups of soldiers dragging their booty behind them. Some of them were so outlandishly clothed after despoiling citizens or cupboards that they 'could only be recognized by their arms!'

This return to Moscow was infinitely sad. The disordered scenes they had just witnessed brought the spirits of Napoleon and his entourage to their lowest ebb. Once they had passed through the gate and entered the town, they found not a trace of the resplendent Moscow that had made the hearts of all who had seen it from the Mount of Salutation beat faster. 'Happy are those who have not seen this terrifying spectacle, this picture of destruction!' exclaimed the Duke of Vicenza. Immediately noisome fumes rising from charred carcases and rotting corpses caught at everyone's throat. In places the acrid smoke was suffocating. 'What an incredible sight!' cried the Emperor, looking around him. 'Is this all that remains of the great Moscow?'

Indeed the vision that unfolded before him and the men returning with him after their very brief absence was most distressing. Here an isolated house rose, intact in a field of ruins: there it was 'a scene à la Piranesi, of ruined walls, the debris of peristyles, half-burnt trees and a great number of chimneys that seemed like tall columns from a certain distance'. Elsewhere, only a pillar or a façade marked the course of a street that had ceased to exist. Haggard, famished-looking men, women and children in rags and tatters, who looked as if they had emerged from a madhouse, wandered about among the rubbish, 'some giving way to a terrible despair, others showing gloomy resignation'. Many of them squatted in kitchen-gardens and grubbed in the earth with their hands in the hope of finding some stray vegetables; when they found a cabbage or a potato they devoured it on the spot, although it was covered with earth and often rotten. In places a church remained untouched and its gold and blue domes seemed just as unreal as the black ruins they dominated.

Before the ventilators of cellars, nearly all intact, French soldiers and Russian civilians quarrelled over a sugar-loaf or a bottle of champagne or brandy. Others 'fraternised' and went off together, rummaging everywhere, breaking in doors and windows, exploring depots and stores. The mansions and palaces that were spared or torn open offered their abandoned riches to all comers; looters had managed to find silver-gilt table services, jewels and even diamonds, not to mention great quantities of clothes and furs in wardrobes and chests-of-drawers. Astonishing and unexpected booty that spoke eloquently of headlong departures and carelessness born of panic. Groups of soldiers were standing about everywhere, sharing or trading their discoveries. The ravaged squares of Moscow-the-Dead had become markets. There was buying, selling and barter. The rarest objects, unappreciated by their new owners, were sold at ridiculous prices. The trafficking was tremendous. The officers were just as keen and, according to Captain Coignet, 'seeking to do good business, ranged through the town like wild beasts in a charnel house'. In fact, the colonel of his regiment spotted Coignet, who was carrying a sable; he hailed him and relieved him of his treasure in return for a small fox fur. (The sable was sold to the King of Naples for 3,000 francs.) Count Philippe de Ségur, who formed part of the imperial escort, noticed soldiers 'seated on piles of sugar and coffee, in the midst of the most exquisite wines and liqueurs, which they wanted to exchange for a piece of bread'. Several, in a state of drunkenness increased by inanition, had collapsed near flames that eventually reached and killed them. Soldiers, *vivandières* and prostitutes were hurriedly putting bales of merchandise in safety.

The looting was then at its height. The French were not the worst culprits and during the days to come it was other nationalities that gave the inhabitants more cause to complain. The Abbé Surrugues, an eye-witness, did the French that justice and blamed the *horrible chaos* on the foreign troops. A certain Beauchamp made the same observation. A German in the service of Russia, he states: 'Justice alone extracts this confession from me, for during the Seven Years' War I imbibed hatred of the French from infancy . . . They did not do pointless damage. Even in the midst of their excesses their courtesy showed through.' In this army, which had the misfortune of being such a mixture, 'Würtembergers and Poles behave like vandals; the French only rob to satisfy the necessities of life, the Bavarians leave nothing behind them.'

The closer they managed to get to the Kremlin, the more conscious the officers surrounding Napoleon became of the indiscipline, but when they tried to intervene they found that the disaster had so inflamed the soldiery that all respect and obedience had gone. They attracted sharp, mocking retorts:

'Do you think we're going to leave all this to the fire?'

'The Muscovites did their best to destroy everything. So much the worse for them!'

'We have a right to take everything we can lay hands on.'

The fact had to be accepted that looting was a necessity. Indeed, according to the Marquis de Fezensac, Colonel of the 18th Infantry Regiment, it was 'the only resource', so he decided to give his soldiers 'tacit permission to take their share'. Many officers shared his opinion and muttered into their moustaches: 'Must we let them perish of hunger and misery when all this is theirs for the taking?'

'Why all this respect for the fire?'

'What's left in this city comes under the same law as the remains of a conquered army's arms, which belong to the victor by right; have not the Muscovites used their capital as an engine of war to destroy us?'

The Count de Ségur, however, showed his disapproval and he was taken to task for it by General Gourgaud: 'How easy it is,' he exclaimed, 'to be scandalized when your place is laid at the Emperor's table twice a day!' There was a great difference between looting and taking provisions! What harm was there in poor regimental officers taking some foodstuffs and a few bottles of wine when they saw a house or a large shop burning.

As they struggled on through the streets—or what had once been streets—obstructed by blackened bodies, broken crockery, books, furniture and debris, everyone was forced to realize that they were placed in a completely new, unforeseen and unforeseeable situation. No comparisons could be made with what had happened elsewhere; Berlin, Dresden, Lisbon and Vienna were not Moscow. In the midst of riches that no longer belonged to anyone and were disappearing under the rubble, the difference between right and wrong was no longer discernible. 'There is no set rule.' At the most they could try to regulate the looting, to organize marauding 'like any other military mission'. There was only one criterion: the operations had to be 'profitable'. In Gourgaud's view, to speak of 'looting' would be 'an abuse of language and an unspeakable harshness'.

But if they imagined that serious control was possible, they were being taken in with fine words and they were blind if they did not foresee the indiscipline, degradation and demoralization that would arise from this legal brigandage. Soon it would be too late to regret that Moscow had become another Capua. 'Moscow is the sponge that will absorb the Grand Army,' Marshal Kutusov had said at the council of war at Fili on September 13th.

But the Emperor's path was not lined with depressing sights only; there were also ludicrous scenes, contrasting bizarrely with the prevailing desolation. Napoleon, mounted on a horse already christened *Moscou*, was surprised to meet men dressed only in their shirts, but shod with new shoes, and others elegantly clad, but bare-foot. Some of them, who had been absolutely destitute, had plundered the French shops of the Bridge of the Marshals that had remained intact. They wore hats with flowers and silk 'palatines' on their shoulders; there were even French officers on horseback wearing satin pelisses lined with fur, in spite of the mild weather.

There was something repellent about it all that made everyone want to depart as quickly as possible. How disastrous it would be to stay in such surroundings! But the Emperor exclaimed: 'I and the Kremlin—we are still standing!'

Yes, the citadel was intact; a battalion of the Imperial Guard had preserved it. Unfortunately preserved it, as Ségur and the others thought. An uninhabitable Kremlin had been their last hope of a prompt departure. With no residence worthy of him, Napoleon would not have hesitated to abandon the destroyed town, 'the fallen colossus'. But now he was quite determined to re-install himself there, for his great preoccupation, his most fervent desire, his supreme goal, was 'the peace of Moscow':

'To leave the old capital of Russia, once I have arrived there, without having signed the preliminaries to peace,' he said to General de Caulaincourt, 'would look like a political defeat, whatever the military advantages of another position.'

Meanwhile, he wrote to Marie Louise, to whom he had sent no news since his departure from Petrovskoye:

'My dear, I have already written to you about Moscow. I had no idea about this town. It had 500 palaces as fine as the Elysée-Napoléon, furnished in the French style with incredible luxury, several imperial palaces, barracks and magnificent hospitals.[1] It has

---

[1] At St Helena, Napoleon described these hospitals to Las Cases, specifying that the big military hospital was 'one of the best built, vastest and most beautiful' he had ever seen.

all disappeared, fire has been consuming everything for four days. As all the small houses of the bourgeois are of wood, they catch fire like matches. It was the Governor and the Russians who, furious at being conquered, set fire to this beautiful town. 200,000 worthy inhabitants are in despair, in the street and in misery. However, there is enough left for the army, and the army has found no lack of riches of all kinds, for everything is exposed to looting in this upheaval. This loss is immense for Russia; its trade will suffer a great shock from it. These wretched people had carried their precautions so far as to remove or destroy the fire-engines. My cold is over. My health good. Adieu my dear. All my love.

NAP.

Moscow, 18 7bre.[1]

'There is enough left for the army...' Was this to reassure Marie Louise, and through her the court and Paris, or did Marshal Mortier already know that the victuals and fodder, mainly collected from the cellars, 'can suffice the whole army throughout the winter'? In any case, that seems to have been true: Daru, who had ten years' hard experience as Quartermaster-general behind him, shared his opinion. Later, Baron Larrey wrote: 'The provisions found at Moscow were adequate to feed the army for six months.'

The army, perhaps, but not the horses. Moreover, Lieutenant-general the Marquis de Fezensac was not nearly so optimistic:

'We were short of nearly everything,' he wrote. 'We only managed to procure black bread and beer with difficulty; meat began to get very scarce. We had to send strong detachments to seize cattle in the woods where the peasants had taken refuge, and often these detachments returned at night empty-handed. Such was the supposed abundance that looting brought us... The army had liqueurs and jam, but was short of meat and bread. The soldiers covered themselves with furs, but soon they no longer had clothes or shoes. In short, with diamonds, precious stones and all the luxury objects imaginable, we were on the verge of dying of hunger.'

However, there were no real difficulties about quarters. Only 5 out of 30,000 dwellings still stood, but they were stone houses and spacious ones, which could house large numbers. Moreover, there

[1] *Lettres*, op. cit. (No. 94).

was still time, before winter, to organize more comfortable camps on the outskirts of the town. There was plenty of room, too, in the untouched suburban convents and the vast outlying domains of the nobility, which had all been spared by the disaster. All, except one: Count Rostopchin's, Voronovo. The Governor had set fire to it with his own hands. On top of that, on the signpost indicating the road to the castle, he had stuck a poster—the last one—that only made Napoleon shrug his shoulders when it was brought to him.

'For eight years I have beautified this countryside and I lived happily here with my family. The inhabitants of this estate, numbering 1,720, leave at your approach, and as for me, I set fire to my house so that it will not be defiled by your presence. Frenchman, I have abandoned my two houses in Moscow to you, with furniture worth half a million roubles; here you will find nothing but ashes . . .'

It was a sort of visiting card, a frank confession of what he had done elsewhere, the small-scale model of his great machine. Like *his* town, he had immolated *his* house.

This poster, which the Emperor had sent to Paris as proof of Rostopchin's barbarity, 'found more admirers than censors', according to some evidence.

This 'silly joke' neither added to nor subtracted from the situation, which, Napoleon was forced to admit, had changed radically within the space of four days because of the fire. The triumphant arrival of the Grand Army in Moscow had been robbed of all its brilliance. They had not marched so far, suffered so much and sacrificed so many men merely to see the flames devouring their rosiest dreams! From this point on, was it necessary to winter in Moscow?

The Emperor hesitated. At times he envisaged falling back on Vyazma and Smolensk, which would have been the wisest course. 'But,' he said, 'they are poor districts that offer few resources and where we would be ill-equipped to spend eight months in winter quarters.' Poland? Perhaps. He gave Marie Louise to understand that he could have her brought there. Of course, he would have to move closer to his operational bases and the reinforcements he had urgently demanded after the hecatomb of Borodino, and also shorten his lines of communication. But . . . his prestige! But . . . to appear, in the eyes of France and Europe, to have yielded to the elements, to the 'uncivilized method' employed by the Russian people to fight the invader. But . . . peace could only be made at Moscow. All these *buts* operated against Napoleon and lost him precious time. When 'General Winter' and Marshal Kutusov finally came to assault him hand in hand, when famine, superhuman fatigue and destruction swept down on his troops, when Berthier cried out in desperation: 'Sire, the army is no more!' then the Emperor gave way to belated regrets: 'Everything has gone wrong because I stayed in Moscow too long,' he admitted to the Duke of Vicenza.

Thirty-five days too long, which were to be the beginning of the end.

'I should have died after entering Moscow!' he confessed to Gourgaud at St Helena, one day when he was feeling melancholic. While on the island he was often to repeat to his faithful companions: 'I defeated armies, but I could not conquer the flames.' In fact, the burning of the town he coveted so much was the Emperor's first great defeat. He was all the more at a loss, because this defeat had not taken place on a battle-field and was not brought about by a gifted strategist. He was well aware of the lesson to be drawn from it. He ought to leave and prepare his revenge. However, he did not take that decision. Every day and several times a day he favoured departure, then decided to wait. He wanted to put people on a false scent to hide his embarrassment and kept saying that he would leave as soon as the Tsar sent him peace proposals:

'Only his fear of finding me demanding prevents him from approaching me.'

Every day he waited, hoping for a message from Alexander. 'The difficulty consists solely in the manner of broaching the subject suitably,' he repeated. And knowing all the time that he was wrong, he prolonged his stay in Moscow.

Napoleon was worried about what the Tsar was doing, but for the moment scarcely bothered his head about the Russian troops. According to him, 'they are in no fit state to conduct a campaign'. In actual fact, he did not even know exactly where they were.

If the French Emperor did not know the movements of the old Russian marshal, the monarch of all the Russias was equally ignorant of them, which was more paradoxical. 'I have not had a line from Kutusov since August 29th (Sept. 10th): it's scarcely credible!' he wrote on September 19th (n.s.). This meant that the commander-in-chief had not written to him since his letter announcing the abandonment of Moscow.[1] He felt as if he were groping his way in the dark.

However, Napoleon was not completely ignorant about what the enemy was doing, but as it was Murat who informed him, the news was unreliable. 'The King still had visions of the Russian army — taking flight on the road to Kazan, the soldiers deserting, disbanding by troops, the Cossacks even preparing to make common cause with the conqueror.' The fact was that the King of Naples was the victim of his own game. It had become a distraction of which he was sorely in need. 'I'm bored, I'm bored,' he confided to an aide-de-camp. 'I want to go to Naples to look after my subjects!' Then, in the absence of Neapolitans, he turned to the Cossack chiefs 'who overwhelm him with continual flattery', while he never stopped giving them 'signs of his munificence'. Once that situation was established, how could he see that they were trying to mislead him?

Although he doubted their veracity, Murat's messages gave Napoleon a certain satisfaction, annoyed as he was at being unable to situate the enemy on a map. He knew his brother-in-law too well! The Cossacks were supposed to be 'on the point of leaving the Russian army'? And the Russians still marching on Kazan, to the east? Indeed!

'Murat is their dupe,' he cried. 'Kutusov cannot possibly have stayed on this road: he is covering neither St Petersburg nor the southern provinces.'

He sent orders to the King of Naples to change his route, move further west and 'reconnoitre in different directions'. But the King merely did as he pleased, idling away his time, advancing casually, pretending to spare the Cossack rear-guard, showing off and not suspecting for a moment that this rear-guard was nothing but a toy offered by Kutusov to amuse him. The Cossack cavalry of General Vassiltchikov had been launched in the direction of Ryazan to confuse the French, at the same time covering the march of the one-eyed leader. The 'screen of Cossacks' was a smoke screen;

[1] At this date, the Tsar does not appear to have received a letter from Kutusov dated September 4th/16th, an extremely important letter, because it says in particular: 'With the troops I have succeeded in saving, I am moving on the road to Tula, which will enable me to defend this town, where the most important arms factory is situated, and Briansk, where there are equally important foundries. I am also protecting all the resources that our most fertile provinces contain . . . as well as my liaison with the armies of Tormassov and Tschitschagov.

Murat and Sebastiani, his right-hand man, were pursuing a chimera.

How had Kutusov fooled his adversary? After he had got his army through Moscow, he had slipped out of the town moving at night by the gleams of the growing fire. His troops, seeing the flames rise over the venerable city, accused the French, making an uproar and crying for vengeance. Their commander took good care not to pacify them. He led them westwards on the road to Ryazan. Murat's cavalry was pointed out to him and he sent Vassiltchikov and his Cossacks towards them as a bluff; he himself edged suddenly southwards and, covered by Miloradovich's vanguard posted along the road to Kolomna, emerged onto the old road to Kaluga.[1] On September 19th he was at Podolsk, on the 20th at Pakhra-the-Beautiful.[2] For a moment he thought of establishing himself there, but estimated that it was too near Moscow. Tarutino, further south, some fifty-five miles from the old capital, was a more favourable position. From it he controlled the three roads which started from Moscow and which Napoleon might take at any minute if he suddenly decided to abandon the devastated town. They were the new and old road to Kaluga and the road to Smolensk via Mozhaysk. It was a splendid position for intercepting the provisioning and cutting the communcations of the French and lastly it guarded the access to the southern provinces—'the food-supplying regions'—and Tula, where arms were manufactured. In addition, liaison with the armies of Generals Wittgenstein, Tormassov and Tschitschagov was convenient and it would be easy, from this strategic point, to deploy forces in any direction in case of enemy attack. Meanwhile they would rest, re-equip themselves, await reinforcements and fortify their position.

The army established itself around the village of Tarutino;

---

[1] He duly informed his Sovereign of this in a letter dated September 6th/18th, but at the time Alexander grasped neither the importance nor the subtlety of what the Field-marshal had disclosed: 'The army, executing a flanking march on this road, after crossing the river Moskva, is plunging the enemy into uncertainty at each halting-place, while making for a definite goal, but at the same time concealing it by sham manœuvres by the light forces. The enemy, having lost sight of our army and being still perplexed, is sending strong reconnaissance missions to various points in order to discover us . . .' (Archives of the USSR. Published, like the letter quoted in the note on p. 93, by L. Beskrovny, in *The Patriotic War and Kutusov's Counter-offensive*, Moscow, 1951, p. 86.)

[2] Or Pakhra-the-Red, because the two adjectives were synonymous in archaic Russian. The Red Square = The Beautiful Square.

Kutusov set up his headquarters at Letachevka, three miles further south. He announced: 'For the moment, not a step further. We are going to prepare for our task and remember that the whole of Europe and our beloved fatherland are watching us.'

So, while the King of Naples (who had tried in vain to catch the Russians at Pakhra-the-Beautiful) continued to flirt with the Cossacks, 'to whom he would gladly have given his shirt', the wily Kutusov had executed on his own initiative what a witness called 'the immortal flanking movement that decided the fate of the campaign'. And indeed this 'march-manœuvre', this 'brilliantly conceived and brilliantly carried out plan' suddenly changed the character of the 1812 war and put all the trumps in Russian hands.

The plan of the old warrior, who had decided to hold on in the south, temporarily allaying Napoleon's suspicions, was not approved by the wrangling generals in his entourage. To them, this passage from the Ryazan road to the old Kaluga road, that strategic high-way, was the fumbling of an incapable leader, 'senseless oscillation'. At the head of his opponents stood Sir Robert Wilson,* British Government Commissioner, 'the eye of London' in a sense, whose mission was to observe the Russian operations. He was supported by Lord Cathcart, Great Britain's ambassador to the Tsar, and by Alexander himself, who had great need of England. The Cabinet in London juggled with the pound sterling to serve its policy vis-à-vis Russia, as had so often been the case since the time when Elizabeth reigned in England and Ivan the Terrible in Muscovy.

Wilson had no confidence whatsoever in Kutusov. 'The Field-marshal's decrepitude would always make him more or less in favour of peace,' he wrote to Lord Cathcart. Well aware of Alexander's dislike of the 'one-eyed satyr', the Englishman adopted an arrogant attitude, but His Most Serene Highness snapped his fingers at perfidious Albion and its 'observers'. He had judged Sir Robert—with his usual perspicacity—for what he was; a narrow minded, malicious and pretentious man, who enjoyed inflating his own importance by inflicting pointless insults and appealing con-stantly to his superiors. He sent the Tsar venomous reports about the old man.

General Bennigsen, the Chief of Staff imposed on Kutusov by the Tsar, was a bad strategist and a man of limited intellect, who also missed no opportunity of criticizing. The choice of the fortified camp of Tarutino seemed 'regrettable' to him and he made no bones about saying so. But Kutusov fired a Parthian shot at him: 'Was your position at Friedland such a good one, then? As for mine here, it suits me and we shall stick to it.'

He kept on asserting that 'the vainglory' of an immediate engagement, of the kind favoured by Wilson, Bennigsen and Barclay, did not interest him in the least. For the moment all he wanted was to prepare his army for a counter-offensive that would be the second phase of his strategic war. Not until September 24th did he make a detailed report to his Sovereign:

'The army has been near the village of Tarutino on the right bank of the Nara[1] for eight days; it is undisturbed there and is receiving reinforcements. The regiments are being completed by recruits arriving from the governments[2] ... These recruits are drilling without respite and are burning to try their strength against the enemy. Good water and abundant fodder are restoring our cavalry. The army is not short of provisions of any kind; all the roads are packed with convoys of victuals coming from the governments with the most supplies. Convalescent officers and soldiers are rejoining their regiments every day.

'The disorder that reigns in the enemy army prevents it from attempting any move against us; Bonaparte's remoteness from the countries under his domination deprives him of any help he could get from them; he only manages to procure provisions with the greatest difficulty. The horses of his artillery and cavalry are suffering even more. The great majority of the cavalry perished in previous combats, especially on the memorable day of August 26th, so glorious for Russian arms[3]; the remainder, surrounded on all sides by our partisans, is experiencing a terrible shortage of fodder. Our main detachments are on the road to Mozhaysk, St Petersburg, Kolomna and Serpukhov; a day seldom passes without more than three hundred prisoners being taken.

'Today the Russians, distinguished at all times by their love for their Sovereigns, are burning to defend the throne of their Emperor and to fight the oppressor of their fatherland. The peasants are

---

[1] A tributary of the Oka.

[2] Russia was divided into administrative provinces called *guberniy*, normally translated by 'governments'. They were created by Catherine II.

[3] August 26th/September 7th: Borodino.

arming and organizing themselves; they post sentries on the tops of mountains and on belfries to spy out the enemy's approach. Every day we see these worthy sons of the fatherland arriving at headquarters and asking for arms.

'The arm of the Almighty, which protects the just and smites the unjust, is showing its wrath against our enemies at this moment. I have just learnt that the Spaniards and the English have driven the French from Madrid. Thus the aggressors are driven back everywhere and, while they are being cut down in their thousands at the other end of Europe, their tombs are being dug in the soil of this empire, which they will have threatened with destruction in vain.'

This picture was perfectly correct. The old man had written the strict truth to Alexander. Obviously his information about Spain came from Wilson. Wellington had recaptured Madrid on August 12th; Soult had abandoned Cadiz on the 25th. Previously, on July 22nd, Marmont had been beaten at the Battle of Arapiles. And Kutusov, that skilful handler of men, announced to his troops in an order of the day:

'The French have been driven from Madrid. The arm of the Almighty weighs heavily on Napoleon. Moscow will be his prison, his tomb and the tomb of his army!'

If Wilson had known the text of Kutusov's report to the Tsar, he would undoubtedly have stopped worrying about the possibility of an arrangement between 'the old dotard' and Napoleon—the insidious Corsican, as he called him. And Napoleon, for his part, would have finally lost the illusion that made him constantly revert to the same theme and repeat: 'It is only necessary to know how to manœuvre to make the peace of Moscow possible.'

'Accustomed to dictating peace when he arrived in the palaces of the sovereigns whose capital he had conquered,' wrote Caulaincourt, 'he was astonished by Alexander's silence.' The Duke of Vicenza dared to ask him what would happen if the Tsar persisted in turning a deaf ear.

'In that case,' cried the Emperor, 'the French army would be like a ship caught in the ice, but with the return of summer we should start the war again!'

But he went on: 'Alexander will not let me go to those lengths.

We shall come to an understanding. He will sign the peace!'

Napoleon seemed to be fascinated by the Emperor of Russia, but knew nothing about him and had never understood him. And how could he guess all the torments that the young Tsar of thirty-five was suffering at that moment?

For the monarch by divine right was criticized by everyone, whereas Kutusov, whom he hated, remained popular in spite of the fall of Moscow! Yes, criticized, he, the *Gossudar*, and most of all by Catherine, his sister, who harried and wounded him pitilessly. In the most exquisite feminine exterior, she had the virile character her brother lacked, and the letters she addressed to him at this cruel period for him and his empire have an epic note. Urging him to resist whatever happened, she lectured him sternly: 'Moscow is taken. It is one of those inexplicable things. Do not forget your resolution: no peace and you still have the hope of recovering your honour ... My dear friend, no peace; even if you were at Kazan, no peace!'[1]

Three days later, Catherine was even harder on him:

'... The taking of Moscow has put the finishing touches to peoples' exasperation; discontent is at its highest and your person is far from being spared. If such news reaches me, you can imagine the rest. You are openly accused of your empire's misfortune and the general and private ruin, in short of having lost the country's and your own personal honour ...'[2]

This second letter crossed the Tsar's letter answering the first one:

'Admittedly there are things that it is impossible to imagine. But be sure that *my resolution to fight is more steadfast than ever*; I would rather cease to be what I am than come to terms with the monster who is causing the world's misfortune ...'[3]

---

[1] *Correspondance de l'empereur Alexandre Ier avec sa sœur la grande-duchesse Catherine Pavlovna*, published by the Grand-duke Nicolas Mikhailovitch, St Petersburg, 1910. (Letter No. XXXII, dated from Yaroslav, September 3rd/15th.) (R. and Fr.)

[2] *Ibid.* (Letter No. XXXIII, dated from Yaroslav, September 6th/18th.) On September 18th/30th, Alexander replied to this dressing-down in a very long letter justifying himself. It is one of the most revealing documents about the psychology of this enigmatic Tsar and I thought it interesting enough to reproduce it in full in the *Appendices*.

[3] *Correspondance d'Alexandre ...'* op. cit. (Letter No. LXXII, dated from St Petersburg, September 6th/18th.)

Alexander knew that the people would forgive him everything: his departure from the army, his absence from the battle-field at Borodino, the surrender of Smolensk and even that of Moscow, everything, except a capitulation, or negotiations with Napoleon. He did not need anyone to tell him that his determination to resist, to refuse to bow beneath the yoke whatever the consequences, would raise his people's courage and at the same time lower the morale of his enemies. The people, to whom Napoleon was clearly 'Apollyon, the angel of the bottomless pit', loudly proclaimed their desire to raise the standard that had conquered the Tartar hordes and, by forming troops of partisans, to help 'our Mikhail Ilariono-vich' to drive the French out of Russia. The national war, the holy war announced in the manifesto which ought to have the Tsar of all the Russias, the 'Father-Sovereign', at its head—morally, at least. As for the manner of achieving his aim, it must be admitted that he had no choice: he had to trust in Kutusov, guardian, so to speak, of the army, the non-occupied territory and their honour. Undoubtedly he would find a way—with God's help—of driving out this 'infernal adversary, who combines the most terrible savagery with the most remarkable talent, and who has at his disposal the whole of Europe and a host of men of genius'.

Alexander informed his sister Catherine of his *steadfast* resolution on the very day on which Napoleon returned to a Moscow destroyed by the fire, i.e. September 18th. The French Emperor's resolution to sign the peace was equally steadfast. As soon as he was re-installed in the Kremlin, with the portrait of the King of Rome, which had been put away in safety, back in its original place and prominently displayed, he summoned Lelorgne.* He told him that while passing in front of the Foundlings' Home he had observed that that handsome building, whose architecture he admired, appeared to be intact and that he had learnt afterwards that it had been spared, thanks to the protecting picket that had been posted there when the first gleams of the fire started on the evening of the 14th.

He ordered his interpreter: 'Go and see on my behalf what became of all those unfortunate children.'

Seeing the Frenchman arrive, Ivan Akinfievitch Tutolmin, a man of fair words and empty promises, exclaimed:

'The protection of your master is a blessing from heaven to us!

The orphans are in good health and good heart. They quickly realized that the French are not ogres, as they had been led to believe. The man whom only the other day they called "the Villain" they now call "our father".'

As soon as Lelorgne had reported on his mission, Napoleon sent for Tutolmin. The Councillor of State was lavish with his flattery:

'Sire, I place at your feet the deep and eternal recognition of these unfortunates. I have informed them of your august kindness.'

And so on. Lots of words, lots of bowing and scraping.

The Emperor asked thoughtfully: 'So this Rostopchin left you there without any warning, without instructions?'

'Sire, back in the month of August we had secret orders from the Empress to leave as soon as danger became imminent. We were to await the warning which would be given us. We went to the Governor's palace every day, but he kept us in absolute ignorance until the last moment.'

After discussing this theme for a moment, Tutolmin asked His Majesty for authority to write to his 'illustrious patroness' to inform her that the home 'has escaped miraculously'.

'Very well, you may write. I will have your letter handed on to the outposts.'

Then he questioned him at length, with his customary minuteness, about the organization of the home, lingering over every detail. Meanwhile, aided by the wind, new fires sprang up on the other side of the Moskva in a vast, hitherto untouched district. On the 15th the intervention of the east wind had increased the disaster considerably, but the counter-effect of the east wind had prevented it from being complete. Now, it seemed, the elements were hard at it again. The Chevalier d'Ysarn saw 'a sea of flame, whose waves rolled through the air'. That was undoubtedly what Napoleon caught sight of from his study, for he broke off his questioning, went to the window and hurled imprecations at Rostopchin:

'The wretch! He has dared to add this atrocious, man-made, cold-blooded conflagration to the calamities of war which are already so great.'

The Governor was the only one of his adversaries for whom he cherished a keen hatred. Alexander was his 'dear brother'; he had measured his strength against the Russian generals in the field, according to the rules of war. But Rostopchin!

'I have never waged war in this fashion. The barbarian! It is not enough for him to abandon these poor children, whose guardian he is, and the 20,000 wounded the Russian army entrusted to his care. And he thinks he is playing the Roman! He is a stupid savage!'

Then, as he had at last found a Russian who asked for nothing better than to listen to him, he exclaimed:

'I would have like to treat your town as I treated Vienna and Berlin, which are certainly not falling into ruins, as far as I know. But your Russians have committed an act without precedent in evacuating the town almost completely. They have set fire to their capital themselves and in their desire to cause me momentary annoyance, they have destroyed the work of several centuries. My soldiers know how to fight, but they are not incendiaries. Since Smolensk I find nothing but ashes!'

On the spur of the moment, he asked the Councillor of State to add a few words—obviously meant to be passed on to the Tsar—to his letter to the august dowager. He dictated the text himself:

'Madame,

'The Emperor Napoleon groans at seeing your capital almost entirely destroyed by means which, he says, are not those that one uses in real war. He seems convinced that if no one interferes between him and our August Emperor Alexander, their former friendship would soon resume its rights and all our misfortunes would cease.'

Here was an advance which was not one. It was a subtle insinuation; the adumbration of those 'manœuvres' on which the French Emperor depended to extract an offer of peace from his former good friend, whom he had described after Tilsit as a 'very handsome and worthy young man'.

PART III

. . . It was a wrench for him to abandon Moscow without having gained the least advantage from the possession of that capital on which he had based such great hopes; he resembled, in some respects, those gamblers who end up by ruining themselves completely in trying to recoup what they have lost.

THE MARQUIS DE CHAMBRAY

Dazzled by glory and the favours of Fortune, he believed that his desires alone and even his mistakes would always harness this goddess to his chariot.

GENERAL LANGERON

7

THE EMPEROR HOPES

*...He feels so committed that he can neither
advance, nor retreat, nor remain, nor fight with
honour and success; in turns driven and held back
...he stays on these ashes, scarcely hoping, yet
still wishing.*

PHILIPPE DE SÉGUR

TUTOLMIN'S letter, addressed to the dowager empress, was soon
taken to St Petersburg by an official of the Home called Rakin,
who was accompanied beyond the outposts by a French escort.
At the same time, the Councillor of State had written to the Tsar
to report his conversation with the French Emperor and tell him
about the disaster:

'I cannot adequately describe to you the horrors and violence of
the fire of September 15th: all Moscow was in flames and the
extraordinarily strong wind contributed to the spread of the
catastrophe in this ruined town.'[1]

Nevertheless, Napoleon was still preoccupied. He suddenly had
the feeling that the postscript to Tutolmin's letter could not produce
the desired effect and that it was certainly an illusion to use devious
routes to achieve a specific end. Surely a direct epistolary offensive
was needed?

Early on the day after this memorable conversation, September
19th, while sporadic fires broke out and died in the whole northern
section of the city, while looting was completely out of hand, while
hundreds of homeless roamed the streets and many perished
beneath collapsing façades, while it was impossible to alleviate
the tragic situation in the three hospitals still standing where
Russian and French surgeons worked side by side,[2] the

---

[1] Tutolmin to Alexander, September 7/19, 1812. (Schilder Archives, No. 4,346,
quoted by Tarle: *The Russian Campaign*, p. 189.)

[2] The three hospitals that escaped the 'fury of the fire', reported the Marquis de
Chambray (*Histoire de l'Expédition de Russie*, Book II, note p. 41), were the Galitzin
and Paul Hospitals and the Hospital of the Dowager Empress. It was in the last named
that the Russian doctors and surgeons who had stayed at their posts united their
efforts with those of the surgeons—far too few in number—of the Grand Army.
Chambray writes: 'I only quote this because it is unique...'

Emperor gave another audience to a very distinguished Russian.

Ivan Yakovlev was a brilliant courtier of the time of Catherine II, Knight of Malta, intimate friend of Grand-duke Constantine Pavlovitch, a big landed proprietor and brother of the Russian Minister to Westphalia. He was a great character, who had delayed leaving Moscow until it was too late, because he had dithered and talked too much instead of acting. Now he found himself caught in the trap with all his family and servants. Remembering that he had known Marshal Mortier, Duke of Treviso, in Paris, he had thought of asking him for a *laissez-passer* and had himself taken to him by an officer in the Piedmontese cavalry, touched by his melodious Italian speech—*la sua dolce favella*. When Napoleon learnt of this, he had the Russian nobleman brought to him.

Yakovlev[1] was received in the Throne Room with great pomp, whereas Tutolmin had simply been shown into the Emperor's study. The ordeals of September 15th had transformed the former courtier, a stickler for the formalities, into a sort of vagabond. He wore a threadbare redingote—his old hunting rig-out—a grey-looking shirt and a pair of odd and muddy shoes. He had no wig and his beard had not been trimmed since the beginning of the disaster, for lack of a barber. Napoleon opened the conversation with more invective against Rostopchin, whom he this time called a vandal.

Then he paraded his peaceful sentiments, his protection of the orphans, and complained that the Tsar was 'abused by the English'. As he paced up and down the great gilded hall in which the Romanoff's banquets had taken place since the sixteenth century, he cried:

'This war is festering because of a relentlessness that stems neither from Alexander nor from me. The English are dealing

---

[1] Yakovlev was the father (out of wedlock) of the famous Russian socialist Alexander Herzen. In Vol. I of his *Memoirs*, Herzen retells the story of events as he had it from his nurse: 'Your father, well, you know what he's like ... always putting things off till tomorrow. He was getting ready, he was getting ready and then there we were. At last we had tied up all our parcels. The carriage was waiting. The masters were seated at table. Suddenly there was the chef coming into the dining room, all in white, and saying: "The enemy has passed through the Dorogomylov gate!" We were flabbergasted ... There was a commotion and groaning and already the dragoons were galloping down the street ... the gates were closed. That is how your papa stayed behind for the party, and you as well ...'

It was not the only case. Caulaincourt had to look after a certain Zagriasski, the Tsar's Master of the Horse, stuck in Moscow because he had hesitated too long before leaving his house, 'on which he had lavished a lifetime of care'.

Russia a blow from which she will bleed for a long time. Since Smolensk I have found nothing but towns reduced to ashes. Peter the Great himself would call you barbarians!'

Then, brusquely changing his tone:

'I do not give *laissez-passers* to anybody. Why do you want to leave? I am having the markets opened.'

Yakovlev replied respectfully that open markets did not replace a house and that family life in the open air, in the public square, among the homeless and the drunken troopers, in the midst of what the soldiers of the Grand Army humorously called 'the Moscow fair', was not the most pleasant in the world.

Napoleon reflected and suddenly asked:

'Monsieur, would you undertake to deliver a letter to your Emperor? On that condition I would give you and all your family a *laissez-passer*.'[1]

Yakovlev hesitated. He explained that it would be difficult for him to guarantee the success of such an undertaking.

'Can you give me your word of honour that you will do your utmost to hand over the letter personally?'

'I promise on my honour, Sire.'

'That is enough for me. I will send for you. Is there anything else you need?'

'A roof for my family, Sire, during the period we remain here.'

'The Duke of Treviso will do what he can.'

Mortier hastened to find lodgings. A few hours later, at four in the morning, he sent an aide-de-camp to wake up Yakovlev and bring him to the Kremlin. Napoleon was pacing up and down his study, snuffbox in hand. He was in his dressing-gown. His mood was gloomy. When he saw the Russian, he took a letter from the table and held it out to him.

---

[1] It seems plausible that the *laissez-passer* reproduced in the *Correspondance de Napoléon*, Vol. XXIV, No. 19,212, is the one that was given to Yakovlev. It comes from the Mortier archives:

ORDER
'*Moscow, September 19, 1812.*

'The Emperor desires the Governor General of Moscow to supply M. (name illegible) with the time and protection necessary for him to travel to his estate of Voskressensk with his family and his peasants.'

In that case, Napoleon had this document drawn up on the same day as his first interview with Yakovlev. This *laissez-passer* is the only one that figures in the *Correspondance* for September 1812.

'I trust your word,' he said.

On the envelope were these words: *To my brother, the Emperor Alexander*. The letter was dated September 20th.

'My Brother, having been informed that the brother of Your Imperial Majesty's Minister in Cassel was in Moscow, I sent for him and talked to him for some time. I have charged him to go to Your Majesty and make my sentiments known to you. The beautiful and superb town of Moscow no longer exists. Rostopchin had it burnt. Four hundred incendiaries have been arrested in the act; all declared that they were lighting fires on the orders of the Governor and the Chief of Police: they have been shot. The fire seems to have stopped at last. Three-quarters of the houses are burnt down, a quarter remains. This conduct is atrocious and pointless. Is it intended to deprive me of a few supplies? But these supplies were in the cellars that the fire could not reach. Besides, why destroy one of the most beautiful cities in the world—the work of centuries —to achieve such a feeble end? This is the conduct that has been followed since Smolensk and has reduced 600,000 families to beggary. The fire-engines of the town of Moscow had been wrecked or removed, and some of the arms in the arsenal handed over to evil-doers who forced us to fire a few cannon-balls at the Kremlin to dislodge them. Humanity, the interests of Your Majesty and this great town required that it be put into my hands on trust, since the Russian army left it exposed. Administrations, magistrates and civil guards should have been left there. That was what was done at Vienna, twice at Berlin and at Madrid. That was how we ourselves acted at the time of Suvarof's entry. The fires authorize looting, in which the soldier indulges, disputing the debris with the flames. If I supposed that such things were done on Your Majesty's orders, I would not be writing this letter; but I find it inconceivable that with your principles, your heart and your sense of justice, you authorized such excesses, unworthy of a great sovereign and a great nation. At the same time that Rostopchin had the fire-engines removed from Moscow, he left behind 150 field-guns, 60,000 new guns, 1,600,000 infantry cartridges, more than 400 thousands of gunpowder, 300 thousands of saltpetre, the same amount of sulphur, etc.

'I have waged war on Your Majesty without animosity: a letter from you before or after the last battle would have halted my advance and I would have liked to be in a position to sacrifice the advantage of entering Moscow in return for it. If Your Majesty still retains some remnant of your former feelings for me, you will take this letter in good part. In any case, you cannot but be grateful for my having informed you about what is happening in Moscow.[1]

Napoleon.'

An ambiguous letter. The tone of the conqueror who would like to wash his hands of all the damage suffered by the conquered and place all the responsibility on him. Napoleon also tried to sermonize the Tsar, at the same time as he appealed to his good feelings. And that curious *leitmotiv*: 'I have waged war on Your Majesty without animosity.' Alexander might well ask himself what the French Emperor was getting at. Was he talking about peace proposals? Then where were they?

This new move by Napoleon, like the preceding one, was unknown to anybody, except, of course, Lelorgne and the Prince of Neuchâtel. He spoke freely about it in their presence and proclaimed his confidence in the success of his messengers.

On the very day when this letter was written by the Emperor, the Tsar received one of his aides-de-camp, Colonel Michaud, in the Winter Palace at St Petersburg. He was of French origin, an ex-officer in the Sardinian troops, who entered the service of Russia after the capture of the Kingdom of Sardinia by Bonaparte. Sent by Kutusov, Michaud had come to give a verbal report of the abandonment of Moscow and the fire.

At the news of this calamity, tears flowed from Alexander's eyes. It took him a long time to regain control of himself. Then, after he and Michaud had bemoaned the disaster together, the Colonel felt emboldened enough to declare:

'Sire, my heart bleeds, but I must confess that I left the whole army, from the leaders down to the last soldier, in a terrible state of fear.'

'What are you saying, Michaud? Would my Russians let themselves be crushed by misfortune?'

'Never, Sire! They are only afraid that Your Majesty, out of kindness of heart, may let yourself be persuaded to make peace.'

At the time of Michaud's departure, the army had not known about the manifesto. Alexander replied:

'You reassure me. Return to the army and tell our brave soldiers, tell all my worthy subjects, that when I no longer have one soldier left, I shall put myself at the head of my dear nobility and my fine peasants and use up the last resources of my empire—and it offers me even more than my enemies think.'

After other assertions in the same tone, he added:

'Colonel Michaud, don't forget what I say to you here; perhaps we shall enjoy recalling it one day: *Napoleon or I; he or I; now we can no longer reign together. I have learnt to know him. He will not deceive me any more.*[1]

Alexander was deeply moved and immediately after this interview wrote to Kutusov, asking him to give Michaud, 'that excellent officer', the task of bringing him the first good news the Marshal might have to communicate, 'so as to console the Colonel for his painful mission'.[2]

This time Alexander had not spoken for the sake of propaganda, nor to impress Europe, but because he was moved to the roots of his being and consequently fired with fierce resolution. Did he believe that Moscow had been burnt by the enemy? Michaud gave no details; he had said: 'It is in ashes at this moment. I left it a mass of flames.' Did he attribute this act to the population? Or had Rostopchin communicated with him? He never said. However, one thing is certain: his impetuous sister would no longer need to infuse him with energy. Later, the Tsar was to confide to his mysticist friend, the Baroness von Krüdener: 'The burning of Moscow has illuminated my soul!'

A profound remark. Everything leads us to think that in spite of his resolutions and his genuine desire to attune himself to a people crying for vengeance, Alexander would not have had the necessary tenacity, if Moscow had not burnt. With his hesitant nature, he needed a violent stimulus in order to find himself. The phoenix was reborn from its own ashes, but the Tsar was born from the ashes of his old capital. Brought up by his old grandmother Catherine II, who called him 'the sublime child', but despaired of his indecisive, mystico-romantic character, he finally showed

---

[1] It is possible that Michaud, reporting this dialogue seven years later, 'embellished' the truth a little. Nevertheless, if the words exchanged are not verbatim, the character of the conversation matches the reality corroborated by documents whose authenticity is unquestionable, beginning with Alexander's letters to his near relations.

[2] It was indeed Michaud who later came to tell the Tsar about Kutusov's brilliant counter-offensive on October 27th.

himself as she had wanted—self-assured and strong. On that day and for some years to come, a new Alexander appeared, the man whom his people called the Liberator. Thus the fire that had devoured most of Moscow came as a blessing to Russia, a calamity to its invader. Clausewitz, who had watched everything closely, wrote with perspicacity: 'The fire has put any idea of negotiation out of the Emperor Alexander's mind and exalted the Russian people. That is the fundamental disaster it has been for the French.'

In the Kremlin, 375 miles away, Caulaincourt watched the Emperor pinning his faith to a favourable reply from *Monsieur son Frère* and remembered that the year before at St Petersburg the Tsar had addressed these prophetic words to him:

'Communicate to the Emperor Napoleon from me this last, sincere declaration: once war has begun, either he, Napoleon, or I, Alexander, must lose his crown as a result.'

Yakovlev had barely left when bad news from Murat reached the Kremlin on the night of September 21st. His unfortunate mistake and Kutusov's wily manœuvre were exposed in full, with all their consequences. The Russians, who had been regarded as discouraged and in no state to fight, were on the flank of the French army and would make an eventual retreat very difficult. A better tactician than any of his marshals, Napoleon raised his hat to the old Russian leader, as he explained to his entourage:

'A march on Mozhaysk on Kutusov's part would be nothing but bravado. Try to shut us up in Moscow? A victorious army would not dare to try it! The enemy's movement is aimed at covering the road via which he expects his reinforcements.'

Besides, he had long foreseen the possibility of a manœuvre by Kutusov on the old road to Kaluga, because, on September 13th (i.e. when the Russian was between Mozhaysk and Moscow at the halting-place of Tatarki), the Emperor had written to Murat via Berthier:

'The Emperor is worried at not having news of the enemy. If you do not find him in front of you, it is to be feared that he is to your right on the road to Kaluga and he would be in a position to hurl himself on our rear. We do not know what Prince Poniatowski, who ought to be two leagues on your right, is doing. Order him to send his cavalry onto the road from Kaluga to Moscow. The

Emperor is keeping the Prince of Eckmühl's and the Duke of Elchingen's corps here until he knows where the enemy is. So His Majesty awaits your news impatiently, with special reference to what is happening on your right, i.e. on the road from Kaluga to Moscow.'

This old Kaluga road obsessed him like an evil omen and his marshals had not been able to make it unusable by the Russians— negligence that was paid for dearly. But did he himself admit the tactical error he had made at the beginning, for which the Russian Colonel Buturlin criticized him? If, on leaving Mozhaysk on September 12th, he had forked right onto the Podolsk road instead of advancing on Moscow by the main Smolensk road, if he had entered the town by the Serpukhov gate in the south and not by the Dorogomylov gate in the west, he would have first and foremost limited the line of Kutusov's retreat, cutting his communications with the south. Forced to retreat by the Vladimir road, to the east, the Field-marshal would have been isolated from his reserves and unable either to reconstitute his army or to receive aid from the army of the South. Buturlin observed: 'The manœuvres that took the Russians first onto the Kolomna road, then onto the Kaluga road, and prepared the downfall of the still formidable legions of the French Emperor could not have taken place.'

To be sure, these 'legions'—some 350,000 men—were still formidable, but they were dispersed over too great distances. The Warsaw–Moscow line of communication was controlled by the Prince of Schwartzenberg and General Reynier with their Austrians, who were unreliable allies. Marshals Augereau and Victor were at Smolensk; General Junot at Mozhaysk. The right flank of the communications was covered by Dombrowski; the left flank, in the direction of Riga, by Marshal MacDonald. Marshals Gouvion-Saint-Cyr and Oudinot were at Polotsk. Although communications were thus protected, the town of Tula, where the biggest arms factory in the country was still intact, was theoretically within Kutusov's grasp. Napoleon had left it exposed, banking on his adversary's discomfiture. Another mistake. He had not foreseen the audacious raids by the Cossacks, either. Yet as early as September 22nd (although it was not known in the Kremlin until the 26th), the Cossacks had intercepted a convoy, two army mail coaches, and captured a courier on the Smolensk road, some twelve miles from

8. As soon as he was installed in the Kremlin on the morning of September 15th, Napoleon had the portrait of the King of Rome painted by Gérard hung in his bedroom: 'Bausset has handed me the portrait of the king. It's a masterpiece.' (*Versailles Museum.*)

9. During the night of the 14th, fires were lit in Moscow. Soon 'a sea of fire floods the town'.

Moscow. On the 25th a hundred dragoons of the Guard were surprised at Mala-Vyazma, in Prince Galitzin's castle on the main Mozhaysk road, to the west. Orders were at once given to Oudinot to control that road; Bessières, with Davout's infantry and the cavalry of the Guard, was to move towards Kaluga, to the south-west; Prince Poniatowski would advance on Podolsk; the King of Naples would finally leave the Ryazan road and turn westwards. But in the Kremlin the generals knitted their brows; the Russians were only one day's march from Moscow!

For a moment the Emperor thought of bearing on Vitebsk and envisaged the means of transport. This whim was of short duration. He said to the Duke of Vicenza:

'In our present state, Moscow offers us more supplies, establish-ments and means than any other position.'

Undoubtedly he wanted to convince himself that this was true and try to persuade his intimates, too. He apparently revealed his innermost thoughts to Philippe de Ségur:

'Don't think I don't know that Moscow is worth nothing, militarily speaking. It is not a military, but a political position. They look upon me as a general there, when I am really Emperor!'

Emperor in the midst of charred ruins, in a place where confusion and despair reigned. But they were the ruins of a city which was still the symbol of his conquest to Napoleon. That is why he wanted to wait there, and nowhere else, for the other Emperor's reply.

Meanwhile, the Cossacks, helped by bands of peasants, con-stantly attacked the troops sent foraging. Every day the latter were forced to move dangerously far from the town in order to provision men and horses. They returned exhausted or did not return at all. 'Each measure of rye, each truss of hay' they procured was bitterly disputed by the Russians. Moreover, the couriers were delayed more and more, and the post was intercepted—the post from Paris, Warsaw and Vilna that was 'the thermometer of the Emperor's good or bad moods'.[1] The secretaries and *auditeurs* of the Council of State, who regularly brought the work of the Ministers in Paris to the Kremlin and, after they had been initialled by the Master,

[1] The 'Emperor's portmanteau' took from fourteen to eighteen days to travel from Paris to Moscow, thanks to perfect organization by the Count de Lavalette, Director General of the Postal Services of the Empire. Here is one example: a courier who left Paris at 8.15 a.m. on September 28th arrived at Moscow at 1 a.m. on October 14th, after fifteen days, sixteen hours and forty-five minutes on the road.

took them straight back, were now in great danger of being killed by the Cossacks. Yet when the Duke of Vicenza showed Napoleon how urgent it was to give couriers military escorts, after the post had been delayed for fifteen hours, he heard the following reply—much to his amazement:

'It would need a large detachment. The cavalry is already considerably weakened. Besides, it's a pointless precaution. The road is quite safe.'

His opinions and moods changed from hour to hour and according to whom he was speaking. To Marshal Duroc, 'as sincere and upright as Caulaincourt, but with more moderation and tact', he said: 'Moscow is a bad position. We should only stay here long enough to reorganize.'

He distrusted the foreign troops in the Grand Army. 'The Austrians and Prussians responsible for defending our rear would become our most dangerous enemies at the slightest reverse.'[1]

As if to prove the Emperor right, the Prince of Neuchâtel, referring to a letter from Schwartzenberg, informed him that the defection of the Austrians was probable, 'if it had not already begun', and advised Napoleon to fall back on Poland. This put Napoleon in a rage and he retorted: 'You want to go to Grosbois to see the Visconti woman.'[2]

Napoleon did not want to admit that the danger of a mixed army was already beginning to make itself felt. Yet at the same time (September 22nd) Maret, Duke of Bassano, wrote to him from Vilna to inform him that the foreign troops were looting and deserting. He added: 'Marshal de Saint-Cyr no longer relies on the Bavarians: the few he has left are smitten by disease and discouragement or a mania for desertion.'

The Emperor persisted in remaining in Moscow. His stupefied entourage watched him forming plans for wintering 'in such a positive way, as if they were indispensable to the success of his undertaking', that they finally believed that the war was over as

---

[1] From the beginning of the campaign it was known that the Austrian troops attached to the Grand Army were unreliable. As early as June 11, 1812, Schwartzenberg wrote to Prince von Metternich: 'We are still very angry with the French. No one wants to accustom himself to the idea of fighting with them; however, out of esprit de corps we do not want to expose ourselves to dishonouring the uniform.'

[2] Joséphine Carcano, the wife (by her second marriage) of François Visconti, mistress of Berthier, Prince of Neuchâtel and Wagram.

far as he was concerned! He seemed to be positive that he would get a reply from Alexander, feeding his hopes on memories of Erfürt and Tilsit. 'Besides, like all men who have long been lucky, he hopes for what he desires,' remarked Ségur.

Nature herself misled him. The autumn was exceptionally mild. Every day Napoleon mounted one of his favourite horses, *L'Emir*, *Courtois*, *Gonzalve* or *Roitelet*, and rode round the town. He visited the hospitals, the artillery depots, the powder magazines and the barracks. Each time he returned he enjoyed teasing the Duke of Vicenza:

'There's a sample of the terrible Russian winter with which M. de Caulaincourt frightens the children!'

Caulaincourt mentioned his experience of the country: 'The season is still fine, Sire, but what will it be like in a fortnight or a month?'

'All the severities of winter do not arrive within twenty-four hours,' retorted the Emperor, shrugging his shoulders.

'Don't be too sure of that, Majesty. Winter arrives here like a bombshell.'

Napoleon laughed and turned to Duroc: 'Caulaincourt thinks he's frozen already!'

Nevertheless, he remained preoccupied, admitting with Berthier and Eugène de Beauharnais that the harrying was perhaps the sign of a new system intended to isolate him.

'What are we to do, then?' they asked him, worried and bewildered.

'Stay in the Kremlin like prisoners in irons, while we wait for news from the Winter Palace.'

A 'fraternal negotiation' seemed to him to be the first condition of a retreat to Poland. Otherwise he would lose face; and then: 'A withdrawal without peace preliminaries would represent a reverse that could be the harbinger of others.'

Yet the days passed and no news came from St Petersburg.

In spite of this, the more Napoleon reflected the more he insisted on staying where he was. He laboured under a delusion about the Russian climate and about his food supplies, which were squandered rather than increased by the looting and hard to renew because communications were harried. He believed in the security of his rear and the possibility of regularly warding off the attacks of the partisans allied to the Cossacks. He was unwilling to believe in the danger represented by Tschitschagov's army of the south, which would swell Kutusov's armies in the immediate future. According to him, these troops were mediocre and few in number; he evaluated them at 20,000 men, whereas they actually numbered 35,000.[1] He thought that they were not very mobile and in no hurry to proceed northwards. In short, he 'clings stubbornly to his opinions with the tenacity that is his leading quality elsewhere, but his main defect here.'

There was muttering in his suite. The refrain was always the same: 'We have been spoilt by the other campaigns. Peace used to be the reward for our hardships!'

With the exception of the arduous campaign of 1806–07, they had always spent the winter in France—and never among ruins! But the Master had decided to hold on in a city that was three-quarters destroyed and overwhelmed everybody with its gloom. He wanted to reorganize it and buckled down to the task with his usual keenness. 'His nights duplicate his days.' His activity was the best remedy for the malady that gnawed at him: impatience. He was everywhere, knew everything, thought of everything and everybody, of provisioning, administration, defence, the hospitals and also the French colony.

Although the district of the Bridge of the Marshals had been spared, many French emigrés, such as Mme Fusil, had had their lodgings in sectors now destroyed and were without a roof over their heads. Their material situation was lamentable, their moral position unenviable. Suspected by the Russians for the past three months, suspected by the victorious French, looked on as spies by both, they no longer knew where they were. Perhaps because he hoped to make loyal subjects out of them, Napoleon took an interest in them after his return from Petrovskoye. In a decree addressed to the Prince of Neuchâtel, dated September 18th, he gave orders that all the French who were domiciled in Moscow—men, women and children—should be placed in a house near the Kremlin. 'Three syndics shall be appointed to act as their leaders and draw up a register of them: they will be given rations. Work will be given to those who are capable of it, and a cash allowance to all the others.'[2]

[1] Cf. his letter to the Prince of Neuchâtel: *Correspondance* . . ., op. cit. (Vol. XXIV, No. 19,258).

[2] *Correspondance* . . ., op. cit. (Vol. XXIV, No. 19,209).

For better or for worse, they were housed in the Academy of Medicine, near the Bridge of the Marshals, and in the Davidov mansion nearby. But the question of employment raised a much more complicated problem. Count de Lesseps, now Town Major, would have liked to see them filling the municipal posts that all but a dozen or so of the Russians who had been approached had refused indignantly. These Frenchmen, settled in Moscow, felt that they were Russians heart and soul. Already they had visions of what would happen to them on the day, which they imagined would be soon, when Napoleon left Moscow to fall back on the Vistula. So they hesitated to collaborate. Finally, thirty-two men accepted jobs, some in the hope of immediate advantages, others, already engaged as interpreters, forcibly recruited by Lesseps, Mortier or Durosnel, and still others 'driven by their fear of the consequences of a prolonged refusal'. Nevertheless, there were a few, who, sincerely or not, espoused the cause of the victor and acted as recruiting agents. The work given to them did not necessarily match their talents. For example, a certain Alexandre Prévost, a seller of argand lamps, was made responsible for municipal lighting and the removal of corpses! Villiers, the Reader in French, was appointed chief of police and so on. A M. Gravez was lucky: a translator by trade, he was attached to the Duke of Treviso as interpreter.

Eleven days had passed since Yakovlev had taken Napoleon's letter to Alexander.[1] The Tsar had not replied. Now it was the the first day of October. The weather was still fine. Admiral Tschitschagov, with the Moldavian army, was already covering the Riga region and threatening Schwartzenberg, whom he was soon

---

[1] It seems odd that no one has tried to find out—or even to relate—what actually became of the letter carried by Yakovlev. However, there does exist a very interesting document of the period, published by Dubrovin: *The Patriotic War of 1812 according to Letters by Contemporaries*, in the Publications of the Imperial Academy of Sciences, vol. XLIII, St Petersburg, 1882 (R.). It consists of a letter written by Baron von Wintzingerode to Alexander I, dated from the hamlet of Davidovka. After giving the Tsar an account of all the events after Borodino, the Baron adds the following PS: 'My letter was already sealed and I was preparing to send it, but at that very moment the outposts sent in to me a Mr Yakovlev, brother of the man who was Minister to the court of Westphalia. He carried a French passport and revealed to me that he was bearing a letter from the Emperor Napoleon to Your Imperial Majesty. I at once replied that after such a revelation I could not consider him as a normal man, that I could not conceive how he had had the audacity to take such a mission upon himself and that I was going to send him and his papers straight to the Minister of Police, which I did without delay.' (P. 140, in Russian.)

to throw back beyond the Bug. A bitter surprise for Napoleon, whose forecasts turned out to be wrong. And the Tsar's silence seemed like an unforgivable insult. He was no longer willing to admit what an officer in his army, called Puybusque, was writing at that very moment to a friend in France: 'How can we count on a peace with people who have nothing to lose, who have chosen to lose everything in order to save everything?' Yet the Emperor had been the first to say this, at Petrovskoye.

But he was never the man to admit defeat and he tried to find a way to scare the obstinate Tsar. In the early morning of October 3rd, after a restless night, he summoned Eugène, Berthier and Davout. His eyes sparkled: 'Listen to the new plan I have just conceived.'

As the others said nothing and looked nervous, he went on: 'We must burn what's left of Moscow, march via Tver on St Petersburg, where MacDonald will come to reinforce us, while the Viceroy and the Prince of Eckmühl secure the vanguard.'

The project elaborated at Petrovskoye had surfaced again. His old companions in arms eloquently expressed their disapproval by their dismayed looks. Then the Emperor lost his temper:

'Well, doesn't the idea excite you at all? Will there ever have been a greater feat of arms? Henceforth this conquest is the only one worthy of us. What will the whole world say when it learns that we have conquered the two great capitals of the north in three months?'

Then the others broke their silence: 'The season, Sire.'

'The shortage of supplies . . .'

'One hundred leagues of marsh between Tver and St Petersburg. A barren road!'

'Drive northwards? Go to meet winter when it is only too close already?'

Napoleon insisted: the plan was realizable, provided that it was carried out immediately, with conviction and enthusiasm. But it was obvious to him that even those he looked on as the bravest and most faithful were disinclined for further adventures. He was not used to such lack of enthusiasm. Didn't they trust him any longer? He did not ask them that question and closed the interview in a rage. In a few years' time, on his rock, he declared to the Count de Montholon: 'My army would certainly have marched on St Petersburg if it had been the month of August.'

After leaving him, his marshals discussed the idea; they preferred to regard this project born of Napoleon's insomnia as 'nothing but an outburst of rage, an inspiration caused by his despair at seeing himself forced to yield and withdraw in the full view of Europe'. Meanwhile, the situation deteriorated every day. The enemy was manœuvring in the rear and on the flanks of Napoleon's army. The army corps of General von Wittgenstein was enlarged every day by recruits and volunteers, and imperilled Marshal Gouvion-Saint-Cyr's corps. Tschitschagov, who had rejoined Tormassov, was moving freely and paralysing Schwartzenberg. The militias in the big towns were large enough to form whole divisions, with cavalry and artillery. A French officer wrote:

'The Russian Grand Army posted in the environs of Moscow closes the circle that is daily becoming tighter round our army. We have to put ten thousand men plus artillery into the field outside Moscow to forage and we are still not certain of success without fighting . . . The enemy is gaining the energy we are losing; audacity and confidence have passed to his side.'

This all confirmed Kutusov's report to Alexander.

However, all was not plain sailing in the Russian headquarters at Tarutino. His Most Serene Highness was still surrounded by hostility and confronted by cliques. First of all, there was Sir Robert Wilson, cantankerous as usual and distrustful, accusing 'the dotard' of being afraid to fight and doing his best to let the enemy escape. The Englishman had a supporter in General Bennigsen who was jealous of His Highness. Generals Ermolov and Toll were hypocritically playing an underhand game; they flattered Kutusov to his face but criticized him behind his back and kowtowed to Wilson. Barclay de Tolly, superseded as commander, preserved an embittered silence and nursed his grudge. However, he was the only man to recognize the masterful skill of the 'march-manœuvre'. So much so that he finally convinced himself that he had suggested the remarkable tactics himself! And he smiled inwardly as he watched Bennigsen intriguing to get Kutusov dismissed, just as he had intrigued in August to get him, Barclay, removed from his post.

Distrusted, abused, criticized and spied on, the Field-marshal stood like a monolith. Misunderstood, but unshakable for the moment, supported by the love of his soldiers, the enthusiasm of the partisans and the militia, and by every Russian who thought only of the salvation of the fatherland, the old man had great patience, great endurance and the precious faculty of not worrying what people thought about him. His greatest strength lay in his self-confidence and the sovereign contempt in which he held most of his colleagues.

Towards the Tsar he displayed a sort of paternal and ironic tenderness.

The Tsar, who kept silence in such cavalier fashion, exasperated Napoleon beyond measure, especially as he was not the most patient of men. On October 4th he summoned the Duke of Vicenza, to whom he had been cool for some time, knowing that he was opposed to the prolonged stay in Moscow. Caulaincourt was still unaware of Yakovlev's mission and Napoleon asked him casually:

'Do you think that Alexander would be disposed to make peace if I made overtures to him?'

The Duke, whom Ségur described as 'more capable of obstinacy than flattery', and of whom Villemain asserted that he was 'endured rather than listened to' because of his spirited language, which was 'sincere to the point of giving offence', replied smartly.

'A man does not burn his capital to sign a peace treaty on its ashes!'

Once again someone had expressed the same opinion that Napoleon himself had upheld at Petrovskoye, but rejected the next day. So he was furious. He took snuff—a sign that he was very upset—and began to pace up and down, with Caulaincourt on his heels. As he walked, he held forth:

'I am going to march on St Petersburg. That is going to grieve you, Master of the Horse! Then Russia will rise against the Emperor Alexander. There will be a conspiracy. He will be assassinated. It will be a great disaster.'

Then, spinning round abruptly, he looked him in the face and said:

'Will you go to St Petersburg? You will see the Emperor Alexander. I shall entrust you with a letter and you will make peace.'

The Duke remarked that he thought the mission was pointless and assured Napoleon that no one would receive him there. The Emperor bristled up:

'You don't know what you're saying. Alexander will be all the

more eager to seize this opportunity because his nobility, ruined by
this war and the fire, desires peace.'

What had put that idea into his head? Neither Tutolmin nor
Yakovlev had said anything of the kind. Had Mme Aubert-Chalmé
been stupid enough to express this opinion and the Emperor been
naive enough to take her opinions seriously? He continued to
denigrate his adversary, which had never been one of his habits:

'The Russian generals are incompetent and the Tsar is well
aware of it. The best of troops can do nothing under such com-
manders. Besides, the Russian army is greatly reduced in numbers
and discouraged, whereas the French army is in a position to march
on St Petersburg immediately.'

Perhaps Caulaincourt, a loyal, well-informed and generous man,
thought what Chateaubriand was to write later: 'We must weep
when the giant is reduced to playing the humbug . . .' At all events,
he defended his attitude with courageous obstinacy:

'The more the season advances, Sire, the more the chances are in
Russia's favour!'

'The season is still fine. If we march on the capital, the Russian
Empire is lost.'

The season was still fine! That was to be one of his strongest
arguments, both then and later. He returned to the subject again:

'Everyone who has been in Russia before has told me fairy-tales
about the climate, beginning with you.'

He insisted on his idea of sending Caulaincourt to the Tsar,
but the Master of the Horse held his ground. He replied fearlessly:

'Such a move, Sire, would reveal all the difficulties of our
position.'

A fig for that! In Napoleon's eyes it was Alexander who was in
difficulties. So, thinking that he detected a personal motive behind
the Duke's refusal—a distaste for showing himself in St Petersburg
where he had recently been a popular and welcome guest—he
suggested a compromise: Kutusov.'

'Sire, I know the Emperor Alexander's character. If I refuse the
mission with which Your Majesty wishes to entrust me, it is because
I am sure that he will not sign the peace in his capital. Since this
move on our part cannot produce results, I venture to think that
it would be more suitable not to make it. Alexander will not listen
to any proposal until Russian soil is evacuated.'

Thereupon Napoleon turned his back on him, growling:

'Very well! I shall send Lauriston; he shall have the honour of having made peace and saving the crown of your friend Alexander.'

A formal dismissal, spiced with ill-feeling that was unfair and unpleasant. But the Duke did not take offence. He was merely secretly astonished that the Emperor still deluded himself by believing in negotiations, although there had not yet been a reply to any of his overtures and the dates of his first moves, as much as his own common-sense cried out that Alexander did not want to negotiate. He could not help feeling—like everyone else—that the Emperor's repeated messages revealed his difficulties. How could a man so shrewd and so level-headed, with the eagle's eye view and such superior judgment, delude himself to such an extent? Caulaincourt was perplexed, but tried to explain these discrepancies 'in such a great character' by that tendency of the human heart to feel sure of what it desires, even against all probability, by the very human need for hope, the last consolation of man in adversity.

Jacques Alexandre Bernard Law, Marquis of Lauriston, one of Napoleon's fellow-students at Brienne, who became his aide-de-camp during the Italian campaign and Brigadier-general at Austerlitz, was forty-four. A good soldier and excellent diplomat, he had been ambassador in Russia from 1811 to 1812. Although he was probably delighted to supplant Caulaincourt, of whom he had a poor opinion (a feeling reciprocated by Caulaincourt) because of old jealousies and questions of precedence going back to the time of the Consulate, he was by no means optimistic about his mission. That is putting it mildly. His categoric and vehement objections went far beyond the Duke of Vicenza's. He thought that it was no time to make advances, but rather to begin the retreat at once, taking the road to Smolensk via Mozhaysk. Napoleon would not hear of it:

'I like simple plans, the least tortuous roads, but there is one road I will not set foot on again unless the peace is signed and that is the road by which I came.'

Then he showed him a letter to Alexander, saying: 'Go and get a safe-conduct to St Petersburg from Kutusov.'

Leaving Lauriston no time to voice any further objections, he dismissed him, emphasizing in a grave tone words that were certainly hard to pronounce:

'I want peace. I must have it. I want it at all costs. Save only our honour.'

8

WASTED TIME

This conquest was going to turn out like so many others—made en masse and lost sight of among the details.

PHILIPPE DE SÉGUR

As soon as Lauriston had left, the Emperor had his adversary informed that a truce-bearer was being sent. At 4 a.m. on October 5th, he ordered the Prince of Neuchâtel to write to the King of Naples:

Since His Majesty has decided to send one of his aides-de-camp to the Russian General in Chief, he wishes you to have your Chief of Staff write to the general commanding the enemy vanguard a letter couched in these words: 'It being the Emperor's intention to send one of his aides-de-camp to the General in Chief Kutuzow, he wishes to know the day and hour when, and the place where, the general wishes to receive him ...' The aide-de-camp whom His Majesty proposes to send will probably arrive at headquarters tonight.

Once the great negotiation had been initiated, Napoleon devoted himself seriously to the organization of Moscow.

Nothing really constructive had yet been achieved by the new municipal officials. In the absence of genuine organization of the provisioning system, looting had become a sort of rite as well as a necessity. Perhaps there had been someting to feed the army on in the beginning, but only if there had been an energetic fight against wastage and individual cupidity, and the assurance of a regular supply of fresh meat. But there had been nothing of the kind and only unnecessary items abounded, as many examples prove. Sergeant Bourgogne, quartered with his company in a big restaurant, found well-stocked cellars in it, with wine, champagne, rum and barrels of excellent beer covered with ice to keep them cool during the summer. The troops made the same heady discoveries nearly everywhere in the cafés and inns that were untouched or smashed open. They drank their fill. Large reserves of sugar were used to make punch! Captain Duverger relates complacently how he had 'taken his share of the booty in the common disaster'. If we multiply this 'share' by the number of officers and non-commissioned officers of the Grand Army occupying Moscow since September 14th, we can imagine that provisions posed a serious problem by the beginning of October in a town that received virtually nothing from outside. 'I was rich in furs and pictures,' says Duverger. 'I was rich in boxes of figs, coffee, liqueurs, macaroni, salted fish and meat . . .,' but there was no white bread, no fresh meat and no table wine. That did not prevent him entertaining his general and he procured (he does not say how) a whole leg of beef! A banquet table was laid for twelve. A health was drunk 'to the entry into St Petersburg'.

The cellars of Moscow, of which their owners had been so proud ever since the eighteenth century,[1] were the ruin of Napoleon's soldiers. Drunkenness was followed by bacchanalia and masquerades, thanks to the splendid wardrobes in the mansions of the nobility. Mother Dubois, a canteen keeper, never went abroad unless wearing a dress of silver lamé; many an infantryman sported 'a French costume of the time of Louis XVI', unearthed, no doubt, in the cupboards of some courtier of Catherine the Great. *Un vero carnevale!* exclaimed the Italian César Laugier de Bellecœur.

At St Helena Napoleon was to recall 'the unexpected abundance' resulting from the troops' 'indefatigable researches'. A misleading abundance; the superfluous took the place of necessities and that was highly dangerous in itself. The luxury of rare foodstuffs was bad for the discipline of the army and the health of intemperate men. 'Moscow became another Capua for our troops,' Napoleon said later.

Each day that passed saw an increase in the waste of provisions. Too much reliance had been placed on victuals arriving from the surrounding countryside. This turned out to be a myth. The peasants supplied nothing, in spite of a proclamation by de Lesseps:

[1] Champagne was introduced into Russia by the Marquis de la Chétardie, ambassador to the Empress Elisabeth Petrovna (1742–62). The other wines of France were already greatly appreciated since the time of Peter the Great, thanks again to an ambassador: M. de Campredon.

'The peasants, farmers and inhabitants of the outskirts of Moscow will be able to bring their foodstuffs into the markets of the capital in complete safety.' What foodstuffs and by what means of transportation? Both had already been forcibly removed or destroyed by the peasants themselves, who preferred to die of hunger rather than supply the occupying forces. Instead, they victualled the flying squadrons of partisans who made ever more frequent and bolder raids, endangering the French foragers daily.

There was little substantial nourishment for the men and scarcely any for the horses. 'The loss of animals is unfailing. They gnaw at their mangers for lack of hay. As for our maintenance, it doesn't cost much for we find nothing to buy,' wrote a non-commissioned officer to his sister on September 29th. 'Our ordinary meals consist of eating the bread which we are very glad to have,[1] sometimes meat, plus our supplies of vegetables, but they are becoming exhausted like everything else.' In spite of all this we discover an astonishing note of fervour in this letter, as we do in the majority of letters written at the time by officers, non-commissioned officers and men: 'Here we do not allow ourselves to reflect about our future situation; the hope of overcoming our troubles bravely buoys us up, adding to that the great confidence we have in the man who brought us here . . .'

Did the man who had brought them as far as Moscow still believe in his star? He could not overlook the feelings of his entourage that ranged from pessimism to discontent, via despondency. Nevertheless, far from preparing for a retreat that everyone wanted or advised—for they were all very afraid that Lauriston would come back empty-handed—he made active preparations for spending the winter. The works he ordered 'loudly proclaimed his intention to stay in Moscow'. He thought that that would scare the Russians and make them feel disposed to bargain. And he tried to convince everyone of it 'by his actions and by his words'.

During these wasted days that precipitated the disaster by completing the work of the fire, he had the town fortified, put the Kremlin in a state of defence and equipped the monasteries around Moscow with cannon. He ordered a daily parade in the courtyard

[1] Caulaincourt was the man who, starting on September 19th, had seen to the organization of the bakeries in the Kremlin, but they were mainly intended for the Old Guard, who were in the Emperor's service.

of the Kremlin and wanted it as impeccable as it had been in Paris.[1]
Standing by the Emperor's side, the Count of Narbonne watched
the march past of 'these regiments that were so decimated, but still
presented an admirable appearance of martial glamour and almost of
elegance in the midst of this horizon of blackened walls'. Napoleon,
who was in an excellent mood, exclaimed:

'Well, my dear Narbonne, what have you to say about an army
like that, manœuvring in bright sunshine?'

The Count had never balked at giving an honest opinion and
let no opportunity of preaching wisdom pass:

'I say, Sire, that it has rested already and can take the road in
order to occupy its quarters in Lithuania, leaving the Russians their
capital in the state in which they left it!'

The army that paraded had rested, perhaps, but the state of the
troops' health as a whole was deplorable. The situation in the
hospitals was critical. Meat was rationed, even for patients, whose
numbers constantly increased. The death rate was frightening. On
top of everything else, these consequences of the fire made life in the
town 'in the state in which the Russians had left it' very precarious.

The Emperor appeared to disregard this. His main concern was
that the army should recover its old morale and discipline; as for
the Court of the Kremlin it was to be established according to the
sacrosanct rules of protocol, 'with the same prerogatives and
order of precedence as at the Tuileries'. Grand Marshal, Master of
the Horse, Chamberlain, aides-de-camp, *maréchaux des logis, four-
riers de palais* and medical officers, all of them being given back or
receiving for the first time their solemn appointment and precise
duties. This went on at a time when the need for reinforcements of
men, horses and materials was making itself felt desperately and the
Emperor was dictating letter after letter to Poland, asking for 'as
many men as possible, horses to remount the cavalry and the
artillery, horses and gun-carriages of the Polish corps'. From France
he demanded the immediate despatch of twenty-two companies of
artillerymen assembled on the Rhine and 14,000 horses; he wanted
'provisions and clothing'.[2]

---

[1] *Tuesday, October 6th :* review of the infantry of the Old Guard; *Wednesday, 7th :*
Roguet division; *Thursday, 8th :* general parade; *Saturday, 10th :* Compans division;
Sunday, 11th : Gérard division; *Monday, 12th :* Morand division; *Tuesday, 13th :* dis-
mounted troopers; *Saturday, 17th :* Delzons division.

[2] *Correspondance . . .,* op. cit. (Vol. XXIV, Nos. 19,218 and 19,234).

However, as the news sent to France was always highly optimistic, the Emperor thought that it would be a good idea to send to Paris some trophies that would catch people's imagination, 'as souvenirs of the success of his arms'. The souvenirs of Moscow the fabulous would be unlike any others. So the order was given to remove the magnificent cross of solid gold that surmounted the historic tower of Ivan the Great: it would crown the dome of Les Invalides! This vandalism did not scandalize anyone—after all, the horses of St Mark had been stolen from Venice—but secretly people thought that it was wasting a lot of time on trifles. Besides it was a veritable labour of Hercules: no Frenchman was willing to climb to that height and naturally no Russian dared to touch an object venerated by all the orthodox. The faithful Berthier himself revolted at depriving a town already destroyed 'of part of the only monument that still remained whole'. Finally, the sappers of the Guard were ordered to carry out the task. A cable broke, the weight of the chains dragged down the cross and part of the colossal scaffolding. 'When it fell, the earth trembled under the tremendous weight.' Contrary to what certain spectators thought they saw, the cross did not break into three pieces. The Emperor, who had come to supervise the work, observed a flock of crows flying in circles round the cross; he went so far as to remark:

'It seems as if these sinister birds want to defend it!'

A remark indicative of his uneasy state of mind.

The gigantic cross was placed in a wagon to be forwarded to Paris, under the supervision of General Claparède, along with other less important trophies,[1] such as flags captured by the Russians in various wars, old armour and a 'sumptuously set' icon.

Meanwhile, M. de Lesseps decided to publish two proclamations addressed to the Russians in Moscow, who numbered about 10,000, according to contemporary estimates. One was displayed on October 1st, before Lauriston was sent off, the other on the 6th, just before his return. Their contents, full of untruths, were unseemly, in the Marquis de Chambray's opinion. He found phrases like the following in bad taste: 'Let the inhabitants return to their dwellings with confidence . . .' Or again: 'Your fellow-citizens are returning to their homes every day.'

'What homes and what dwellings?' he asked himself. Those that

---

[1] This cross, which certain writers have claimed was not made of solid gold, disappeared in the turmoil. No one ever saw it again after the retreat from Russia.

had not been devoured by the flames were occupied by the troops.

'Let the workman and the hard-working craftsman return to their trades . . .' Or: 'Inhabitants of towns and countryside, and you, workers and craftsmen . . . you are called on to respond to the paternal plans of His Majesty the Emperor and King and to contribute with him to the well-being of all . . .'

The result was nil.

Another trial of incendiaries had taken place on September 24th, 'following the orders of H.M. the Emperor and King, for the purpose of judging the authors and instigators of the fire that broke out spontaneously (*sic*) in the various districts of the town of Moscow on the fourteenth and fifteenth days of this month, and then continued during the sixteenth, seventeenth and eighteenth'. The examination and judgment were under the presidency of General Count Lauer, assisted by the army's Provost Marshal, Michel, with General Count de Montholon acting as *procureur impérial*.

Throughout this period, the situation improved very little. The vice closed round Moscow, thanks to the joint efforts of the partisans and the Cossacks, whose sole task was to infiltrate the flanks and rear of the enemy, cause him the maximum amount of trouble and follow his every movement. 'Thus,' wrote Ségur sadly, 'war was everywhere: in front, on our flanks and behind us; the army grew weaker; the enemy became more enterprising every day.' The Tsar said nothing. The Marshals thought only of departure. Time was frittered away. A radiant sun shone on 'the mournful silence of "Moscow-the-Dead".' The soldiers were bored to death. An insurmountable melancholy reigned over everyone, hence the drunkenness, the carousing, abuses of every kind, the frightening waste and the general slovenliness.

On October 3rd the Emperor sent a laconic but revealing note to the Duke of Bassano at Vilna: 'We have nothing new to report from here. The enemy is in the direction of Kaluga. We are trying to restore a little order in the town.'[1]

It was not easy to establish order. The delights of Capua were not conducive to work. Napoleon increased his memoranda and inspections. He complained of slowness, delays, lack of zeal, feeling

[1] *Correspondance* . . ., op. cit. (Vol. XXIV, No. 19,240).

10. (a) 'No serious historian has tried to depict Rostopchin . . . looking at his work through an enormous telescope.'

(b) The fire reached the Kremlin and on the 16th Napoleon gave the order to depart: 'Their departure from the citadel ringed round with flames was something of a gamble.'

11. (a) From Petrovskoye, to which the Emperor had withdrawn, the burning of Moscow was 'a terrifying and grandiose sight'.

(b) 'During the night of September 23rd the Muscovites were awakened by a tremendous explosion.'

shocked and handing out reprimands.[1] However, as 'his genius has this faculty which consists in interrupting his greatest pre-occupation when it pleases him, either as a change, or even as a rest,' he ordered M. de Bausset, Prefect of the Court, to make enquiries about the company of French actors who had been playing in Moscow. Already, on August 22, 1799, when leaving Egypt, General Bonaparte had written to Kléber: 'I had asked for a company of actors several times; I shall take special care to send you one. This article is very important for the army.' Obviously, Napoleon considered 'this article' just as important at Moscow as at Cairo.

It was either through Tutolmin, Caulaincourt's protégé Zagriasski (who truckled to the French), or Marie-Rose Aubert-Chalmé that Napoleon discovered the existence of the actors. Bausset unearthed the Italian tenor Tarquinio, who had been resident in Moscow for two years, and engaged him to sing before the Emperor in the Kremlin. The Italian put the Prefect of the Court in touch with Mme Fusil, who had finally found quarters, for better or worse, with some friends in the outbuildings of the Gagarin palace, where Bausset came to seek her out. Her toilette was freakish in the extreme and she appeared quite put out about it. What was her astonishment when her eminent visitor announced:

'We want to reassemble those artistes still left here to give a few performances and play music for His Majesty. Tarquinio assured us that you were a charming singer.'

'Me?' she protested. 'Me, sing before the Emperor? But, Sir, I am a very modest singer of light songs.'

'Haven't you sung duets with Tarquinio?'

'Certainly, Sir, but that was in the salons of some grand Moscow ladies—Mmes Davidov, Galitzin and Countess Stroganov—and

---

[1] The following memorandum is a good example:

'To General Count La Riboisière
'Commandant of the artillery of the Grand Army, Moscow.

'Monsieur le comte La Riboisière, today I paid a visit to the depots of light and smoke devices; I found little activity and little order there. All the information we have reveals that the enemy had 100,000 cannon-balls in this park and we believe that he threw them into a stretch of water that is easy to dry out, since it is a pond. During the fortnight we have been here, only 10,000 cartridges for cannon-balls have been made. It is my wish that as from the day after tomorrow you have this workshop equipped to produce 6,000 rounds of cannon ammunition a day, to be stored in the Kremlin as soon as they are made.'

Correspondance. . . ., op. cit. (Vol. XXIV, No. 19,242).

those ladies knew that we made no pretentions. To sing for His Majesty, who is hard to please and an expert, would paralyse me! For goodness' sake, leave me in my obscurity!'

'Then, madame, we fall back on vaudeville and comedy.'

'Well, that's a different story.'

In other words, it would be possible to stage a comedy, except that Mme Fusil's house had burnt down. She had lost her furniture and clothes. Her companions were equally badly off. The ladies had neither dresses nor shoes, the men had lost their clothes and boots. And then there were no nails for the scenery and no oil for the lamps.

'Mere trifles!' declared M. de Bausset. 'We will arrange all that.' He knew only too well that a minor annoyance was more likely to make Napoleon furious than a major one. His mood would be terrifying if the Prefect of the Court returned with a negative reply.

Mme Fusil was the first to laugh at the rig-out of the French company when they presented themselves at Bausset's to rehearse the programme. The leading man wore an old military coat over his naked body; his head-gear was a militia-man's cap picked up in the street. The juvenile lead was clad in a seminarist's cassock, with a Russian general's plumed three-cornered hat on his head. The 'noble father' was barefooted; he wore a pair of patched trousers and a dirty white satin fop's waistcoat. The 'traitor', on the other hand, had no trousers at all; he was shod in magnificent Louis XIII boots and proudly draped in a grey Spanish coat that he had managed to sneak from the theatre wardrobe at the last minute. Mme Aurore Bursay[1] sported a red jacket lined with rabbit fur, of the kind worn by Russian women of the lower middle classes, but had neither skirt nor petticoats, and her jacket only went to her knees; by way of contrast she wore the red velvet Maria Stuart bonnet, embellished with large false pearls! In a word, according to Mme Fusil, they looked as if they were 'dressed up to go to a masked ball for madmen and beggars'. They presented a bizarre, tragi-comic spectacle that astounded the distinguished Prefect of the Court. He at once ordered

---

[1] In 1814, Aurore Bursay told Aimé Martin of the *Journal des Débats* that she was 'manageress of the Imperial Theatre of Moscow'. This fact has been rightly denied by A. Gadaruel, annotator of the Chevalèir d'Ysarn's memoirs of the burning of Moscow. Mme Bursay was simply a member of the company. The stage-manager was a certain Louis-Antoine Domergue, known as 'Saint-Amand', born at Auxerre, who published his *Souvenirs* in 1835.

General Count Dumas, Commandant of the Kremlin, to 'clothe all these people suitably'.[1]

There was scarcely any underwear, but satins, brocades, lace and braid appeared as if by magic, materials that had been 'found' in the French shops of the Bridge of the Marshals, private houses and a church where objects snatched at random from the fire had been hastily deposited, and lastly among the treasures of the Kremlin.

In normal times, the performances had taken place in turn in different Moscow theatres that were now all destroyed or badly damaged. The only one left was the theatre of a rich patron of the arts, Pozniakov—a small admirable planned hall, celebrated for its luxury and beauty. The spectacles given in it were considered the best in Moscow. There must have been systematic looting or the beginnings of a fire in it, for it needed a thorough clean up. No sooner said than done. When it was cleaned and whitewashed, when the boxes were superbly draped and a curtain made out of a single piece of brocade, a solid silver candelabrum with 1,700 candles, taken from a sanctuary, was hung from the ceiling. The stage was arranged with great taste and elegance. It contained furniture, bronzes, marbles and curios that many a Muscovite noble would have been surprised to see there. The whole theatre was surrounded with barrels and buckets of water—one never knew. Lastly, a handsome poster, 'just like in Paris', was printed by the army printing-works:

THE FRENCH THEATRE IN MOSCOW ←

The French actors will have the honour to present on Wednesday next, October 7, 1812:

the first performance

of the JEU DE L'AMOUR ET DU HASARD

Prose comedy in 3 acts by Marivaux

followed by

[1] 'All these people' formed part of the regular company of the Imperial French Theatre of Moscow, reorganized by decree of Alexander I in 1808. On June 18, 1812, the French company, wishing to prove its pro-Russian feelings, organized an anti-Napoleonic show, in which Mme George, then on tour, took part. The public gave it an icy reception. After this fiasco, the French gave no more performances. Some of them left for St Petersburg. Other young artistes followed their Russian 'protectors' at the time of the exodus. Among those who remained we may mention Adnet, former leading man at the Porte-Saint-Martin, Lekain, a descendant of the great actor and Mlle Lamiral, a teacher of dancing and deportment at the Catherine Institute for the daughters of the nobility. During the performances given for the Grand Army, she was the star attraction in her Russian dance number.

L'AMANT AUTEUR ET VALET
Prose comedy in 1 act by Céron

In the *Jeu de l'Amour et du Hasard*: MM. Adnet, Péroud, Saint-Clair, Bellecœur, Bertrand, Mmes André and Fusil.

Prices of seats

Dress circle	..	..	..	..	5 roubles or 5 fr.
Stalls ..	..	..	..	..	3 roubles or 3 fr.
Upper circle	..	..	..	..	1 rouble or 1 fr.

The performance will begin at 6 o'clock precisely

The excellent orchestra was composed of the best soloists of the Guard. The company, to be sure, was not distinguished by its youth or beauty, especially where the ladies were concerned, and Mme Fusil made no bones about admitting the fact: 'Misfortune had willed it that the oldest and least attractive had stayed behind.' She even had a 'black' enough sense of humour to suggest putting on *L'Ile des Vieilles*, a play written by Aurore Bursay! So perhaps the performance would be no more than the 'sad parody of a real play', but they would do their best not to disappoint an almost exclusively male audience. There were, in fact, very few female spectators: some canteen keepers, a few milliners from the Bridge of the Marshals and some French schoolmistresses. As a specialist in such matters, Mme Fusil noted that: 'There was no claque in the hall and no competition on the theatre (stage) where all selfish personal rivalry had vanished.'

Altogether eleven performances were ultimately given, with varied programmes, and they played to packed houses. Soldiers of all ranks and all branches alternated frenziedly between applause and shouts of '*Vive l'Empereur!*' He himself was never present. Tarquinio and the young pianist Martini, son of the famous author of *Plaisir d'Amour*, came fairly frequently to give concerts 'at the Court'.

On the night before the première, October 6th, Count Lauriston returned from his visit to Kutusov. It had not been the most pleasant of interviews.

9

'THE BEGINNING OF THE END'

*He could not convince himself that fortune, which
had smiled on him so often, had completely forsaken
him at the moment when he had to ask miracles of
her.*

PHILIPPE DE SÉGUR

WHEN Lauriston arrived at the Russian outposts at dawn on
October 5th, in a carriage preceded by a French officer carrying a
white flag, there was tremendous excitement at Kutusov's headquarters. Sir Robert Wilson opposed an interview altogether, storm-
ing and sending an immediate letter to the Tsar:

'I have the honour to inform Your Majesty that this morning
Field-marshal Kutusov communicated to me his intention to grant
an interview at the Russian outposts to the aide-de-camp general of
Bonaparte. I have believed it my duty to put forward very firm and
clearcut objections to this idea, the realization of which is not in
keeping with Your Majesty's dignity, for it will encourage the
enemy, sow discontent in the army and provoke the distrust of
foreign States.'

A denunciation in due form, accompanied by a veiled warning
against any idea of toying with an armistice on the part of Alexander,
who was well advised to fear England's wrath. Two days previously
(October 3rd), 50,000 English guns had been unloaded at Kronstadt.
At the same time, the British observer informed his ambassador at
St Petersburg, saying that in his opinion it would be indecent and
harmful to receive the Frenchman. (At all events, as his letters
took eleven days to reach the capital, neither the Tsar nor Cathcart
could have changed anything that happened!)

Kutusov had no need of mentors. Personally, he had no desire to
talk to Napoleon's emissary, so he sent General Bennigsen to meet
Lauriston at the Russian outposts. The General was accompanied
by Prince Peter Volkonsky, Alexander's personal envoy, who had
come in his master's name to ascertain what was happening in the

camp of Tarutino. These two men were merely to hear the French-man and report what he said to His Most Serene Highness. But a snag cropped up here: Lauriston had received orders to address no one but Kutusov. There were to be no intermediaries! He refused categorically to see the two delegates and withdrew to the head-quarters of the King of Naples at Vinkovo, behind the river Tschernitschnaya, an hour's ride from Tarutino. This threw the Russian camp into some confusion. The Field-marshal did not want to let the French General go without having received his message, but insisted on seeing him alone. Wilson at once shouted 'treason' and demanded that witnesses should be present. As solid as two columns, two relations of the Tsar, the Prince of Oldenburg and the Prince of Würtemburg, ranged themselves beside the Englishman. This trio of foreigners (so much more 'German' than Barclay!) harassed and exasperated the Field-marshal by showing their arrogant distrust. There must be no secret tête-à-tête! (One never knew with the old one! He might yield out of sheer weariness.) However, there had to be a compromise; Kutusov agreed to receive the envoy of Bonaparte in his study, in such a way that the other three could see and hear the speakers from a neighbouring room, but without intervening.

So Bennigsen set off alone for the headquarters of Murat, with whom, claimed Murat, he talked in the most friendly and in-sinuating way, trying hard to seduce him by praise, to 'deceive him with soft words that were eloquent only of weariness with war and hope for peace'. The King of Naples, for his part, who had become an expert in the art of conversing with the Russians from outpost to outpost, greatly appreciated this intermediary.[1] After a conversa-tion in which each in turn let themselves be 'enchanted, seduced and deceived', Murat transmitted Kutusov's new proposals to Lauriston, who was brooding in his tent. When the Count learnt that witnesses were to be present at the interview, he rejected the proposal with disdain. Perhaps he was glad to seize the excuse for

[1] So much has been written about this conversation between Murat and Bennigsen! Ségur goes so far as to claim that the King of Naples allowed himself to be seduced by the promise of becoming 'King of the Cossacks', or King of Poland, which General Gourgaud sensibly and indignantly refuted. It is much more likely that the King of Naples, who had made no secret of his weariness with the war for a long time, insisted rather too much on his imperial brother-in-law's desire for peace. Thiers has certainly interpreted the affair accurately: 'Bennigsen, by expressing to Murat a desire for peace that was feigned, induced him to express his own desire that was not feigned and, indeed, only too obvious.' (*Histoire du Consulat et de l'Empire*, Vol. XIV, p. 240.)

not beginning negotiations, since he disapproved of the move as much as Caulaincourt. He reckoned that this humiliation inflicted by the Russians was providential. He would be able to return to the Kremlin empty-handed to relate how the *missus dominicus* had been received and the furious Emperor, hurling himself on the enemy without losing a moment, would overthrow him by surprise.

Nevertheless, he finally yielded to the pleas of Murat and Bennigsen. At midnight he was taken to Kutusov.

As soon as their nocturnal encounter was over, Kutusov reported it in detail in a letter to the Tsar. He hated writing, as was well known, but on this occasion there was no time to be lost. He gave his Sovereign a very clear picture; besides, the written content of his pages would be given a verbal commentary by Prince Peter Volkonsky, who left for St Petersburg without delay to take the Field-marshal's letter to Alexander, together with a copy of the French Emperor's letter.

In this long epistle, dated: 'From the village of Tarutino, the 23rd day of September of the year 1812,' the Field-marshal related in detail the conversation between him and Lauriston, 'the former ambassador at St Petersburg', and explained to the 'All-powerful Sovereign' that for this reason he had had 'to retain aide-de-camp general Prince Volkonsky for a further twenty-four hours'. After a lengthy preamble he went on:

'At last he (Lauriston) came to the real point of his mission, that is to say he began to talk about peace, saying that the friendship that had existed between Your Imperial Majesty and the Emperor Napoleon had unfortunately been broken by purely external circumstances; the present moment offered a good opportunity for re-establishing this friendship. 'Must this strange war, this unique war, last eternally, then? My master the Emperor has a sincere desire to end this dispute between two great and generous nations, and to end it for ever.'

'I replied that I had no instructions on this subject and that at my departure to join the armies even the word peace had not been mentioned once; moreover, I had no desire to communicate one iota of all this conversation to my Sovereign, regardless of whether all the words that I had heard from his mouth came from him, as the result of his personal reflections, or of whether they had a higher source; that 'I would be cursed by posterity if I was regarded as the prime mover in any kind of settlement, for such is the prevailing frame of mind of my nation'. At this moment, he handed me a letter from the Emperor Napoleon, a copy of which is enclosed,[1] and asked me to request Your Majesty's authorization for him, Lauriston, to go to St Petersburg with it; and proposed an armistice (which I refused him) while waiting for a reply. Here he impatiently calculated the time it would take for a reply to arrive.

'I promised to comply with his request, which amounted to making the Emperor Napoleon's desire known to Your Majesty . . .'

At the same time that the wily old man had his letter taken to Alexander by Prince Peter Volkonsky, he sent another, by an aide-de-camp, to inform the Sovereign that the Moldavian army's movement on Boruch and Minsk was proceeding satisfactorily.[2] He also referred to the 'parleys entered into with the leaders of the French army'. (He was referring to the conversations between the outposts.) They had only taken place, he made clear, 'with a view to maintaining the pernicious security' in which the French lived at Moscow 'at such an advanced period of the season'.

Some of these parleys were certainly not of a nature to reassure the French. When General Baron Korf met the French General Armande at the outposts 'by chance', the latter declared without more ado:

'We are really very tired of this war! Give us the chance and we will leave.'

Korf retorted sharply: 'Certainly not, General, you came without being invited, so you must take "French leave", without formal goodbyes!'

Upon this, Armande launched into jeremiads about the 'war of

[1] As no trace of this letter from Napoleon has ever been found, certain historians, including Jean Hanoteau, have doubted its existence. (Cf. *Mémoires de Caulaincourt*, Vol. II, note 1, p. 48.) It seems hard to disbelieve in it, in view of what Kutusov wrote above. We may suppose that the Field-marshal destroyed the original and that the Tsar did the same with his copy. We may also accept the theory that both of them were lost. The fact that Kutusov sent his Sovereign *a copy* of Napoleon's letter proves the lengths to which he would go in refusing to transmit any proposal for negotiations. Sending the original would have been to play the intermediary between the two Emperors.

[2] This was disclosed in 1814 to Baron Denniée, in Paris, by 'a high Russian personality, Baron Z . . .', who has always remained anonymous. General Buturlin, in his *Mémoires*, has his doubts about this letter. However, the mysterious Z . . . claimed to have been the bearer of it.

extermination' that 'two nations who hold each other in mutual esteem' were waging. Korf stuck to his guns and played cat and mouse with Armande:

'I admit that you have learnt to hold us in esteem recently, but would you be able to keep that esteem, General, if we let you go as easily as that, arms in hand?'

Elsewhere, Miloradovich declared to a French general, who could only have been Sebastiani:

'Our people are terrors. They would kill on the spot anyone who dared mention peace proposals to them.'

What *der alter Herr*, as Barclay de Tolly nicknamed him, did not relate in his letters was the humorous, or rather the malicious way in which he tormented Napoleon's unfortunate emissary. He was polite, to be sure, and extremely courteous, but brimful of 'that artfulness which particularly distinguished his character', according to one of his aides-de-camp, General Langeron. He placed the letter from the French Emperor nonchalantly on the table and then began to talk—enjoying Lauriston's impatience—of the 'good old days' in St Petersburg when Lauriston had been so welcome in the home of Mme Kutusov. He spoke of the Russian climate, the roads, of this and that. Lauriston could not stand it any longer and urged him to study the letter. The Field-marshal skimmed through it, as if reluctantly, with his one eye and put it back on the table without comment. The exasperated Lauriston burst out:

'His Majesty the Emperor, my master, wants to see the end of this cruel war!'

There was no reply.

The French envoy then dwelt indignantly on the cruelty of the partisans: 'In their fury they sacrifice all the French who fall into their hands!'

Kutusov looked at him calmly and said, with something resembling a smile: 'Our peasants are not yet as civilized as yours, Count, and they have heard stories of the ancient invasions by the Tartars and barbarians whom their ancestors destroyed.'

Tartars, barbarians! These words made the Frenchman spring up. What an insult! 'Not at all,' said Kutusov, 'where is the insult?' The rough peasant 'who sees the enemy bringing fire and the sword to his country' could not help comparing him to 'the enemy of bygone days'.

All right. Let it pass. It was not the essential thing.

'I insist on a decision, Your Most Serene Highness.'

'I will send a letter to His Majesty the Tsar by Prince Volkonsky.'

'When?'

'Tomorrow. You have my word.'

As regards an armistice, they came to a curious arrangement. The front of the two camps (the outposts) would cease sniping for a fortnight, but the two wings would be free to do as they pleased. To break this truce, it would be enough to give two hours' notice.

There were a few more spiteful exchanges before they parted; Lauriston, who had obviously not swallowed the 'tartars', said coldly:

'All the same, there is a difference between the French and the warriors of Genghis Khan!'

The old man retorted ironically: 'The Russian people do not see any.'

The former ambassador persisted: 'It was not the French who burnt Moscow.'

Needless to say, Kutusov had never had the slightest doubt about that. There was something that this Frenchman had not understood:

'The Russians are not more attached to Moscow than to any other town in their empire. What matters is to save the fatherland.'

Napoleon's envoy wanted to have the last word.

'Do not believe,' he said, 'that our affairs our hopeless. You are nearer your provisioning centres, but we have our reserves.'

'What about Spain?' asked Kutusov. 'Fortune has ceased to smile on Napoleon in Spain, as it has in Russia.'

Of course! It must have been Wilson who had informed him. Because of that accursed Englishman, the Count did not have the last word. Yet he made a supreme effort:

'We have indeed suffered reverses, owing to Marmont's stupidity, but everything will be settled, for several army corps have already been sent to Spain. His Majesty places great reliance on the Dukes of Albufera and Istria.'

The interview was over. Lauriston was taken back to Murat's headquarters. From there, he returned to Moscow.

In Napoleon's study in the Kremlin, Lauriston gave a very succinct résumé of the preceding day's tête-à-tête, stressing only the

parts calculated to please the Emperor. First point: the letter had
left for St Petersburg. At once, His Majesty smiled joyfully and
triumphantly at his entourage. This time, he assured them, there
would be a reply; a fortnight would be long enough for it to arrive;
he alone knew the Russians.

'On receipt of my letter, bonfires will be seen in St Petersburg!'
Lauriston did not dampen his ardour. He even confirmed that in
his opinion the Russians' state of mind seemed 'absolutely satis-
factory'. Strange! Only a week ago he had been just as opposed to
any form of negotiation as his bête noire, Caulaincourt, and the
inveterate moderators, Narbonne, Daru, always firm and precise,
and the Count de Lobau, who was accustomed to pass censure
authoritatively, putting forward accurate facts 'in few words'. And
here was Lauriston holding the diametrically opposite view. We
must believe, with Ségur, that he retained 'a stronger impression
of Bennigsen's soft words than of Kutusov's thrusts and reticences'
or that, like Murat, he was now persuaded that the Russians 'display
nothing but weariness with the war and hope of peace'.

As he spoke, horizons broadened and his whole tone became more
optimistic. He no longer said simply that Prince Volkonsky had left
for the capital to take Napoleon's letter to Alexander, but that the
Field-marshal had told him to urge the Emperor of Russia to adhere
to the peace proposals of the French Emperor! Everyone repeated
'Count Lauriston met with a very good reception,' and they allowed
themselves to be carried away by a vague feeling of hope. On
October 10th, the Marquis de Méjan wrote to a Piedmontese
friend: 'For three days there have been rumours of peace here that
I think a little *precocious*, although I don't think they are *absurd*.'
He, too, had been won over by the atmosphere which Napoleon
was trying to create at all costs: the hope of a peace was not absurd.
In this highly critical 'military position', complicated by 'the most
delicate ever political situation', the Emperor, 'hitherto so great
because of his unswerving perseverance', could not accept a prompt
renunciation of the goal he had set himself. That was how Philippe
de Ségur, in his blissful loyalty, interpreted the situation as
Napoleon had created it; he was not the man to risk raising objections, nor to confess that henceforth all argument was specious and
that hope was not only absurd, but *senseless*.

Yet the weather was so fine! The very day of Lauriston's return,
Napoleon had written to Marie Louise: 'The weather here is

beautiful, as warm as at Paris. We have just had those lovely *Fontainebleau days*.'[1] The unusual, mild, superb weather was the sole topic of conversation and everyone was amazed by it. But it was another illusion, like the armistice.

Had Lauriston been taken in by the armistice, that patched-up truce? Certainly not! He was not Murat. Napoleon was even less deceived, that was clear. But the idea, the very word 'armistice' pleased and cheered them up, for, in a sense, an armistice is the anteroom of peace. So the word was seized on like a fetish, while everyone knew perfectly well that the Cossacks' raids continued worse than ever, that they could not bring in a convoy or go on a foraging expedition without leaving men and horses behind. And, in any case, this truce did not even touch the partisans, who were bolder and more aggressive every day, because they were more numerous, better organized and better armed, inspired by heroic temerity, with numbers of extraordinary daredevils in their ranks, including many women.

Napoleon was so well aware of all those facts that on the same day as Lauriston's return he ordered Marshal Victor, Duke of Belluno, to concentrate on Vilna and then take up a position between Orcha and Smolensk. It was a 'precaution'; these troops were to supply a 'general reserve', either for Gouvion-Saint-Cyr, or if he found himself in difficulties at Polotsk, for Schwartzenberg, if he was pressed by Tormassov's army, *or even for the Grand Army of Moscow*.[2] In this way, he envisaged using all the means at his disposal to support himself and meet the dangers that might threaten his rear. So there was no excessive confidence, in spite of appearances. He continued to keep an eye on everything, but at the same time launched into optimistic speeches again, using the Duke Vicenza as an audience. Caulaincourt had the stubborn look of his bad days. No one would make him change his mind now, any more than they had been able to before. Perhaps even less. The Emperor embarked on a diatribe against Alexander:

'He is stubborn. He will be sorry for it. He will never have such good conditions as those I would have given him at this moment. Giving Poland back all its former frontiers and creating three grand duchies there; closing all the Russian ports to the English, pro-

---

[1] *Lettres . . .*, op. cit. (No. 105, October 6, 1812).
[2] *Correspondance . . .*, op. cit. (No. 19,258, of October 6, 1812).

posing a defensive and offensive alliance between the Tsar and the Emperor to drive the Turks out of Europe permanently; lastly, sending about 40,000 Cossacks to India to attack the English.'[1]

But Caulaincourt was unshakeable.

'Perhaps,' he retorted, 'Kutusov is trying to lull Your Majesty to sleep in Moscow? They must be feeling the advantages of our difficulties at St Petersburg.'

Incensed, Napoleon got on his high horse. 'What do you call our difficulties?'

'Why, the winter, Sire, the lack of magazines, of horses for your artillery, of transport for your sick, the poor clothing of your soldiers, the interruption of your communications . . .'

A pause, then: 'So you think that I should leave Moscow?'

'Yes, Sire.'

'If I went, I would prevent the reply from arriving and having a result. The Russians cannot put up with this state of affairs for long. Kutusov and his generals are so well aware of it that they want peace.'

At this moment Prince Volkonsky was on the point of arriving at St Petersburg, carrying Kutusov's letter. Another few miles and there was the gate, the broad avenues, the Neva between its granite quays, the monumental staircase and the Tsar's study. And there was Alexander buttoned up tight in his white and green uniform. Very tall, very erect. His eyes deep blue. He held out his hand. A white, feminine hand. The hand of his grandmother Catherine II. He read Kutusov's letter and the copy of Napoleon's letter, and said:

'Peace? But we haven't waged war yet. My campaign is only beginning!'

A rather grandiose phrase and undoubtedly one of the few great phrases he ever pronounced. The flame that inspired him and burnt purely at that moment was the flame inspiring all his people. The fact that he was the man of a fleeting moment did not matter: he was that man to the full and the future could not tarnish that deep and sincere impulse, that obstinate determination and that mani-

[1] This had been one of Napoleon's ideas before he was Emperor and when Paul I was reigning in Russia. A start was even made on this crazy expedition. 20,000 Cossacks had left under the leadership of Hetman Platov, but the assassination of Paul I had stopped everything.

festation of energy—fleeting though it was—by a man whose
weakness of character was his worst curse.

He replied belatedly to Kutusov on October 9th/21st, in an
imperious tone:

'Prince Mikhail Larionovitch! by your report sent with Prince
Volkonsky, I learnt of the interview that has taken place between
yourself and the French aide-de-camp general, Lauriston.

'At the very moment of your departure for the armies that were
entrusted to you, you knew, from the explanations I gave you
personally, of my firm and insistent desire to abstain from all
negotiations and all relations with the adversary that might have
tended to produce a peace.

'But today, after these events, I must repeat with the same
firmness that the rule established by me must be respected strictly
and resolutely in its entirety.

'By the same occasion, I learnt with extreme displeasure that
General Bennigsen has had an interview with the King of Naples
and, what is more, without any urgent motive.

'Pointing out the unseemliness of his behaviour, I demand you to
exercise strict and effective supervision to prevent the other Generals
from having any interviews, and if the possibility of interviews
should arise, I ask you to see that they try to avoid them by all
possible means.

'All the news you receive from Me, all My exhortations, all the
Ukases issued in my name, in a word everything convinces you of
My firm resolution: at the present moment no proposal by the
adversary will incite me to cease battle and in so doing to weaken
our sacred obligation to avenge the injured fatherland.

'I remain, your ever well-disposed,

                                                        'Alexander.

'St Petersburg,
October 9, 1812.'

As for Napoleon, he had taken similar measures as early as
September 27th. Through the Prince of Neuchâtel, he had expressly
forbidden his high-ranking officers to parley with the Russians, or
to receive anyone at the outposts. 'All parleys with the enemy
always turn to our disadvantage and the man who provokes them
has a reason for them . . . That reason is obviously our demoralization!' he wrote.

Sending Lauriston stood for something quite different. A higher parley, as it were, on the imperial level. According to the Emperor, it could not but bear excellent results.

Of course, no answer came from the Tsar and none would ever come. He had nothing to say to Napoleon.

The French Emperor's nervous irritation was mingled with a dull anxiety and melancholy, which everyone observed in gloomy silence. Baron Fain, his devoted secretary, sighed when he saw his master, who was 'so accessible to the proposals of his enemies', repulsed at the first attempt he had believed he could make. 'And by whom?' he exclaimed. 'By the Prince from whom he had received a letter scribbled on a rag on the field of Austerlitz, whose truce-bearing boat he had welcomed on the banks of the Tilsit and who only recently had claimed to be his best friend!' And he watched Napoleon pacing through the Kremlin, night after night, and he saw on his roll-top desk one single book: *L'Histoire de Charles XII* by Voltaire. For some time it had been the Emperor's only reading and he constantly went back to the pages concerning the defeat of the King of Sweden by Tsar Peter I, beneath the walls of Poltava.

He planned to leave Moscow between October 13th and 18th. They would fall back on Smolensk. They would winter there. In the spring, they would march on St Petersburg in force.

'There is absolutely no question of a retreat, it is a strategic march,' commented Napoleon. 'My army is not beaten as far as I know!'

He had had all the almanacs for the last forty years consulted, and had concluded that the severe frosts did not arrive until the first days of December. That was twice as much time as he needed to reach Smolensk. Once this plan was studied and developed, he turned to another and enthused about it:

'I am going to attack Kutusov. If I beat him, as is probable, the Emperor Alexander will run great risks. He could end the war immediately, by one single word. If he reflected, he would see that that can go a long way with a man of my temperament, because his refusal to reply to any of my offers will mean that I no longer have to handle him with kid gloves.'

His great temptation was a rapid battle with the old Field-marshal 'to remove him to a distance and be left in peace'. If anyone pointed out the absolute lack of everything necessary to protect the troops from the cold, he replied as if he was talking to foreigners:

'You don't know the French. They will have everything they need; one thing will take the place of another.'

During this time, his soldiers were writing morose letters, which, with a few exceptions, were all strangely alike: 'We are not well off here, I assure you. Very often we have neither bread nor meat. We eat what we can . . .'

Snow fell on October 13th. This perplexed Napoleon. Had the bad weather arrived without warning and had Caulaincourt, whom he had mocked so much, been right after all?

'We must hurry!' he said. 'We must be in our winter quarters in twenty days.'

He decreed that they should move towards Kaluga. The King of Naples would continue to hang on at Vinkovo, where he had been since October 4th, beyond the river Tschernitschaya. The Russians were six miles to the north in the retrenched camp of Tarutino; if the King's position became untenable, he was authorized to fall back on Voronovo, Rostopchin's estate, some eleven miles north of Vinkovo, on the old road to Kaluga. The Emperor informed him of this urgently by letter at two in the morning, saying specifically: 'the position of Voronovo is excellent and compact, and can be defended by the infantry, who could easily cover the cavalry.' But Murat remained obstinately at Vinkovo, against all common sense and to everyone's misfortune.

The trophies, those famous trophies intended to commemorate the glorious capture of Moscow in Paris, were dispatched under the supervision of General Claparède. Convoys of wounded were put on the road to Mozhaysk where Junot, Duke of Abrantes, was in command. He had been kicking his heels there since the month of August. He went mad as a result, in the strictest sense of the word. His passionate attachment to Napoleon (his friend since the siege of Toulon) had at all times made him touchy, sensitive and jealous. The fact that the Emperor had not summoned him to join him in Moscow was sufficient proof for Junot that he no longer liked him!

On October 14th, the weather seemed more promising. Napoleon wrote to Marie Louise: 'We have had the first snows; yet it is not cold.' However, a semi-confession burst through at the end of the letter: 'I do not think I can come to Paris yet and to bring you to Poland is a very long way.'

He ordered Berthier not to let any artillery convoys go beyond Smolensk; the cavalry and artillery corps were to halt at Mozhaysk, Gzhatsk and Vyazma, while awaiting further orders.

The faithful Count Daru, whose 'profound knowledge of details' the Emperor had always admired and whose 'work was as rapid as his own thoughts' in his estimation, declared that it was too late to march against Kutusov:

'His army is re-established, ours is weakened, our victory forgotten.'

'What are we to do then?' cried the Emperor.

'Stay here. Turn Moscow into a great fortified camp and spend the winter in it. In the spring our reinforcements and the whole of the Lithuanian army will come to free us, join forces with us and complete the conquest.'

Napoleon brooded for a while, then he said:

'That is the advice of a lion! But what would Paris say? We cannot foresee the effect of six months without communication! No, France would not get used to my absence; Prusssia and Austria would take advantage of it.'

Nevertheless, he could not make up his mind whether to stay or go. 'Conquered in this battle of stubbornness, he put off admitting his defeat from day to day.' On October 15th, he signed the first and only decree from Moscow, he who had dreamed of issuing so many—it was the decree that gave the Comédie Française a statute intended to be permanent. He had drafted it in three evenings.

To his Minister of Police, Savary, Duke of Rovigo, he wrote:

'The war will probably be prolonged throughout the winter and only the capture of St Petersburg will open the eyes of Emperor Alexander. Moscow no longer exists. This is actually an important loss for this empire, whose centre and pride it quite rightly was. All the officers in the Russian army seem to be in despair because of the Muscovite catastrophe, which they attribute to the senseless and furious passions of a sort of Marat, Rostopchin, the Governor General of the town. I have evacuated all my hospitals that were installed in the houses among the ruins. I have only fortified the Kremlin, which is now safe from sudden attack. 2 or 3,000 men could hold out there for some time. I have installed all my munitions and food supplies there ...'

Then he made an abrupt allusion to his departure: 'I shall soon be leaving to prepare my winter quarters and my operations for next year ...'

On top of this, he belittled the enemy's infantry, saying that it was 'insignificant'. According to all his information, it numbered only 15,000 regular soldiers; 'the remainder consists of militiamen of the territorial reserve'. However, 'the enemy has reinforced his cavalry. He has quadrupled the number of his Cossacks, the countryside is flooded with them, which causes a lot of very troublesome minor skirmishes'. Once again he was watering down the facts by this brief allusion to the continuous harassing by the Cossack cavalry and their understudies—the light squadrons of mounted partisans. Napoleon pretended to treat them with scorn when writing about them to the Duke of Rovigo, but was worried nevertheless at noting that one out of two convoys was attacked and often captured!

The letter to Savary was dated October 16th. That same night, the Emperor lost his patience and sent Lauriston back to the outposts, after he had written to the Duke of Bassano that he would *probably* set up his winter quarters between the Dnieper and the Duna.

At Vinkovo, Lauriston rejoined the King of Naples, who obstinately insisted on staying there, merely keeping a rather inattentive eye on the Russians and, by his negligence, allowing his cavalry, which had already been so roughly handled since the beginning of the campaign, to deteriorate.[1]

It was agreed that Murat's aide-de-camp, Colonel Berthémy, should take Prince Kutusov the 'dispatch' that the Emperor had dictated to the Prince of Neuchâtel.

'*The Prince of Neufchatel and Wagram to the General in Chief Kutusoff.*

[1] There is no lack of evidence on this subject. Here is the opinion of a captain in the 16th Light Cavalry who went through the whole of the 1812 campaign under Murat's command: 'The King of Naples, who is very brave personally, has little military talent. He is primarily responsible for the ruin of the cavalry, not only by exposing it often and quite uselessly, but also by placing it far from water and forage.'

'Moscow, October 16, 1812.

'General Lauriston was given the mission of proposing to Your Highness the making of arrangements to give the war a character in conformity with the established rules and the taking of the indispensable measures resulting from the state of war. In fact, the devastation of her own country is harmful to Russia, as much as it affects the Emperor painfully; Your Highness will readily feel the interest I have in ascertaining the definitive decision of his government.

'Respectfully, etc. . . .

(Signed): Alexandre.'[1]

(*Berthier*).

In short, it was a text in which Berthier committed himself as little as possible and which was apparently meant to refer to the actions of the partisans. In reality it was a veiled question: 'Had a reply been received from the Winter Palace or not?'

For, in spite of the emphatic rebukes of his entourage, rebukes whose justice the Emperor understood, he insisted on making this new and humiliating move. He had merely agreed to spare Lauriston any risk of being insulted; hence the dispatch of Colonel Berthémy to Russian headquarters.

Once the message had been transmitted to Kutusov, who obviously could not keep it secret, Sir Robert Wilson flew into another of his Britannic rages. He sent Lord Cathcart a malicious report:

'I know,' he wrote, 'that the Field-marshal would not dare to begin negotiations, without risking his life; I am convinced that the Emperor [the Tsar] would consider anyone who should propose negotiations to him as a traitor; but the impression of these reports is so harmful from the internal, external, political and military point of view that their consequences may become disastrous . . . and the most reasonable people are filled with distress by them.'

This text, which was obviously meant to reach Alexander I, became more and more venomous as it continued:

'The Field-marshal is undoubtedly disposed to woo the enemy,

[1] *Correspondance . . .,* op. cit. (Vol. XXIV, No. 19,277).

the French compliments delight him. He esteems these birds of prey who have come to seize Poland from Russia, to foment a revolution in Russia itself and to provoke the Cossacks of the Don, whom they greatly appreciate and whose good-will they seek to ensure by advances and favours . . .'

The English observer even went so far as to play Achilles sulking in his tent and threatened to leave headquarters 'if the Field-marshal kept the supreme command and if the Emperor did not forbid him to maintain personal relations with the French.'

Wilson's attitude to a large extent influenced a decision that Kutusov was preparing to take—somewhat owing to the effect of exasperation. His decision would be that *surprise*, which, as the Duke of Vicenza sadly noted, 'was going to open everyone's eyes so cruelly'.

Lauriston, his mission accomplished, returned to the Kremlin on October 17th, only twenty-four hours after he had left it. He had no reason for delaying.

The reply of His Most Serene Highness Prince Mikhail Ilariono-vich Kutusov was not to reach Napoleon until six days later. In the interval, the future of the Grand Army was decided.

PART IV

Thus finished this gigantic enterprise that had begun under such happy auspices ... History cannot show the example of a similar disaster. I ask those who will read me to join me in admiring so much courage and bemoaning so many misfortunes.

COLONEL MARQUIS DE FEZENSAC

The glory of Kutusov is inseparable from the glory of Russia, from the memory of the greatest event in our contemporary history. His title—the saviour of Russia; his monument—the rock of Saint Helena.

PUSHKIN

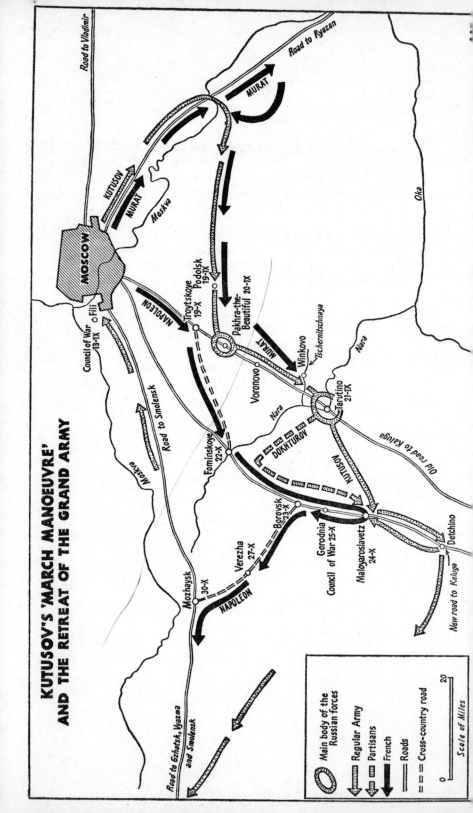

KUTUSOV'S 'MARCH MANOEUVRE' AND THE RETREAT OF THE GRAND ARMY

Road to Vladimir

Road to Ryazan

MURAT

KUTUSOV

MURAT

Moskva

MOSCOW

Oka

Council of War 13-IX · Fili

NAPOLEON

Troytskoye 19-X · Podolsk 19-X

Pakhra-the-Beautiful 20-IX

MURAT · Winkovo · Tschernitschnaya

Voronovo

Nara

Nara

Tarutino 21-IX

Road to Smolensk

Fominskoye 22-X

DOKHTUROV

Old road to Kaluga

Moskva

KUTUSOV

Borovsk 23-X

Gorodnia · Council of War 25-X

Maloyaroslavetz 24-X

Detchino

Verezha 27-X

Mozhaysk · 30-X

NAPOLEON

New road to Kaluga

Road to Gzhatsk, Vyazma and Smolensk

Legend

Main body of the Russian forces
Regular Army
Partisans
French
Roads
═ ═ ═ Cross-country road

Scale of Miles

0 _____ 20

10

A SUDDEN DEPARTURE

So the essential fault was the enterprise itself. To look for the faults of execution that could also be added to the main fault would be unprofitable, if nearly all the faults of execution had not flowed from the main fault.

THIERS,
Histoire du Consulat et de l'Empire

AT noon on October 18th the Emperor attended the daily parade in the courtyard of the Kremlin. That day he was reviewing the 3rd Corps, commanded by Marshal Ney, Duke of Elchingen. People thought they caught the rumble of cannon fire in the distance, carried by the south wind. At one o'clock in the afternoon, a horseman arrived, looking dog-tired. He dismounted and handed dispatches to Napoleon; it was M. de Bérenger, one of the King of Naples' lieutenants. Immediately the order was given to break up the review.

The news brought by Bérenger was serious. Murat reported that at daybreak—the moment when he least expected it—the Russians had left their fortified camp at Tarutino and attacked him 'with all their forces' (which was inaccurate). The King's forces had been very roughly handled; he had lost 3,000 men, 36 cannon, 50 cases of ammunition and the few cavalry he had left. Only a desperate counter-attack had enabled the French troops to regroup on the left bank of the River Tschernitschnaya, mainly owing to Generals Claparède and de Latour-Maubourg, commanding a division of the Imperial Guard and the 4th Cavalry Corps respectively.

The day before, the Emperor had decided to order the departure for October 20th. Now, everything was suddenly, brutally changed. Once again events had decided for the man, who, before this campaign, had always been the master of his decisions.

After a long silence, the Emperor addressed the Prince of Neuchâtel:

'We must wash out the insult of this surprise.'

So he considered this unforeseen attack as an insult, and was already thinking of the effect it was going to have on his empire.

'They must not be allowed to say in France that a set-back has forced us to retire.'

As for the unforeseen nature of this event, he hastened to throw the blame on his brother-in-law:

'What stupidity on the King's part! No one looks after himself.' This upsets all my plans. Everything is being spoilt for me. The honour of our arms must be re-established on the battle-field. We shall see if the Russians make the same showing there as in this surprise attack. It seems as if the King has inflicted some damage on them, too, for they have not dared to follow him. At all events, we must march to support and avenge him!'

It was true that the Russians had suffered some damage and lost one of their best leaders, General Bagovut; it was also true that Platov and his Cossacks had pursued Murat, but had not persisted. The truth was that they had by no means deployed 'all their forces'. At all events, their position remained just as solid.

Once back in his apartments in the Kremlin, the Emperor betrayed very noticeable physical agitation. He repeatedly opened the door of the salon where his duty officers were, asking now for one person, then another, speaking quickly, in a dry, brusque tone, in broken sentences, as he had always done when he experienced annoyances or dissatisfaction. He seemed unable to remain still for a moment. At mealtimes, he rose from the table almost as soon as he was served. M. de Bausset, who watched him with concern, felt that the victor of Austerlitz had only just understood all the fatal consequences of such a long stay in Moscow.

Indeed, the Emperor seemed to have realized all of a sudden that the die was cast, since the Russians had passed to the offensive for the first time in the campaign. That was the unexpected but decisive factor that forced the French Emperor to leave Moscow, he who had said to Daru such a short while before: 'That would look like flight! Imagine the repercussions in Europe!' Henceforth there could be no question of beating about the bush, waiting for a reply from Alexander or constructing plans for next spring. Now he was forced to embark urgently on a course he had been reluctant to choose and to set in motion the dangerous machinery of a retreat.

It was indeed, as Talleyrand was to say, 'the beginning of the end'.

However, the most important thing of all was to depart 'in the manner of an enemy who is performing a manœuvre, and not that of an enemy who is beating a retreat'. Napoleon insisted on that point in all his discussions with his general staff. He reverted to it in a letter to Maret, Duke of Bassano, who was guarding Vilna. Yet even to that old comrade the Emperor was set on painting reality a little differently from what it really was:

'I already warned you several days ago that I was counting on leaving to take up my winter quarters between the Borysthenes (the *Dnieper*) and the Duna. The time has come. The army is on the move. I shall leave Moscow on the 19th. I shall depart by the road to Kaluga. If the enemy wants to cover this town, I shall defeat him; then, depending on the requirements of the season, I will make a surprise attack on Tula, or I shall return directly via Vyazma. In any case, towards the first weeks of November, I will have brought my troops into the square which lies between Smolensk, Mogilev, Minsk and Vitebsk. I am deciding on this movement because Moscow is no longer a military position. I am going to seek another more favourable one at the beginning of the next campaign. The operations will then be directed towards St Petersburg or Kiev.'

A by no means pessimistic letter, which presented the facts in such a way as to make the recipient believe that the departure was foreseen and planned. In other words, Maret had no need to be alarmed! However, at the end of the letter, written on the very day when the Emperor had learnt of the disaster of Vinkovo, a phrase slipped in that resembled a sigh: 'Moreover, in affairs of this nature, the event often turns out to differ greatly from what has been envisaged . . .'

The event also differed from what had been envisaged for Field-marshal Kutusov, because the attack on Murat's vanguard did not enter into his plans.

From the beginning, i.e. Smolensk, he had made it his fixed intention to husband his troops and material. Borodino had been 'an inevitable evil', but another battle as atrocious had to be avoided at all costs. In fact, the old man was not bent on the total destruction of Napoleon and the Grand Army, but on driving them from

Russian territory. Until his death, which was not so far away,[1] he would never cease repeating that the destruction of the French emperor could only be to the advantage of England. Besides, the old man considered the burning of Moscow as a veritable defeat for Napoleon, as important as a battle lost. The rest, he estimated, would follow of its own accord. But the Tsar did not see the situation in the same light, so that to the very end the Monarch and the Field-marshal would be opposed in a bitter controversy about the aims of war. And the Grand-duchess Catherine Pavlovna would continually point out to her brother 'the ineffectiveness' of the old warrior, who, according to her, was 'a contemptible man, to whom honour is a word devoid of meaning'. Here she was purely feminine in her inability to modify her passionate and subjective judgment. She wrote: 'The physique [of Kutusov] must be prejudicial to him in his present post, for, with that massive body, he cannot like activity, and the inaction of the army is only the result of his personal laziness.'[2]

Meanwhile, Kutusov, firmly implanted at Tarutino, watched his general staff growing impatient and grumbling. For several days now—in fact since Murat had taken up his position at Vinkovo on October 4th—the Russian generals had been pestering their chief to attack the French vanguard, which was only some 22,000 strong. It was within striking distance, poorly defended and badly situated. (The King of Naples, disregarding Napoleon's advice, had not fallen back on better positions.) Their scouts? It was obvious that they were doing nothing. They appeared to be entertaining themselves. It was high time to change over to action. That was the sort of talk that the old man heard buzzing in his ears from morning to night. Though tired of war, he finally let himself be swayed. He had had more than enough of Wilson's denunciations and the jeremiads of the general staff, who with the exception of Ermolov and Miloradovich, detested and criticized him. All right! He would throw them a bone to chew—those impatient, short-sighted generals, those bad chess players.

If operations were properly planned, thought Mikhail Ilarionovich, there was no need for large troop concentrations to swoop on the enemy and destroy him. Consequently, the Field-marshal only allowed General Bennigsen a fairly small body of men and scanty

---

[1] Kutusov died on April 16, 1813, at Bunzlau, in Silesia, during the German campaign.
[2] *Lettres d'Alexandre . . .*, op. cit. (October 3, 1812, pp. 93–6).

material. The attack was swift, the battle fierce, but finally, in spite of big losses on the French side and heavy enough losses on the Russian side, the skirmish fizzled out and Napoleon had been alarmed for nothing.

Bennigsen was beside himself with rage. The whole of Murat's army corps could have been smashed if Kutusov had sent reinforcements, he asserted, not without reason. But reinforcements had been categorically refused. Foaming at the mouth, Bennigsen wrote to his wife on October 10th/22nd:

'I can't get over it! This magnificent, this brilliant day could have had incalculable consequences if I had been supported. Before the eyes of the whole army, Kutusov forbids the sending of even a single man to my aid, those are his own words . . . Imagine my situation: I have to wrangle with him whenever it is a question of making a move against the enemy. His cowardice exceeds even the limits accepted for poltroons . . . He has become ridiculous in the eyes of the whole army . . .'

It was a lie and Bennigsen must have known it. As for what he said about cowardice, it was a disgraceful calumny, and he knew that, too. But this did not stop him from addressing a treacherous memorandum to his supreme commander:

'The troops of His Imperial Majesty had won this victory in a style such as one only sees on manœuvres. It is regrettable that Your Highness was much too far from the battlefield and could not see the splendid spectacle of the enemy's defeat!'

It was true that the Old One—as they called him more than ever at his headquarters—had refused Bennigsen reinforcements, mainly, it was also true, out of a sort of vindictiveness. He had yielded to this individual whom he despised merely to put a stop to his recriminations, but expecting him to look after himself. If he could not, so much the worse for him. But this petty motive, though quite in keeping with His Most Serene Highness's character, was not the only one in this affair. Dorokhov and his partisans had come to warn him the day before (October 17th) that Napoleon seemed to be on the point of leaving Moscow. So, in the Field-marshal's view, the important thing was not to waste his troops in a battle that was not imperatively required by any strategical need. He was satisfied with the success gained by the Russians. He regretted nothing. He knew that this Tarutino–Vinkovo skirmish marked an important date, because the Russians had taken the initiative. The giant chessboard had been placed by them and they had made the first move.

But Bennigsen was not pacified and sent a letter denouncing his chief to the Tsar. He accused him of abandoning the army to its fate, of not attending to anything and 'living in ease and luxury'. Alexander sent this letter to Kutusov after he had read it. To put him on his guard against his entourage? To play him a dirty trick? Alexander dare not, could not discharge this detested old man, but perhaps he was satisfied with letting him know what Bennigsen thought of him—Bennigsen whom the Tsar valued so highly! And perhaps it was also a devious and rather hypocritical way of showing Kutusov what his Sovereign felt about him.

Once more, the Field-marshal shrugged his shoulders, but all the same the insult was too flagrant this time. He sent for Bennigsen and ordered him to leave the army. Then he devoted himself to an urgent task. Sesslavin and Dorokhov had just informed him that Napoleon had left Moscow immediately after the news of Murat's defeat. The French army had taken the old road to Kaluga, so apparently it was making straight for the fortified camp.

Well and good, let them come! The Russian army, fortified and equipped, was ready for anything; so were the partisans. And soon 'General Winter' would emerge from the woods.

On October 18th, the poster at the Pozniakov Theatre announced *Les Amants Protées*. For most of the day the company had rehearsed *Le Sourd*, which was billed for two days later. Night fell. *Les Amants Protées* had a great success. When she reached home after the show, Mme Fusil was unable to go straight to bed. First she had to patch up the costume of 'Petronilla', a part she was to play on the 20th. It grew late. She was sleepy. Suddenly there was a knock on the door. It was a French officer who lived in the same house. Louise Fusil opened her eyes wide when she saw that he was 'armed from head to toe' and seemed to be in a daze. He stared at the actress in bewilderment and asked:

'What are you doing, Madame?'

'As you see, Sir, I am getting a dress ready for my part.'

The soldier uttered inarticulate cries, then said impatiently:

'If you'll take my advice you'd do better to get your bags ready for tomorrow morning! We're leaving in two hours.'

That was how Mme Fusil came to be the first of the 'Franco-Muscovites' to be warned of the departure of the Grand Army, the first person to be confronted with the dilemma of whether to leave or to stay. The question was going to arise urgently for everyone 'who had been compromised by their trust in Napoleon's luck', noted the Chevalier d'Ysarn, who stayed on the spot, since he had nothing to reproach himself for. But a large number of people, as innocent of collaboration or compromise as he was, were seized with panic all the same and believed that they would be lost if the Russians found them there on their return. None of them were left much time for reflection and consequently, with fear as their only counsellor, some 3,000 men, women and children fled from imaginary dangers and rushed to meet ordeals that were only too real. The majority disappeared completely in the tragic collapse of Napoleon's army. Miraculously, Louise Fusil was among the fugitives who saw France again; all she brought back with her was a little orphan girl she had picked up at Vilna. Later she skilfully (and profitably) managed to interest high Parisian society of the Restoration in the girl's fate.

'On the evening of October 18th,' wrote Sergeant Bourgogne, 'when several of us non-commissioned officers had met together as we did every day, stretched out like pashas on ermine, sable, lion and bear skins, smoking tobacco of the Indies perfumed with roses in exquisite pipes, with a monster punch made of Jamaican rum flaming in our midst, at the moment when we were talking about France and the joy it would be to return there as conquerors . . . we heard a great commotion in the big salon where the soldiers of the company were sleeping. At the same instant, the *fourrier* of the week entered to tell us that, by order, we must get ourselves ready to leave . . .'

The vanguard, commanded by the Viceroy, Ney's 3rd corps and the 1st corps of Davout left during the night. They were to be followed at dawn by the Roguet division, responsible for escorting the headquarters' equipages and the convoy of treasures and trophies. Then came the Old Guard, behind it the Young Guard, and lastly the cavalry. The Emperor was preparing to leave in person on the morning of Sunday, October 19th. Forced to leave Moscow before the date envisaged, he decided to leave some troops there and accordingly dictated an order for Marshal Mortier to the Prince of Neuchâtel:

'*Moscow, October 18, 1812.*

'My cousin, inform the Duke of Treviso that I leave tomorrow morning with the army to pursue the enemy; that it is my intention that the Duke of Treviso reside in the Kremlin and quarter there:

'1 the Laborde division;

'2 the brigade of General Carrière, composed of four battalions of dismounted cavalry, 4,000 men strong;

'3 two companies of sappers;

'4 one company of artillery;

'5 the artillery of the Laborde division.

'Lastly a brigade of 500 troopers; with this force the Duke of Treviso will be able to guard the town, but with the appropriate prudence . . .'

He ordered Mortier to fortify and mine the Kremlin, and 'to keep a post' in the convent occupied by Davout, the position of which was important because it commanded a bridge over the Moskva. The sick soldiers who could not be evacuated were to be assembled in the Foundlings' Home. Lastly, the Emperor came to a question that was of capital importance to him:

'Tomorrow, after the army has left, the Duke of Treviso will have a proclamation made by the municipality warning the inhabitants that the rumours of evacuation are false; that the army is moving on Kaluga, Tula and Briansk to seize those important points and the arms factories they contain; and binding the inhabitants to maintain public order and prevent anyone from trying to complete the destruction of the town.'

That was what he had set his heart on: neither Russia, nor Paris, nor Europe must believe that Napoleon was abandoning Moscow for good. Moreover, it was not a pretence, for in the Emperor's view, this retreat was by no means definitive. His immediate aim was to rejoin Murat, who had finally fallen back on Voronovo, the place where his brother-in-law had directed him to take up a position at the very beginning of October. With the remains of these troops and Junot's army corps (which was to come from Mozhaysk), the army would number about 140,000 men capable of fighting. They would march straight on the enemy in order to drive them ahead, push them back and occupy the fertile provinces and the factories at Tula.

What was it like, this army that was leaving Moscow? The Marquis de Chambray asserted that the infantry was excellent, composed almost entirely of experienced soldiers, who had 'recovered from their fatigue'—which was less certain. At all events, it was enervated by the delights of Moscow and had been short of wholesome food. The artillery was eager for the fray, but 'very poorly equipped with horses, gun-carriages and wagons'; the cavalry was 'in the worst possible state'. So Napoleon's hopes rested almost entirely on his infantry.

Another hope was that Kutusov would refuse battle and strike camp on the enemy's approach. That was why it was necessary to march on him by the old Kaluga road, as recommended by the Duke of Eckmühl a few days previously, but rejected at the time by Napoleon. Now this choice was forced on him and in order to achieve his plan, he had the new road cleared—a fatal blunder, as he would very soon realize, when his expectations were frustrated; but at the time, the movement represented very specific tactics to him.

When all the orders had been given, the Emperor prepared to leave the town which he had dreamed of possessing in all its splendour, but which he had found transformed into a mass of smoking ruins, a month ago to the day, on his return from Petrovskoye. This town had conquered him. The wily Kutusov had been quite right: the burning of Moscow was a defeat for Napoleon; a battle lost—the most important before Waterloo. It contained the seeds of the retreat that turned into a debacle and the annihilation of the army. 'I defeated armies but I could not conquer the flames'—this declaration, made much later, when everything was over, was not empty rhetoric, but a statement of fact. The Emperor had succeeded in conquering the ancient capital of Russia, but he had taken it in flames—an immense pyre that symbolized the refusal of the Russian people, which 'illuminated the soul' of every combatant, as it did the Tsar's. 'Scythians! Vandals!' Napoleon had exclaimed. Perhaps. But those barbarians had conquered 'the grand general leading the grand army' by fire, as surely as by arms.

True, it was not directly because of the fire that they were leaving today, but the fire was responsible for the departure, nevertheless. Because of it, thirty-five days had been spent divorced from reality and everything had been distorted by this incredible conflagration. Kutusov ought to have been overthrown long before and Napoleon's army installed in the south; but Napoleon had persisted obstinately, wishing to prove to the world that even the flames could not oust him. During that time, Kutusov had made his counter-attack possible. And Napoleon finally left Moscow.

It seemed as though he withdrew regretfully, as though his sudden decision weighed heavily on him. As he left these pathetic ruins he was still obsessed by another vision that he could not help recalling even at the moment of departure—a vision of Moscow as he had seen it for the first time on a radiant September afternoon, from the top of the Mount of the Salutation. And in the last letter he addressed to the Empress, before passing through the gate, he spoke again of the city he was abandoning, the city which, such a short while ago, had seemed to him 'so much the more beautiful and so much the more astonishing because it was almost the only one of this size in this immense country.'

11

TOWARDS THE CATASTROPHE

That is where the Russian catastrophe began.

PHILIPPE DE SÉGUR

IN his critical situation Napoleon really needed a mobile army ready for rapid marches, because the success of the operation depended exclusively on the speed and suddenness of the manœuvres. But the Grand Army that left Moscow from October 18th to 19th was a sort of monster that could only move clumsily and slowly.

It seemed as if an ironic destiny had chosen to enact here the counterpart of the Russian exodus on September 14th: the civilian 'Franco-Russians' obstructed Napoleon's rearguard just as the Muscovite civilians had held up Kutusov's rearguard. Large numbers of the French colony—the small world of the Bridge of the Marshals and the parish of Saint-Louis-des-Français—were escaping from the hatred of those who had recently made much of them and who would very soon be returning to their town. All these bewildered folk had crammed their bundles, cases and furniture into carriages or onto carts. Each one of them might well think, as during the preceding exodus: 'This is no longer the march of an army, but the migration of a whole people!'

The civilians were not the only hindrance to the troops. None of the soldiers wanted to give up his finds and every officer or non-commissioned officer had managed to lay hands on a vehicle—droshkies drawn by the little Russian horses, barouches and light carts. 'The most elegant and most magnificent carriages,' relates M. de Fezensac, 'were jumbled up with the vans, wagons and carts that carried the provisions.' It all looked like an immense caravan advancing laboriously along the Russian high roads. Anatole de Montesquiou, describing this traffic of carriages of all shapes and sizes, exclaimed: 'You cannot imagine what it was like!' And the Count de Ségur stated: 'The fighting men still recalled the terrifying array of world-conquering warriors, but the rest resembled a horde of Tartars after a successful invasion.'

Many generals, who had always been satisfied with a single

carriage, took away several, while a great number of officers 'who had not had one before now all had their own'. Soldiers and canteen-keepers had piled the fruit of their pillage in many of these unusual equipages. Their acquisitions were tucked into every available corner: in private carriages, on provision wagons, even on artillery wagons and ambulances. The trooper had loaded his horse with them, and that was in a cavalry force where every mount was worth its weight in gold, in view of the desperate shortage of saddle-horses; 'the infantryman, victim of his greed, bends beneath the weight of his sack'.[1]

Obviously each man was very determined to guard what he had obtained by looting and to take his trophies home. One had heaped up piles of rugs, another canvases by old masters, rolled up to make them easier to transport. This soldier was jealously huddled over jewels, medallions and 'the Grand Crosses of Russian princes, embellished with diamonds', that one over silver plates, spoons and forks, and candelabra. They took with them whole suites of furni-ture, musical instruments, complete libraries or piles of books 'gilt-edged and bound in morocco'. Sergeant Bourgogne had even taken the nut-brown skirt of a lady's riding habit, lined with green velvet. He did not know what it was for and thought that the woman who wore it was over six feet tall! Many had loaded themselves with what Captain Duverger called 'comforts': rice, sugar, coffee and other rare foodstuffs. One of his friends carried three large pots of jam on his back, 'two of which were cherry and the third goose-berry', he made a point of specifying, with an attention to detail that is stupefying in an account relating the greatest and most tragic retreat of the Grand Army. (Later, back in their homes, each man boasted shamelessly about what he had stolen in Moscow —the nostalgic memory of treasure 'gloriously won' and lamentably lost in the debacle.)

This procession was swelled by the convoys of the wounded and of the official trophies—flags, crosses, icons and so on. Not to mention the *heavy impedimenta* described by Caulaincourt: a berlin for the Emperor, two for his suite, a spare barouche, two carriages for the secretaries, one for the wardrobe, two catering carriages,

[1] All these details of the Grand Army's exodus are taken from the memoirs of French officers and NCO's. Even Russian memorialists have not painted a blacker picture. Both sources emphasized that this frightening caravan was almost as responsible as the hunger and cold for the terrible retreat from Russia, which began on October 26th, after the battle of Maloyaroslavetz.

eight vans for the household, bread, pantry, cellar, provisions, linen and silver plate.

And the army itself? Under a sun almost as lovely as the one that had shone on the troops marching rapidly towards Moscow, the army advanced: the formidable infantry, 'whose appearance is so martial', the remains of the cavalry and lastly the artillery 'which trailed along languidly'. Bottle-necks that overwhelmed the troops with fatigue and finished off the destruction of the cavalry formed at all the bridges and gorges. Captain Lyautey tells us: 'The artillery columns had to clear a passage through a confused mass of carriages, pack-horses and pedestrians that cluttered up the road to Kaluga.'

Many carriages had great difficulty in advancing over sandy terrain, getting stuck in it, losing a wheel or two, breaking an axle. Then the drivers were heard 'shouting in French, swearing in German, calling on God in Italian and the Holy Virgin in Spanish', in an army which had become an amalgam of nationalities to its own misfortune. At each incident, women wailed and children squalled; there was tumult and disorder, and 'the din was fit to split your head open'.

Perhaps this sight was 'extraordinary, at the same time imposing and bizarre,' but many anxiously asked themselves how the head of this column could trail behind and protect such an awkward mass of carriages over such a long route. The Emperor himself 'had difficulty in clearing a way through this immense throng'. Most unwisely, he would not take what Ségur euphemistically called 'the fruit of so many labours' from his soldiers; besides 'the booty was smothered beneath stolen foodstuffs, so how could he order them to abandon it all when he himself was unable to supply them with their normal rations?' Thus he let the moment slip when he could still have dealt severely with 'the immense baggage train he was trailing behind him' and considerably reduced it.

He finally won free and, pushing on along the old road to Kaluga, he reached his first halting-place: the castle of Troytskoye, near Desna.

Before leaving 'the modern Pompeii' at 7 a.m. on October 19th, Napoleon had hurriedly scribbled another note to Marie Louise:[1]

[1] *Lettres . . .*, op. cit. (No. 112).

'My dear Louise, I write to you as I am just about to mount my horse to visit the outposts. It is hot here, with beautiful sunshine, as beautiful as it can be in Paris during this 8bre. We have had no cold weather at all, we have not yet experienced the rig[ours] of the northern climate. It is my intention to take up my winter quarters soon and I hope to be able to have you come to Poland so that I can see you . . .'

He did not say in so many words that he was leaving Moscow. The fine weather was still the *leitmotiv* of his letters, for he was obsessed by it. At the hour of the great departure 'beautiful sunshine still lit up the domes of the holy city' and the Emperor asked General Rapp:

'Don't you recognize my star in this brilliant sun?'

But he put the question with 'a sinister expression' and there was something pathetic about this 'appeal to fortune', as Ségur called it.

At Troytskoye, the Emperor was informed that Kutusov showed no signs of retreating and was awaiting the enemy resolutely. Warned about Napoleon's movements as early as October 19th, the Field-marshal sent General Miloradovich to keep an eye on the King of Naples, to the north of the river Motcha. So Napoleon became convinced that the old Russian warrior would no longer refuse to give battle. Then, faced with the prospect of a battle, the outcome of which was uncertain, which would oppose 30,000 completely fresh Russian cavalrymen to some 14,000 rather battered French cavalrymen—faced with the vision of serious losses of men, horses and material, let alone all the wounded he would have to carry behind him—the Emperor suddenly modified his plan. He would steal a march on the enemy by branching off towards the new road to Kaluga.[1] This was the road from which he had imprudently ordered the Broussier and Ornano divisions to withdraw; now he gave orders that the troops were to move onto it, reaching

[1] Perhaps it is pertinent to point out that the question of the road taken by Napoleon to leave Moscow has been the subject of many controversies. Thiers had commented at length on the departure by the *old* road and the unforeseen forking onto the *new* one. Subsequently, many historians, including the scrupulous Tarle, have claimed that Napoleon left directly by the *new* road, 'for the old one was completely devastated'. The Soviet Academician L. Beskrovny, in his masterful work *The Patriotic War of 1812*, published in 1962 on the occasion of the 150th anniversary of the Russian Campaign, has proved irrefutably the passage of the Grand Army from one road to the other. His conclusions agree with those of Thiers in all respects.

it by cross-country roads, and go to Fominskoye, while Ney continued to march towards Murat along the old road. This was a ruse, by which Napoleon hoped to deceive the Russians and conceal the new direction he had just taken, for the space of one or two days' march. He behaved as if he had no idea that Platov's Cossacks, as well as the partisans of Dorokhov, Sesslavin and Figner, who were constantly on his flanks, could follow and signal his every movement to Tarutino.

He sent his wife a letter from Troytskoye intended to reassure her and consequently reassure Paris:[1]

'My dear, I am on the way to take up my winter quarters, the weather is superb, but it cannot last. As Moscow was completely burnt down, it was not a military position to suit my subsequent plans. I shall abandon it and withdraw the garrison I left there. My health is good, my affairs are going well . . .'

What a lot of reticences in this missive dated October 20th! None of the essential facts was mentioned; as for the surprise attack at Vinkovo, the immediate cause of his sudden departure, it was covered by this single sentence: 'The vanguard had a skirmish with the Cossacks.' He admitted that he had abandoned Moscow permanently. That had not been his original plan; had he not had a letter written to the Quartermaster general at the moment of departure: Since the Emperor intends to return here, we shall retain the main stores of flour, oats and spirits.' But now everything had changed. He could no longer count on surprising and overthrowing Kutusov in his fortified camp; therefore he no longer ought to leave Mortier in Moscow, with his garrison of 10,000 men. He would find himself cut off by the Russian troops that remained intact in his rear.

So he dictated a letter to Berthier, dated from Troytskoye, October 20th:[2]

'My cousin, order the Duke of Treviso to have the tired and lame men leave tomorrow at daybreak . . . and send them all to Mozhaysk. On the 22nd or 23rd at 2 o'clock in the morning, he will arrange for setting fire to the warehouses containing spirits, the barracks and the public buildings, except the house of the Foundlings. He

[1] *Lettres . . .*, op. cit. (No. 113).
[2] *Correspondance . . .*, op. cit. (Vol. XXIV, No. 19,292).

will arrange for setting fire to the Kremlin. When these expeditions have been carried out, the Duke of Treviso will leave the Kremlin and move along the road to Kaluga. He will take care to remain in Moscow until he has personally seen the Kremlin blow up. He will take care to set fire to the two houses of the former governor and the house of Razumovsky.'

This time it was the French Emperor who had Moscow burnt, in imitation of the 'vandal', the 'Scythian Rostopchin'.

When the order was sent, he set in motion the arduous operation that would take his troops from one road to another, without previous preparation—a movement 'that accentuated the difficulties of a march hampered by such a scandalous number of carriages', noted Captain Lyautey. To make matters worse, fine rain began to fall and put the roads in a very bad state. In addition, the troops had to cross numbers of small, narrow rotten bridges, which collapsed. This difficult manœuvre meant two days lost to the French, two days pregnant with consequences that could not be made good, but which were skilfully exploited by the Russians.

On the night of October 20th, Dorokhov came to inform the Field-marshal of the passage of the enemy troops onto the new road to Kaluga and their advance on Fominskoye. Kutusov dispatched Dokhturov's 6th corps in that direction, giving it the mission of attacking the Ornano and Broussier divisions. The old man was not duped by his adversary; he was a past master of bluff and sudden bifurcations. Napoleon was trying to steal a march on him in order to outstrip him rapidly and occupy Kaluga. It was obvious that the French were now trying to avoid a large-scale battle as long as possible.

Arriving at Fominskoye in person on October 21st, Napoleon granted the Viceroy a whole day to rest his troops, harassed by their arduous cross-country march. Another day wasted during which General Dokhturov came together with Hetman Platov and Dorokhov's *franc-tireurs*.

It was the next day, the 22nd, when Colonel Berthémy, armed with a safe-conduct, reported to the Emperor Kutusov's reply to the letter that the Prince of Neuchâtel had addressed to him on October 16th. Since then, everything had changed. The Emperor could no longer lose himself in vain conjectures about the Field-marshal's plans; Kutusov's letter was merely a terrifying confirmation of his intentions:

'Prince Kutusof to the Prince of Neuchâtel and Wagram.
'At headquarters, October 21, 1812.

'My Prince, Colonel Berthémy, whom I received in my own quarters, has handed me the letter with which Your Highness had entrusted him: everything that forms the subject of this new approach has already been submitted post-haste to the Emperor, my master, and, as you must be aware, Prince Wolkonsky was the bearer of it. However, in view of the distance between the places and the difficulty of the roads at the present time of year, it is physically impossible for a reply to have reached me as yet. So I can only refer personally to everything I have had the honour to say to General Lauriston on the same matter. However, I will repeat here a truth, the full force of which you will undoubtedly appreciate, my Prince, namely that it is difficult, however much one may desire it, to stop a people embittered by what it sees, a people that has never known war on its own territory for three hundred years, that is ready to sacrifice itself for its fatherland and that is quite insensitive to those distinctions between what is or is not customary in ordinary wars. As for the armies I command, I flatter myself, my Prince, that everyone will recognize, in the way in which they act, the principles that characterise every loyal, brave and generous nation; I have never known others during my long military career and I flatter myself that the enemies I have had to fight have always given me credit for my maxims in this respect. Please accept, my Prince, my sincerest regards.

'The Marshal and Commander in Chief
of the armies,
'Prince Kutusof.'[1]

Thus everything was stated here quite clearly, even though some tact was used. 'These people do not want to negotiate!' cried the Emperor, but he thought that the reply was 'very dignified'.

The French left Fominskoye on October 23rd to march on Kaluga, via Borovsk and Maloyaroslavetz.[2] Sesslavin's scouts informed Kutusov, who sent Dokhturov to occupy Borovsk. Milo-

---

[1] This letter was written in French.
[2] It was 36 miles from Kaluga to Maloyaroslavetz.

radovich would secure his rear, now that he no longer needed to
keep an eye on the King of Naples. He and Marshal Ney had now
abandoned their positions behind the Motcha and in the outskirts
of Voronovo, and rejoined the main body of the army.

But Dokhturov was narrowly beaten to Borovsk by the enemy.
The Field-marshal at once ordered him to go to Maloyaroslavetz
by forced marches. He himself also moved in the direction of that
town at three o'clock in the afternoon of the same day. His army
was about 110,000 strong. He explained his operation to his
Sovereign: 'The enemy is doing his utmost to circumvent me in
order to hurl himself on Kaluga and penetrate into our fertile
provinces.'

Simultaneously, Napoleon installed his headquarters at Borovsk.
It was from there that Berthier wrote to Junot, who was still at
Mozhaysk:

'As the town of Moscow has been burnt to ashes, the Emperor
has thought it advisable, after having had the Kremlin blown up,
to evacuate it in order to be master of his movements, since this
corpse of a town requires 15 to 20,000 men to keep public order
among its ruins. If the enemy army means to cover Kaluga, the
Emperor wants to join battle with it.'

Relying on what Berthémy had told him and not receiving any
other reports, the Emperor believed that Kutusov was still en-
trenched at Tarutino. He was deprived of all information because
the French were not taking any prisoners and no spy dared to
penetrate the Russian lines. Lulled into false security, he planned
to reach Smolensk and his reserves, passing through Kaluga and
the rich regions which had remained untouched.

During the afternoon of October 23rd, Napoleon had personally
carried out a reconnaissance on his left and had returned from it
completely reassured. At six in the evening, he learnt that General
Delzons and his division had found Maloyaroslavetz, four leagues
ahead of them, empty, as well as the woods that dominated it. All
was calm along the Luzha, a river that flowed at the foot of the town.
So the Emperor passed a quiet night, certain that no danger
threatened him at the one point where Kutusov could bar the road
to Kaluga to him. And then at 5 a.m. on October 24th, General
Delzons was attacked out of the blue by General Dokhturov!

Napoleon had been outstripped. With an army relieved of all

its superfluous paraphernalia, he would have been able to reach Maloyaroslavetz two days earlier. Moreover, the day of rest granted to Eugène's vanguard on October 22nd now turned out to be a new and regrettable error.

The battle for Kaluga—for so it appeared to the spectator—was a fierce and murderous combat that was prolonged into the night of the 24th, with dramatic ups and downs. Fortune changed hands as many as seven times. Delzons met a heroic end there. 'A fatal field'—wrote Ségur later—'where the conquest of the world came to an end, where twenty victories came to grief, where the great collapse of our empire began.'

There were more than 5,000 dead on the French side, against 2,000 on the Russian side. A battle for nothing. The Russians, descending further south, positioned themselves on all sides to cut off any advance by the French and were ready to give battle again. Kutusov wrote to the Tsar: 'This day will remain one of the most memorable in this bloody war, for the loss of the battle of Maloyaroslavetz would have produced the most disastrous consequences and would have opened the road to our most fertile provinces to the enemy.' So it was a victory in Russian eyes and a French victory according to the 27th bulletin of the Grand Army. The French had won the day over the Russians; the army was 'pursuing its way to Vereya without being bothered by the enemy'; it was twenty-five miles nearer to St Petersburg. In fact, Napoleon's troops did hold their own at Maloyaroslavetz, but Napoleon said to Caulaincourt: 'This is getting serious. I still beat the Russians, but that doesn't settle anything!'

A decisive battle, an undisputable victory could have settled everything, guaranteed excellent winter quarters and made it possible to prepare a lightning advance on St Petersburg for the first fine days; but was the army in a state to fight this battle that Napoleon still considered as necessary as the battle of the Moskva? That was the agonizing question that the Emperor put to his companions in arms on the evening of October 25th in an *isba* at the hamlet of Gorodnia, situated a little way behind the Luzha.

Napoleon had spent the whole day in rash reconnaissances and had very nearly been caught by a Cossack patrol. He did not return to Gorodnia until five o'clock in the evening—yet another day wasted! In a log cabin a council of war was being held by an

Emperor, two Kings, two Princes and a Duke, all army com-
manders who had proved themselves many times: Murat, Eugène
de Beauharnais, Berthier (Prince of Neuchâtel and Wagram),
Davout (Prince of Eckmühl) and Bessières (Duke of Istria). This
council of war was one of the most dramatic and certainly one of
the most decisive in Napoleon's career, just as the council of Fili
had been in Kutusov's career. And just as his adversary had done
on September 13th, the French Emperor, with despair in his heart,
was forced to give the order to retreat.

For the first time in his life, he refused to give battle. Napoleon
asked the five men assembled in the miserable hovel to speak frankly
to him and give their opinions without evasions or ulterior motives.
Seated at a small rustic table, he put his question:

'Should we fight a second battle to pierce a way through to
Kaluga, or should we march to Borovsk, turn off to the right to
Mozhaysk, and then onto the main road from Moscow to Smolensk?'

This familiar road, the 'undisputed property' of the French,
guarded by numerous posts, was the road which, in August, had
been ravaged first by the Russians and then by the Grand Army.
What a dilemma! The new road to Kaluga was barred by Kutusov;
the road to Smolensk, via Mozhaysk and Vyazma, promised hunger
and privation. Napoleon, huddled in his chair and dejected, listened
with his head in his hands—obviously as much to hide the expression on his face as to reflect. Opinion followed opinion and so did
the altercations, for Murat, always ready to act on impulse, burst
out:

'What do I care for the threat of the Russians and their impenetrable forests? I despise them! With the remains of my cavalry,
I am going to overthrow Kutusov and open the Kaluga road to the
army.'

But the others protested vehemently. They invoked the reasons
that reason itself imposed on them:

'We shall weaken ourselves tremendously at a time when every
soldier is precious.'

'We shall lose at least 10,000 men and trail the same number of
wounded behind us!'

'When the enemy sees us ready to pounce on him, he will mass
on our right and bar the road to Mozhaysk!'

'Then everything will be irrevocably lost, for that road is our
last resort.'

These were weighty opinions which the generals found distressing to utter, but they were unanimous, except one—Murat.

The Emperor had not stirred. It was hard for him not 'to re-establish the ascendancy of his arms, already rather compromised', hard to give up the idea of wintering in a rich region. The army, supplied with fresh provisions and shielded from the winter, would recover its dash. Its numbers would be reduced, to be sure, but it would be reinforced morally. Perhaps, with his former reliable instinct, he had a presentiment that a general battle, whatever the cost, would be more profitable than a retreat on a road that was no more than a desert and at a moment when the provisions brought from Moscow were running low. And winter, also an enemy, was going to move to the attack at any moment.

But all around him they insisted and repeated:

'We must take the shortest route out of a country where we have stayed too long!'

At last the Emperor raised his head. His face was livid; his features distorted. 'Falling back' and 'beating a retreat' were words that revolted his whole being. And yet . . .

He said wearily: 'All right, gentlemen, I will decide.'

During the night, he confided to Berthier, as if he was talking to himself: 'We have done too much for glory. It is time to concentrate on saving the remains of the army.'

He said to the Duke of Vicenza: 'I see that it will be indispensable for me to draw closer to my reserves, for even if I drive Kutusov out and make him evacuate Kaluga and its fortifications, the Cossacks will still hamper my communications so long as I am without my Poles.'

The order was given to withdraw towards Borovsk on the next day, October 26th, at 9 a.m. The Emperor himself would take the road about 11 a.m. His decision, so novel for him, was such a blow to his pride that it made him feel ill.

However, Napoleon had a presentiment that he could still have swooped on Kutusov and overthrown him. Impressed by the arguments of his generals, he had made a choice that struck him as regrettable. Later—too late—he told Gourgaud that he would have avoided some great reverses if he had relied solely on his own judgment. Perhaps, too, 'because of having ventured too much in undertaking this war, he is not venturesome enough in his way of prosecuting it'. That was the opinion of some of his intimates. But he would have ventured everything if he had been able to guess that the Field-marshal, too, was refusing to risk a large-scale battle. Neither the Emperor nor Kutusov knew that the other was guided by prudence and prudence alone.

They were strange hours, those twenty-four hours, a critical period when everything hung in the balance. The French Emperor had taken his decision so as to spare 20,000 men, and in doing so had condemned 100,000 men to die of hunger and cold. The Russian generalissimo wanted to avoid bloody combats, the outcome of which was uncertain, because the forces confronting each other were more or less balanced at that date. He was of the opinion that winter, fatigue and misery would wipe out the Grand Army, whereas at the moment it was still able to turn on him 'like a wild boar harried by hunters'. Beat the enemy? No, destroy him! That was his obsession.

That was how the two armies turned their backs on each other on October 26, 1812, and withdrew, one to the north, the other to the south. From that day on the one-eyed commander was to justify to the full the nickname that Mme de Staël, transported with admiration, gave him in a letter to Princess Kutusov: the *Fabius Cunctator of Russia*.

As if to prove Kutusov right, the cold suddenly clamped down, beginning on October 27th. It was 24·8° F (−4° C). The fine autumn weather that had deceived the Emperor was really over. 'General Winter' had made up his mind, too. The Russian catastrophe had begun.

Naturally, the 'Old One's' plan met with nothing but resistance. Sir Robert Wilson pounced on him with his claws out. He announced that the Field-marshal had gone beyond the permissible limits. The Englishman complained directly to the Tsar that the armies of His Majesty, which were fighting so intrepidly, 'deserved to have a more skilful commander'; the Prince's age and 'physical decrepitude' could serve him as an excuse at a pinch, but it was regrettable that his weakness 'made him limit his desires to seeing the enemy leave Russia, and that at a moment when the liberation of the world was in his hands!' But there it was; the liberation of the world was a matter of supreme indifference to the old man. He did not see—did not want to see—beyond the frontiers of his own fatherland. Short-sighted tactics, undoubtedly, which took no account of the inevitable battles in the future that the united sovereigns would have to fight to rid themselves of the man they so hated and feared. Then the Russians, victims vowed to new hecatombs, would lie on foreign soil in their thousands. No. Kutusov did not think about the difficulties that might lie in wait for Russia in the near future and that 'would be laid at his door', according to Wilson.

The observer heaped the old man with reproaches and insolence. The imperturbable and obstinate Field-marshal retorted:

'I would give the enemy a chance to escape rather than compromise my army and the fate of the Russian empire.'

'Then you want to give the Corsican a free passage?' cried Sir Robert, turning purple with rage. 'You want to let him escape with his victory. Imagine the cry of indignation that will go up all over Europe.'

'First and foremost I am Russian. I want my country to be liberated. As for Europe, let France and England decide between themselves who will dominate it.'

He even imagined—showing a trust that was most unlike him—that the Tsar would approve of his sentiments, if he knew the whole story. He was in for a bitter disappointment. Alexander, who heard the vociferations of Lord Cathcart, his dear Bennigsen and almost all the general staff, raged and fumed. He scoffed at Kutusov's explanations, seeing only the facts, which had no justification in his view. So he sent Kutusov a severe reprimand. He blamed him for his negligence, his incomprehensible inactivity, after the Tarutino skirmish and his 'useless and harmful' retreat after the battle of Maloyaroslavetz: 'You have wiped out all the advantages of our position. Everything should have ended in the capture of Napoleon and the immediate destruction of his army. The last paragraph was blazing with anger: 'Drawing your attention to all our well-justified fears, I remind you that you will bear personal responsibility for all the misfortunes that may arise.'

Meanwhile Napoleon and his army had reached Mozhaysk in three days. There they rejoined Marshal Mortier with his garrison from Moscow, which he had left at dawn on October 24th.

12

THE END

Their tombs are dug in the soil of this empire.

KUTUSOV

AT 4 a.m. on October 24th the inhabitants of Moscow were suddenly awakened by a tremendous explosion. Window panes shattered into smithereens. Ceilings fell in. The untouched houses split open and those that had been half-ruined by the fire collapsed completely. Three more explosions occurred at irregular intervals. It all happened in the vicinity of the Kremlin.

Impenetrable obscurity enshrouded the town. A cold autumn rain fell in torrents. The ragged, haggard Muscovites hurled themselves into the street *en masse*. There was a general panic. From all sides in the district adjoining the citadel of the Tsars rose strident shouts, fearful shrieks and groans. Many of the victims were pinned beneath beams or blocks of stone and were calling for help. Others ran in all directions, wounded by flying glass, broken timber and debris. The Kremlin was lit up by sinister gleams. 'We thought it was the end of the world,' related a witness. Everyone was asking what was happening. Was there going to be a battle in this town that had already been so sorely tried?

The hypothesis did not seem absurd to several citizens—the day before some Russian officers and a patrol had ventured into the town!

In fact, General Wintzingerode, who commanded a detachment of mounted partisans and was making constant raids within a radius of twelve miles around Moscow, had learnt something strange: the French troops left behind in Moscow were digging trenches beneath the walls of the Kremlin, placing mines in them and recruiting peaceful Russian citizens to help them. The Russians refused to work. They said: 'Come what may, we will not be responsible for this crime!' They were severely beaten. Many of them had fled into the country and some of them who reached the hamlet of Tschachkino met Wintzingerode's partisans there. On hearing their story, the General exclaimed:

'I am going to tell Marshal Mortier that if a single church blows up, I shall hang my French prisoners!'

He had captured several recently—forage parties and couriers.

No sooner said than done. Wintzingerode, accompanied by his aide-de-camp, Narychkin, and a small patrol, entered Moscow without a bugler or a white flag. He was stopped in the Tver Boulevard by Leleu de Meuperthuis, Lieutenant of the 5th Riflemen of the Line, who refused to consider him as a truce-bearer and took both him and Narychkin to the Duke of Treviso. The Duke did not accept the Russian's explanations: that was no way for a truce-bearer to present himself! He held both officers prisoner and said to them:

'The Emperor himself will decide your fate. We are taking you with us.'

For Mortier was going to carry out his Emperor's instructions to the letter and evacuate Moscow, leaving it in flames.

There was another alarm at midnight: some detachments of Cossacks were attempting to invade the suburbs in their turn. They were intercepted and driven back by the French vanguard, which was beginning to leave Moscow by the Kaluga gate. When he was ready to leave with his rearguard at two o'clock in the morning, Mortier had ordered his men to set fire to the mines placed beneath the palace of the Tsars and elsewhere. The actual combustion did not take place until later. Those Muscovites who were brave enough to approach the Kremlin saw the arsenal collapse in flames, as well as the gate and the tower of St Nicholas, several adjoining buildings and a sanctuary. The heart of Moscow was burning once again. This time Rostopchin had nothing to do with it.

Pointless, incomprehensible destruction, which the Marquis de Chambray himself called 'senseless vengeance' that could only help to fan the hatred of the Muscovites.

The fifth and last explosion occurred about five o'clock in the morning. The noise it made resounded all over the town. A group of Cossacks, patrolling nearby under the orders of Second-lieutenant Yazikov, at once decided to go to see what was happening.

Entering the town at dawn by the Dorogomylov gate, they found their 'little mother Moscow' plunged in deathlike silence. There was no one in the rain-lashed streets. The civilians had fled to the suburbs or hidden themselves. There was not a Frenchman in sight!

Everywhere they found the same desolation, the same silence. But they were dismayed by what they discovered by the light of the flames. The palace proper was badly damaged. The Palace of the Facets had collapsed. Several towers were decapitated or breached. The tower that had stood at the corner of the citadel, opposite the stone bridge, had disappeared, leaving a deep hole. Two turrets placed on the wall bordering the river had blown up, making breaches in the great embattled defence wall. A miracle had saved the whole Kremlin from being turned into a pile of stones and debris—the rain had wet the fuses. There was another miracle for the amazed spectators to look at. Although the tower and gate of St Nicholas had been badly damaged, the venerated image of the Thaumaturge was intact.

The whole picture was distressing and shocking, and yet the Cossacks were not completely dismayed by it. The truth they had just discovered—*they had left!*—was so incredible, so wonderful that they could not feel too dejected. Perhaps Moscow was even more destroyed than before; it would be rebuilt. But it was free! And Yazikov's group, which, along with so many others, had done its best to make the French army's stay untenable, thought that it had well deserved being the first to announce the extraordinary news.

Yazikov made contact with Dorokhov, who told Kutusov in the outskirts of Maloyaroslavetz. The Field-marshal could hardly believe it. Had Napoleon really given up the idea of leaving a garrison in Moscow? But the partisans had captured some stragglers from Mortier's units and brought them, slung across their saddles, to General Dokhturov. He questioned them; they told the story of their departure and the explosions. The general dispatched a staff officer, Bolgovsky, to the Commander-in-chief. Kutusov received him seated on a camp bed, but, the officer related, 'in full-dress uniform with all his decorations'.

He asked him: 'Tell me, my friend, what is this story? Have the French abandoned Moscow? Is it true?'

As Bolgovsky wanted to go into detail, the Marshal burst out: 'Faster! Don't keep me on tenter-hooks!'

When the officer had told him everything, Kutusov made as if to speak, but choked. He gave an old man's sob. He snuffled, then, turning to an icon of the Saviour, he cried fervently:

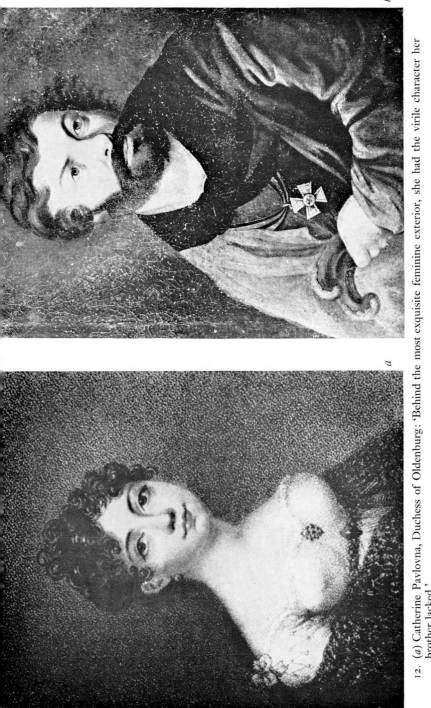

12. (*a*) Catherine Pavlovna, Duchess of Oldenburg: 'Behind the most exquisite feminine exterior, she had the virile character her brother lacked.'
(*b*) Denis Davidov: 'He led the partisans, that scourge of God that the Grand Army feared even more than fire and frost' (*painting by V. P. Langer*).

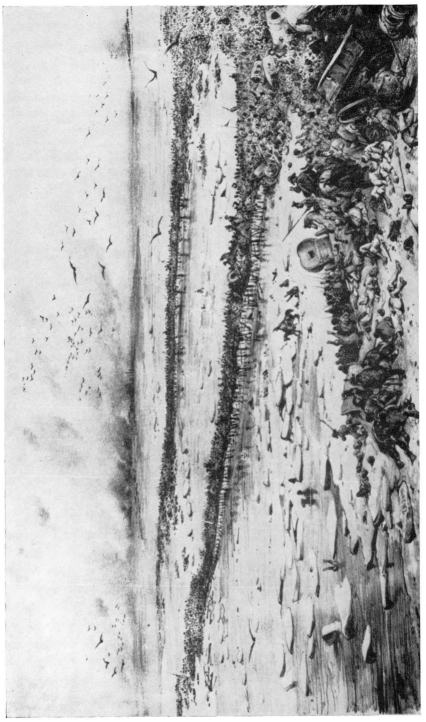

13. 'The Beresina! The last glorious fling by the Grand Army that saved its honour.'

'God, my Creator! Thou has granted our prayer at last! Russia is saved!'

Napoleon had given up the idea of guarding Moscow. That meant that he was fleeing, that he could no longer hope to hold out. All that was needed now was to lead him back to the frontier, decimating his army in the process.

The Duke of Treviso had left behind him 400 or 500 wounded who could not be transported, entrusted to the efficient Ivan Akinfievich Tutolmin. He had rejoined the Grand Army at Mozhaysk and was moving towards Vyazma with it, along the too familiar Smolensk road.

The cold grew more intense. The horses, which had not been shod for ice, fell and never got up again. It was impossible to avoid passing the battlefield of Borodino, still littered with rotting corpses that were devoured by stray dogs, while birds of prey hovered above them—a sight that did not help the troops' morale. What a disaster and for what purpose! wondered the shivering, starving men. Many young soldiers and foreign troops threw down their arms, disbanded and hid themselves in the anonymous straggling crowd that trailed behind the army, increasing its difficulties. For twenty regiments of Cossacks under Platov and two infantry corps under Miloradovich were pursuing it. On its left flank, the majority of the Russian forces, initiating the 'parallel march' decided on by Kutusov, were advancing through regions where food and fodder abounded. Their aim was to make constant, sudden, small-scale attacks.

There was a lively engagement between the vanguards at Vyazma to force the passage of that town. Davout succeeded, but he lost 2,000 men and abandoned large numbers of wounded. From then on, the army was forced to leave the wounded behind, delivering them to the vengeance of the peasants, who had all taken up arms. A pitiless decision, dictated by absolute necessity, which lowered the combatants' morale still more.

Shortages were felt even more after Vyazma and the army consoled itself by thinking that it would find plenty of everything at Smolensk.[1] The Cossacks embarked on sudden raids, sabreing the troops who left the columns on marauding expeditions. The baggage train was looted, the van drivers killed or carried off. Discipline

[1] It was 90 miles from Vyazma to Smolensk.

M

relaxed. In order to advance more quickly, escorts got rid of the wounded they had transported all the way from Moscow by throwing them into the ditches. 'All hearts were closed to pity,' said the Duke of Vicenza later. Soldiers ate dead horses; 3,000 had perished in a few days. But that was nothing. When they were three days' march from Smolensk, half the total strength had already been lost as a result of minor assaults and skirmishes, hunger and cold. 'During the day, there were constant combats, and during the night, famine; there was never any shelter; only bivouacs that were even more murderous than the fighting: the rest, which should have refreshed us, finished us off,' wrote Ségur. The army continued to traverse 'regions that were exhausted'. All the cavalry, except the cavalry of the Guard, was dismounted.

On November 5th at Dorogobuzhe, the weather changed again. Now they met snowstorms driven by a violent wind. The next day, two disastrous pieces of news reached the Emperor: Admiral Tschitschagov and General von Wittgenstein had driven back the army corps of Marshal Gouvion-Saint-Cyr and those of Marshal Victor, Duke of Belluno, onto the Duna and the Upper Beresina; the link up that Napoleon had hoped for so much became improbable and the reinforcements coming from Poland would be cut off.

The news from Paris, brought by the first courier who had managed to reach the Emperor for ten days, was even more serious: on October 22nd, General Malet had carried out a *coup d'état*, arresting the Minister of Police, Savary, Duke of Rovigo, and Pasquier, the Prefect of Police. His triumph had only lasted twelve hours and Napoleon was informed about it when it was all over and the conspirators judged and executed. But what had struck the Emperor 'to an extraordinary degree' was that such a thing should have been possible.

He said to Caulaincourt: 'The French are like women: one must not stay away from them too long. I really don't know what intriguers would manage to convince people of and what would happen if the French were without news of me for any length of time!'

And the Duke of Vicenza remarked: 'The proven possibility of such an undertaking, even though the result proved the impossibility of success, already seemed to him a serious blow to his power.'

From that moment, Napoleon became sombre, taciturn and almost indifferent. An emperor at Moscow, as he had said himself, turned general again during the first stage of this retreat, he was once again an emperor who thought more about his empire than his army.

On November 9th the army was at Smolensk, on which it had been advancing as if to the Promised Land. It was a terrible disappointment: the stores of provisions did not live up to expectations and could not meet the needs of so many famished and sick soldiers. The governor of the town, General Charpentier, warned too late of the departure from Moscow, had only been able to assemble small quantities of supplies.

On November 14th, Baron Larrey consulted the thermometer that he always wore pinned to his uniform. The temperature was 6·8° F (−14° C). That was still not excessive for well-fed men, but it was a terrible ordeal for harassed and starving soldiers.

After Smolensk, the retreat began to resemble a rout. 'We no longer looked anything like conquerors,' an officer wrote to his wife. The Marquis de Fezensac described the road from Smolensk to the Beresina as 'a continuous battle-field'. And yet, Caulaincourt tells us, the Emperor still tried to deceive himself: 'He flattered himself that he could still re-establish everything and even take up an impressive position,' once he had the storehouse of Minsk at his disposal.

'I shall find reinforcements at every step, whereas Kutusov will weaken himself like me by his marches and move farther away from his reserves. He is left in a countryside that we have exhausted. The storehouses are waiting for us. The Russians will die of hunger there.'

But at the same date Tschitschagov had taken Minsk, pushing back the Dombrowski division responsible for protecting that town, and Wittgenstein had captured Vitebsk! Kutusov and his army were moving in the direction of Orcha and Borissov. They had been fighting at Krasnoye for three days. Further losses of men and material. The Austrian 'allies' had decided not to budge and to dig in behind the Bug. From then on it was the inexorable march of 40,000 combatants (out of the some 100,000 who had left Moscow) advancing with a mob of 25,000 disbanded soldiers and 1,000 civilians in their wake.

It was true that the Russians had also lost a lot of men, that, being ill equipped, they suffered from the cold. They were also feeling the lack of forage, owing to the severe frost, but their morale was intact. However, in such conditions, Kutusov was more resolved than ever to avoid the clash of a battle, despite the Tsar's orders and the shrill protests of the general staff. Nevertheless, he now had on his side, not only Generals Ermolov and Miloradovich, but also Dokhturov, Rayevsky and Toll. Their faith in their Commander-in-chief never faltered.

On November 22nd, the Emperor published an order of the day:

'The baggage train will be reduced.

'Every general or administrative officer who has several carriages will burn half of them and hand over the horses to the artillery park.

'The Major-general is responsible for the execution of this order.'[1]

It was a little late.

The Beresina! The Grand Army's last glorious fling, which saved its honour. A desperate, heroic crossing. Great valour was shown by leaders and soldiers, although it was accompanied by extreme cruelty. At this critical hour, all pity was set aside. Civilians, including women and children, were pushed back, jostled, trampled underfoot and abandoned on the bank where they were crushed by the wheels of the carriages and the horses' hooves or hit by bullets or cannon-balls fired by the Russians who were lying in wait for the French at this crossing. Later, at dawn after the terrible night of November 28th, they were stripped by the enemy and thrown naked onto the ice in the river.

After this crossing, the French burnt the bridges hastily built thanks to the courage and endurance of the troops of General Eblé, and Napoleon's army—or what was left of it—trailed, an inchoate mass, through the marshes, over a narrow area, without supplies, without shelter, in the midst of a snowstorm. On November 29th, the Emperor wrote to the Duke of Bassano, who was still at Vilna:

'The army is numerous, but terribly disbanded. I need a fortnight to return them to the colours, and where shall we find a

[1] *Correspondance* . . ., op. cit. (Vol. XXIV, No. 19,346).

fortnight? We shall be at Vilna: shall we be able to hold on there? Provisions, provisions, provisions! without them there are no horrors which this indisciplined mob may not commit against this town. Perhaps the army will only be able to rally beyond the Niemen. In these circumstances it is possible that I may believe my presence in Paris necessary for France, for the Empire, for the army itself.'[1]

And on December 6, 1812, at Smorgoni, after assembling his faithful companions, he declared: 'In the existing state of affairs, I can only dictate to Europe from the Palace of the Tuileries.'

Dictate to Europe, and especially France. For on December 2nd, he had sent Anatole de Montesquiou, Berthier's aide-de-camp, to Paris with the 29th bulletin, that terrible bulletin in which he had 'said everything', according to him at least, and he was anxious to be in Paris when the text was made public by *Le Moniteur*. So he left by sledge, taking the Duke of Vicenza with him and leaving the army to Murat. That was one last unfortunate error he could not avoid, since 'the King takes precedence of the Viceroy, who takes precedence of the Prince, who takes precedence of the Marshals'. Murat led the remains of the Grand Army to their ultimate destruction. He abandoned Vilna and then Kovno. He abandoned his general staff, who were filled with rage and shame, and the unfortunate troops that had been entrusted to him, and fled to his kingdom of Naples.

Then, in an 'annihilating' cold, 'the miserable remnants' dribbled away to Prussia as best they could, protected by the rear-guard of Marshal Ney, 'who upholds the honour of our arms to the last moment'. And the Prince of Neuchâtel, 'sick with misery and fatigue', wrote to his emperor:

'Sire, I must tell you the truth: the army is in complete disorder. The soldier throws down his gun because he can no longer hold it; both officers and men think only of protecting themselves from the vicious cold which still remains at $-7.6°$ to $-9.3°$ F ($-22°$ to $-23°$ C). The officers of the General Staff and our aides-de-camp are no longer able to march.'[2]

He concluded this last report with these words: 'Sire, the army is no more!

[1] *Correspondance* . . ., op. cit. (Vol. XXIV, No. 19,362).
[2] *Archives Nationales*: A.F. IV, No. 1,643.

13

MOSCOW RISES FROM THE ASHES

INDESCRIBABLE disorder reigned in Moscow. There was absolute anarchy and violence as well. Thirsting for vengeance, many citizens rushed to the Foundlings' Home where, heedless of Tutolmin's exhortations, they massacred the defenceless wounded. Everywhere looting began again worse than ever: the people fought to snatch everything that the French had abandoned. This only lasted for twenty-four hours, but total licence prevailed. Fortunately, some Russian troops, stationed to the north-east of the town, were warned of the departure of the occupying troops and entered Moscow commanded by Generals Khovaysky, Benkendorff and Schakhovskoy. They restored a degree of order, but had great difficulty in calming the over-excited and also famished population.

Rostopchin's first move, after leaving his sacrificed town on September 14th, had been to join the general staff. Throughout the flanking march and at Tarutino, he had made himself obnoxious to Kutusov, who in turn had made him realize that he was undesirable. He had left, after addressing an insolent letter to the Field-marshal, in which he described his departure as voluntary and ended with this piece of calumny:

'Your most Serene Highness having thought fit to abandon the province as you abandoned the town, my duties came to an end with the departure of the troops. As I do not wish to remain inactive nor contemplate the destruction of the province of Kaluga, nor hear all day long that you are busy sleeping, I leave for Yaroslavl and St Petersburg. In my capacity as a loyal and true servant of the Fatherland, I desire you to pay more attention to Russia, the troops entrusted to you and the enemy. As for me, I thank you that it does not fall to me to deliver a capital or a province to anyone, and that you do not let me enjoy your confidence in any way.'

The Governor had in fact gone to Yaroslav to see his protectress, that Grand-duchess Catherine, but had not travelled to St Petersburg. He had settled at Vladimir, from where he addressed a constant stream of 'manifestoes of encouragement' to the Muscovites. Very few of these messages reached their destination. It was at Vladimir that Rostopchin received the good news of the liberation. He at once dispatched to Moscow a commissioner of police called Helman, who was a friend of his. When he had informed the governor that a semblance of order seemed to be re-established, the Count appeared in 'his town', flanked by the Chief of Police, Ivachkin.[1]

His Excellency at once reinstalled himself in his palace of the Lubianka, which had not blown up, in spite of Napoleon's strict orders. Had Mortier wanted to spare one of the few untouched districts and the Church of Saint-Louis-des-Français? Had the fuses been wet there, too? We do not know. He began to work with his usual energy. There was plenty to do: lodging the homeless, feeding the population, caring for the wounded who had escaped the massacre and putting an end to brigandage. For this last named task and, incidentally for the others, he resorted to his special fad —posters:

'You refused to obey Bonaparte, but you listen to gang leaders and blackguards! The Commissioners of Police are in office again and the heads of the Ministries. Come, my children, live henceforth in peace and honour!'

The removal of the bodies was a very difficult task. They were found everywhere in the streets and squares, and under the debris. During the winter of 1812 to 1813, 23,000 were burnt!

Untouched buildings were replastered, the ruins were cleared, shops and booths were hastily built; the markets were opened; the restoration of the Kremlin was begun. Already a large number of aristocrats who had taken refuge on their distant estates had returned. The first arrivals hastened to inform relations and friends about the state of their residences and sent them lists of burnt-down houses. Soon there was a general return. Then the governor's palace was flooded with countless claims for lost property. More trouble for Count Rostopchin. He was asked to arbitrate in thousands of law-suits, because a large number of pieces of furni-

[1] Count Andrei Rostopchin has the following story to tell about General Ivachkin: 'He and his wife spoke devilish bad French. Madame was rather greedy by nature and when, after the French had departed from Moscow, an inventory was being made of objects found in ruined houses and not claimed by anybody, she never failed to put in an appearance and, choosing what she fancied, called to her husband: *'Cher! Puis-je?'* And the husband replied: *'Pouvez, ma chère, pouvez!'*

ture, *objets d'art* and curios had been transported from one house to another by the French and sometimes they were claimed by several people at once! But that was not the worst of Rostopchin's worries. He expected to be complimented and now all these injured proprietors held him responsible for the destruction of their property. Henceforth he was exposed to the reproaches and vindictiveness of his subjects and found himself spurned by everyone.

It was a complete waste of time when he tried to defend himself in a virulent article that he had inserted in *The Russian Courier*, in which he declared coldly that the defence of Moscow had not depended on him. But no one had forgotten what he had claimed in his posters in the month of September.

The Tsar was absent from Russia. He was travelling through the battle-fields of Europe. However, the lamentations of the Muscovite nobility reached him *en masse*, and apparently made him determined to dismiss the man for whom he had always felt deep antipathy. On his return, the Verestchagin affair was laid before him by the father of Rostopchin's unfortunate scapegoat and he ordered an enquiry. On August 30, 1814, he signed a decree dismissing Counf Fyodor Vassilievich Rostopchin from his post as Governor ot Moscow. Nevertheless, throwing him a bone to chew (no doubt on his sister's intervention), he appointed him member of the Imperial Council. A purely honorary function, which reduced the ex-governor to despair and filled him with bitterness. He never stopped railing against his fellow-citizens, taxing them with ingratitude and meanness. After a brief stay in St Petersburg, where he felt overwhelmed by the hostility of the Court and all the aristocracy, he left for abroad—Berlin, London and Paris—as a voluntary exile. He did not return to Russia until 1823 to die there in January 1826.

Before these events and while he still presided over the destinies of Moscow, the Count had buckled down to another task, which he specially enjoyed: that of unearthing and judging everyone— French and Russian—who had worked in the service of the enemy army.[1]

After the arrest of a tradesman called Nakhodkin, who had

<hr>

[1] Chtchukin, in *Papiers relatifs à la Guerre patriotique de 1812* (Vol. II, pp. 12–19 and 33), publishes a list of French subjects innocent of all collaboration and desirous of remaining in Moscow, and the list of sixty-seven 'collaborators' drawn up by Ivachkin: 'These unworthy people, who, during the enemy's stay, formed part of the Municipality and the Police, have all been taken and kept a close watch on'.

accepted, although a pure Russian, to fulfil the duties of Deputy Mayor, a complete list of the employees of the municipality was found at his home. A ukase dated November 9/21, 1812 designated a commission of enquiry 'into the affair of employees and persons of all classes having held employment under the enemy'. The first session of this commission, presided over by the Governor in person and by two senators who had come expressly from St Petersburg, had taken place on December 3/15, 1812. It was to sit for three months. The sentences were inspired by the degree of culpability of each of the accused. The Senate transmitted the following text to the Government of Moscow:

'The fault of the majority of the accused stems from their weakness of character which did not enable them to put up a firm resistance to the threats and pressures of the inhuman enemy, to whose power they had to submit by virtue of the law of the strongest.

'Nevertheless, among them there are some whose acts are prejudicial and tainted with suspicion; in the execution of the obligations and duties that were imposed on them by the enemy they have displayed a dubious morality, contrary to the sanctity of the oath of a faithful subject and to the duties of a good citizen.'

It followed that the only people who could be considered as traitors to the fatherland were the naturalized Russian Frenchmen and the few authentic Russians who had served under the orders of Lesseps and Durosnel. For them the verdict was deportation and prison. The other Frenchmen who had collaborated with the Grand Army, but had not fled with Marshal Mortier, were taken back to the frontier. Some of them, however, were discharged, because they had been brought to trial on pure suspicion or as the result of denunciations.

The sentences delivered were not carried out: on August 30, 1814, an Imperial ukase announced 'the good news of the re-establishment of peace in Europe' and pardoned all the condemned.

At the end of the year 1812, 70,000 inhabitants of the destroyed town were re-installed in their homes or in temporary housing. And one Muscovite wrote to a friend:

'Moscow risen from its ashes, beautiful, illuminated by the glory of an immense sacrifice, will always remember the day of its misfortune, but she will remember it as a source of pride.'

CONCLUSION: WHO BURNT MOSCOW?

'IT is one of the most singular facts in history that an action to which public opinion attributed such a great influence on the fate of Russia remains without a father, like the fruit of a forbidden love affair, and will always remain shrouded in mystery, according to all the probabilities!' Thus wrote Clausewitz in his important work, *La Campagne de 1812 en Russie*.[1] And it is true that the file on the burning of Moscow in September 1812 is still not closed. For 150 years people have argued about whether Count Fyodor Vassilievitch Rostopchin set fire to the town of which he was Governor or not.

The polemic began when Rostopchin published a pamphlet in Paris in 1823 entitled *La Vérité sur l'incendie de Moscou*.[2] The Count had been living in France since November 1816. He had been warmly welcomed by the Bourbons and all the society of the Restored Monarchy, which saw in him a sort of hero who had made a large contribution to defeating Napoleon. 'You cannot imagine all the marks of esteem and consideration they show me,' he wrote to his wife. 'The phrase on everybody's lips is: Without you, we would not be here.' And elsewhere: '... I am having a success here such as no other foreigner has had; the English and the Spanish have joined the emigrés, the men of letters, the lawyers and the journalists, and my praises are sung everywhere. I am known here simply as the "Governor" and I have been told that for some months the takings at the *Variétés* are higher than usual, because it is the only theatre that I frequent and people go there to see the "Governor" in the ambassadors' latticed box.'

One evening they even came to recite an extempore bit of doggerel to him in the box:

> *Rostopsin, in his ardent courage,*
> *Burnt Moscow to avoid seeing us!*
> *We are more polite, for everyone, I swear,*
> *Burns with desire to receive him.*

[1] French translation, Paris, 1900 (p. 154).
[2] *Chez* Ponthieu, at the Palais-Royal (Galerie de Bois, No. 252, 1823).

Before his arrival in Paris he had been entertained by all the countries in Europe liberated from the 'Corsican': the King of Prussia had received him with great pomp in Berlin. In London he had been presented to the King of England; on this occasion he had even solicited 'a title or a distinction' through the intermediary of the Russian ambassador, Count Simon Vorontzov. George III had refused, but the British people had offered him an engraved vase. His portrait was on sale everywhere, with the inscription: *Rostopchin the incendiary*; below one of them he had amused himself by writing in his own hand:

> *I was born a Tartar*
> *And I wanted to be a Roman;*
> *The French made me a barbarian,*
> *And the Russians . . . Georges Dandin!*

The elegant women of Paris, Vienna and Berlin wore coiffures *à la Rostoptchine*. All this seemed to delight the governor. He swaggered in the salons, where he continued to make his witty remarks, enjoying rallying the French, whose guest he was. One of his sallies is celebrated: 'With the French, illusions become realities. That is why they are convinced that they are invincible, that they are wise and that the Bois de Boulogne is a forest!' In July 1819, he married off two of his daughters in Paris. The eldest, Nathalie, married Dmitry Narychkin; the younger, Sophia, married Count Eugène de Ségur, grandson of the ambassador to the court of Catherine II, nephew of Napoleon's aide-de-camp.

And then he suddenly wrote and published the famous pamphlet, two memorable pages of which precede the detailed refutation of the 'accusation' that had weighed on him since 1812:

'Ten years have elapsed since the burning of Moscow and I am still pointed out to History and posterity as the author of an event, which, according to accepted opinion, was the principal cause of the destruction of the army of Napoleon, his downfall, the salvation of Russia and the delivery of Europe. Certainly such fine claims were something to be proud of, but, never having usurped anybody's rights and tired of hearing the same fable constantly repeated, I am going to tell the truth, which alone ought to dictate History.

'When the fire destroyed six-eighths of the houses of Moscow in three days, Napoleon appreciated the full importance of this event and foresaw the effect that it would have on the Russian nation, which was justified in attributing this disaster to him because of his presence and that of 30,000 soldiers under his command. He thought that he had found a sure method of diverting from his person all the odium of this act in the eyes of the Russians and Europe, and laying it at the door of the leader of the Russian government in Moscow. Then Napoleon's bulletins at once proclaimed me to be the incendiary. The newspapers, the pamphlets of this period repeated the accusation in emulation and authorized all those persons who have written since about the campaign of 1812 to present an entirely false fact as authentic.

'I am going to recapitulate the principal proofs that started the belief that the burning of Moscow was my work. I shall reply by facts known to all Russians. It would be wrong not to add by faith, since I am renouncing the finest role of the epoch and am personally bringing down the edifice of my celebrity.

Then follow some very feeble refutations written in an airy, ironical style, very much in the Rostopchinian vein.

The Parisian newspapers were the first to express their astonishment. They criticized these forty-five pages stuffed with specious arguments and pointed out that the author was suddenly rejecting, as he would a worn out garment, the homage that had been unanimously paid him by all the enemies of Napoleon. Le Miroir attacked the pamphlet violently:

'The burning of Moscow, if it had been the result of the will of the conqueror, would have vowed its author to the execration of centuries. Considered as the result of the determination of the conquered, does it not inspire a quite different sentiment? Is it not one of those acts which we admire though we tremble. Which assumes a more heroic character as time throws into relief its salutary consequences? Themistocles delivering Athens to the torches of the Persians and saving the Greeks at the cost of his own fatherland was proclaimed great by his own fellow-citizens. So was it calumniating Count Rostopchin to see in him the Themistocles of modern times?'

The article finished with this witty paragraph:

'Conclusion: The truth about the burning of Moscow is that Moscow has burnt. We cling to this idea until a more luminous dissertation makes us change it. All men of good sense will do the same. Jocrisse himself, whose name the author we are crossing swords with sometimes recalls, if he was pressed to explain the explanation given by the governor of Moscow, would probably say: *I see nothing but fire in it!*'

Count Rostopchin's children and grandchildren never accepted the Governor's belated and strange denial. His son, Count Andrei Fyodorovitch Rostopchin, has left us the following important text:[1]

'My father never gave a direct order to anyone to set fire to Moscow, but he took all kinds of measures to see that it did burn. When they came to tell him that the French were entering the town by one gate, he left on horseback by another and, a hundred paces from the gate, he turned round, raised his hat and said to my brother, who was accompanying him: "Salute Moscow for the last time. In an hour, it will be in flames."

'To begin with, the Muscovites applauded the destruction of their homes, but once they had returned to the capital they began a chorus of complaints and bitter recriminations against the author of this disaster. It was under the pressure of these reproaches that my father wrote his pamphlet, saying: "Since the Muscovites are complaining of this aureole of glory with which I have ringed their heads, all right then, I'll take it away from them!" Contemporaries did not wish to believe in the abnegation of a man rejecting the glory of a heroic action, but posterity will confirm this judgment in bronze and marble.'

Count Andrei, then, was anxious for his father to preserve his 'aureole of glory', but, at the same time, displayed the governor's refutation as a sort of revenge on his ungrateful subjects, who had shown themselves neither solidly behind his action nor happy with the glory he had wanted to bestow on them. But why did he wait so long to express his irritation in this curious fashion? Since the year 1815, when he left Russia, he had had all the time he wanted to show them his rancour openly and 'punish' them in this way!

[1] Brussels, 1864, and P. I. Chtchukin: *Papier relatifs à la Guerre patriotique de 1812*, Moscow, 1897 (Vol. I, p. 55).

Count Anatole de Ségur, in the biography devoted to his grand-father,[1] considers that the pamphlet of 1823 'exists as a shadow in this noble life, as a proof . . . that the proudest minds and the most independent characters have their moments of weakness'. He states:

'After a detailed examination of the facts and evidence, my conviction can be summed up as follows: Count Rostopchin is not the sole, but he is the principal author of the burning of Moscow. He did not carry it out, nor order it positively, but he premeditated it, wanted it and laid the preparations for it. So it is with reason that contemporaries attributed to him the honour and responsibility for it, and it is with justice that the History begun for him fifty years ago has indissolubly linked his name with the burning of Moscow.'

Countess Lydia Andreyevna Rostopchin is even more categorical than her father and her cousin. In her *Chroniques de Famille*,[2] she enumerates all the long researches to which she devoted herself, including studying 'the most secret archives of the Ministry of Foreign Affairs, those of the general staff and the Muscovite archives of the Lefort Palace' (during the reign of Nicholas II) and she writes:

'My mind is made up. It corroborates all my family traditions, all my youthful and adolescent memories, and those of friends of my parents: it was certainly Count Fyodor Rostopchin who set fire to Moscow and gave the order for it immediately after receiving, at 11 p.m. on September 13, the letter from Prince Kutuzov announcing the retreat without a battle . . . Why then did he reject this heroic deed in his celebrated pamphlet, *La Vérité sur l'incendie de Moscou*, published by him in Paris in 1823? Why did he deliberately snatch from his head the crown that Fame had placed on it? Why, alas, did he not tell the truth in this supposed "Truth"?'

To this 'why' a Russian contemporary had replied that Rostopchin 'thought it a cunning move to flatter the Bourbons by blaming Napoleon'. But the answer to that is that he could have done so as soon as he arrived in France, adding his voice to the chorus of

---

[1] A, de Ségur: *La vie du comte Rostoptchine*, Paris, 1871.
[2] Countess Lydia Rostopchin: *Les Rostoptchine* (*Chroniques de Famille*), Paris, *chez* Félix Juven, 13, rue de l'Odéon, 1905.

imprecations against the prisoner of Saint Helena. He had not done so and, on the contrary, accepting 'the finest role of the epoch', had watched 'the edifice of his celebrity' being built, with apparent satisfaction. In 1823 Napoleon had been dead for two years and the climate had changed. Scholars have imagined that, tired of living in exile, tormented by deep nostalgia for his beloved fatherland, he wanted to be reconciled with his compatriots, who, as Anatole de Ségur wrote, 'had forgotten the glorious side of his action and saw only the disastrous consequences from the point of view of their material interests'. (Had he not burst out, when he was first attacked by the Muscovite nobility: 'I was wrong to worry about them so much. Furniture, that's what's dearest to a man!') He has been credited with the hope that his fellow-citizens would pardon him their material losses, forget their grudges and welcome him with open arms if he proclaimed his innocence in print.

But Countess Lydia gives an entirely different and very curious explanation, saying that the Governor acted under the pressure of his wife, Countess Catherine Rostopchin, 'whose influence had gradually sapped the eternal principles of truth in him'. The Countess was secretly converted to Catholicism. 'The discovery of this well hidden secret was a terrible blow to the Count and he kept silent about it until his death, but he also retained the lasting bitterness it inspired.' And Countess Lydia, a fervent member of the orthodox church, who could not forgive her ancestor this *apostasy*, accuses her of having been 'perverted by the Jesuitic spirit' and of having persuaded her husband that 'to suppress a part of the truth is not a lie'. So, she wrote,

'Tired, turned irritable and morose, soured by the complaints and whinings of Muscovites ruined by the fire, who did not spare him the most threatening letters, the ex-Governor wanted to explain one day the real facts about this fire that provided material for so many controversies; he grabbed a pen . . . but alas he dipped it in Jesuitic ink . . . with which his home was always well supplied.'

A little known, original and interesting interpretation, but certainly a subjective one that is unverifiable today. Doubtless it contains its share of truth, like all historical theories. What is certain is that the children and grandchildren of the Governor had absolutely no doubt about his action and praised it. The evidence of Count Andrei—'he took all kinds of measures to see that it did burn'; that of Count Anatole—'he premeditated it, wanted it and laid the preparations for it'; and finally that of Countess Lydia, quoting a letter from the Governor in which he wrote: 'In the past I have exceeded the duties of a faithful subject and I have acted like a demoniac or an Asiatic intoxicated with opium . . .',[1] all that was published so that no doubt should continue to exist in the minds of future generations.

It is obvious that no serious historian has ever tried to depict Rostopchin running round Moscow with a blazing torch, or looking at his work through an enormous telescope, as we see him in contemporary caricatures. As far as the preparation is concerned, the Governor's order to the Chief of Police, Ivachkin, about the departure of the fire-engines, has been found and published.[2] The Soviet historian, Eugene Tarle, has quoted the official report of Voronenko, the Commissioner of Police, to the tribunal of Moscow, at the time of the Russian authorities' enquiry into the fire: 'On September 2nd/14th, at 5 a.m., Count Rostopchin sent me to the Wine Market, the Mitny Markets and the Central Police Station, and instructed me to try to destroy everything by fire, should the enemy enter suddenly; which I did until 10 p.m., in various places, to the best of my ability, in the presence of the enemy . . .'[3] This important statement could not be ignored by General Mikhailovsky-Danilevsky, one of the first to have studied the Russian Campaign in detail, but he tried to clear Rostopchin of all responsibility for the fire.[4] Voronenko, according to him, had misunderstood the orders and was only responsible for the first fires, in any case; the great conflagration of September 15th was comparable to the looting and acts of violence committed by the occupying army. It was partly deliberate, partly caused by negligence. Developing this theme, the memorialist Dmitry Sverbeyev[5] writes:

'How can we help admitting that Moscow would have been more likely to burn than to remain intact, in the midst of such atrocious

---

[1] Rostopchin to Mr Bulgakov, from St Petersburg, June 11, 1816, op. cit. (p. 47).
[2] P. I. Chtchukin, op. cit. (Vol. I, p. 96).
[3] *La Campagne de Russie, 1812*, French translation, Paris, Gallimard, 1950. After the Schilder archives copy, Scientific and Military Archives, No. 4,346, Moscow/N.
[4] *Account of the Patriotic War of 1812*, St Petersburg, 1840 (R.).
[5] *Memoirs*, Moscow, 1889 (Vol. I, p. 447). (R.).

14. In an 'annihilating' cold, the miserable remnants of the army dribbled away to Prussia. 'The army is in complete disorder . . . . The army is no more.'

15. On December 6th, the Emperor left by sledge with Caulaincourt: 'I can only dictate to Europe from the Palace of the Tuileries.'

disorders? Let us recall that there were neither municipal authorities, nor police, nor any means of extinguishing the fire in the town [he does not say why!] and what contributed most to the spread of the fire was the complete lack of discipline in the ranks of the enemy army.'

Although certain historians of the Stalin period have squarely laid the blame for the destruction of Moscow by fire on Napoleon's shoulders, Tarle is more subtle: 'True,' he writes, 'Rostopchin made a very active contribution to starting the fire, although he denied it in the pamphlet published towards the end of his life, when he was living in Paris . . .' But: 'It is more than probable that among the people who remained in Moscow there were individuals who had decided to act independently of Rostopchin's orders, even at the risk of their lives, obeying this watchword: *May all perish rather than fall into the hands of the enemy!*' Nevertheless, he adds: 'On the other hand, it is certain that many fires were the result of the negligence of the French soldiers in abandoned shops and houses, where they found enormous stocks of alcoholic drinks.' That is very possible, but does not explain such large conflagrations, enveloping whole districts at the same time, or almost. We may also admit that some desperate Muscovites, remembering what had been done at Smolensk, may have acted spontaneously. However, that does not take into account the men who did act on instructions, nor the common law criminals whom the governor had set free at the eleventh hour, an action he did not deny when he gave his explanation of the Verestchagin affair.

The opinion of Count Rostopchin's contemporaries as to the responsibility for the fire seems to us to be of exceptional interest.

Colonel D. Buturlin asserts in his *Histoire de l'Invasion de l'empereur Napoléon en 1812*:[1]

'The most positive information permits of no doubt that the burning of Moscow was prepared and carried out by the Russian authorities. As the fire only burst out after the arrival of the French, it was easy to persuade the mob that the French had started the

---

[1] Published in French in 1824, this book was translated into Russian the same year, published at St Petersburg and re-issued in 1837 (Vol. I, p. 369).

fire. This opinion, by exasperating the country people, gave a more pronounced character to the national war.'[1]

Buturlin specifies that the authorities had had inflammable materials placed in a number of houses and had distributed round the town 'a troop of paid incendiaries, directed by some officers of the former Moscow police force ... Rostopchin had taken the precaution of taking with him the fire-engines and other fire-fighting appliances. These measures had the success desired ...'

Let us emphasize that Buturlin's work was published one year after Rostopchin's pamphlet, which had stupefied and enraged the veterans of 1812. To them, as Langeron (a French emigré and General in the Russian army) had not hesitated to write, the fire was 'a heroic act, a terrible and superb decision, motivated by extraordinary abnegation, by the most burning patriotism.' Therefore he 'believed in it' firmly, like Buturlin, who wanted to assert in writing what he considered to be the strict truth, at the risk of displeasing the Bourbons, Prussia and England. An interesting fact is that he published his book in Alexander I's lifetime, without being subjected to his dreaded censorship, and the second edition appeared under Nicholas I, who was an even stricter censor and a much more narrow-minded man!

This reign also saw the publication of the book by the Russian Councillor of State, Liprandi: *Neither Hunger nor Cold were the cause of the destruction of Napoleon's troops.* (Sub-title: *Was it the Russians or the French who burnt Moscow?*[2]) It was a detailed and rather venomous refutation of the 'official' work by General Mikhailovsky-Danilevsky quoted above. According to Liprandi, Danilevsky was unable to prove Rostopchin's 'innocence', in spite of all his efforts, and he jeers at this truism by the author whom he is criticizing: 'Napoleon is really responsible for the fire, because if he had not invaded Russia, Moscow would never have burnt!' Nevertheless, two of Liprandi's arguments may be criticized:

1. In support of his thesis that Rostopchin is an incendiary, he quotes a letter from the Governor to the Tsar: 'I am in despair because he [Kutusov] concealed his intentions from me; for I,

---

[1] Clausewitz's opinion resembles Buturlin's in that he declares that the burning of Moscow was a misfortune for Napoleon because it excited a veritable patriotic fanaticism throughout the whole Russian people.

[2] St Petersburg, 1855 (R.).

not being capable of guarding the town, I would have burnt it . . .'
In that he sees not only the proof that the Governor set fire to
Moscow, but also that he had no doubt of Alexander's agreement,
without which he would not have dared to express himself like that.
We see a regret in it, but not a proof. Nevertheless, it is true that
it must have taken much assurance on Rostopchin's part to write
to the Tsar so categorically—even if it was in the conditional tense
—'I would have burnt it!' But surely he had this assurance, because
Alexander had conferred full powers in him and had said when
pinning his diamond 'cipher' to his epaulette: 'Now you must carry
me on your shoulders!'

2. As regards the agreement of Alexander and the fact that the
Sovereign knew the author of the fire, Liprandi refers to the
Manifesto of which we have spoken.[1] The Tsar, he says, does not
accuse the French of having burnt the old capital, 'which he
would obviously not have omitted to do if he had believed them
guilty of the crime'. Therefore, he knew the man responsible and
approved of him, as this passage in the Manifesto proves: '[Moscow]
offers a tomb rather than a resting-place to the cruel aggressor.'
Liprandi has made a mistake in the date. The Manifesto was dated
September 17th and Alexander was not informed of the fire until
the 20th, by Colonel Michaud. He was only alluding to the evacuation of the town. Otherwise we would have to admit that Liprandi
knew positively that the Tsar had received the horrible news at a
date and from a person that have remained unknown to us. A
seductive theory, because scholars have always been surprised that
Alexander learnt about the burning of Moscow so late, but it is
invalidated by a letter published by Dubrovin in his important
compilation: *The War of 1812 according to Letters by contemporaries.*[2]
Alexander wrote to Rostopchin on September 5th/17th:

'I have received your letters punctually up to that of August 29th
(Sept. 10th) inclusively. I cannot tell you how satisfied I am with
the way in which you are filling your post . . . Keep me up to date
about everything that happens.'

On the 17th, therefore, the Tsar still did not know anything about
the disaster; but such a letter could explain the governor's assurance
even better.

Among other verdicts by contemporaries, we must mention the

[1] Pp. 74–76.
[2] St Petersburg, 1882, letter no. 119, p. 124. (R.).

memoirs of Colonel (later General) Ermolov, the future conqueror of the Caucasus. On the subject of Rostopchin's pamphlet, he wrote:

'Why strip ourselves of the glory of having sacrificed our capital, when a fair adversary does not snatch this glory from us? Each individual Russian, all the people together, made a generous sacrifice for the common good.'[1]

This is a new aspect of the situation: Rostopchin incarnating the will of the Russian people. And it seems clear that apart from some spiteful Muscovites, many people in Russia held the same view. We find an echo of it in numerous letters of the period where we find statements like these: 'The fire was the deed of a small number, but the idea of all.' 'It is the testament of a generation for posterity,'[2] etc.

As for Clausewitz, he at first attributed the catastrophe not to the French, but to 'the Cossacks' habit of looting in earnest everything that had to be abandoned to the enemy and then setting fire to it'. But: 'after all that has been said about it, especially after the rather unsatisfactory defence that Rostopchin had printed', he became convinced that it was Rostopchin who had had Moscow burnt on his own authority, without warning his government in advance.

'His disgrace and his long absence from Russia are perhaps the consequences of his independent initiative—something a Russian autocrat does not easily forgive . . . It is not likely that Alexander wanted or ordered the fire. It is not in keeping with his flabby character. On the other hand, Rostopchin's responsibility was enormous, because he had to give instructions from his own lips to certain underlings, who were his tools . . . So we must believe that if he did it, it was because the degree of bitterness and passion that he seemed to have reached at that moment gave him the necessary strength.'

That is reminiscent of the governor's letter to Bulgakov quoted above, a letter which, writes Lydia Rostopchin, had 'suppressed

[1] Ermolov: *Materials for the War of 1812* (*Memoirs*), written in 1815 and published in Moscow in 1863 (2 vols.). (R.).
[2] Cf. *The War of 1812 according to Letters by contemporaries*, op. cit.

her last doubts', because of these extraordinary words: 'I have acted like a demoniac or an Asiatic intoxicated with opium!'

Let us add, so as to omit nothing, that at the time, several people imagined that the fire had been lit for a strategic purpose by soldiers of the Russian army which abandoned Moscow. Prince Eugene of Würtemberg, a contemporary witness of these events, as we know, has shown the absurdity of such a supposition.[1] The mere fact that the Russians left 10,000 to 15,000 soldiers who had been wounded at Borodino in the town would be enough to prove that their leaders did not imagine for a moment the danger to which these unfortunates were going to be exposed.

As for knowing what Alexander I thought of the fire, it is yet another mystery surrounding that enigmatic Sovereign! During the last century in Russia it was generally written that the Tsar had 'disowned Rostopchin without disapproving of him'. That was quite in keeping with his chameleon-like, fickle character. But we must never lose sight of the hate he bore for the man he appointed Governor under the pressure of his entourage and events. He could not forgive him—and that is understandable—for a certain letter not intended for him that fell into his hands. After the defeat of Austerlitz, Rostopchin wrote to his relation, Princess Galitzin: 'How do you expect God to protect the arms of a parricide?'

We find it impossible to attribute the burning of Moscow to chance, as Tolstoy did, or to the carelessness of unruly soldiers in Napoleon's army. We think that Count Fyodor Rostopchin, whatever one may think of his character, was indeed 'the ardent and fierce patriot, the unforgiving and merciless Russian, who did more to conquer Napoleon by fire and flight than the united armies of England and Germany.'[2] We think that, together with Kutusov, he was the architect of the defeat of the Grand Army, and we choose to share the view of the Prince of Würtemberg, who said: 'It is no longer possible to rid its author of the responsibility for this tragic event, as difficult to judge, incidentally, as the action of Brutus, but which cannot in any case be laid at the door of either the Russian or the French army.'

---

[1] *Memoirs*, Breslau, 1846.
[2] Jean de Bonnefon, Preface to the *Oeuvres inédites du comte Rostoptchine*, Paris, Dentu, 1894 (pp. IV-V).

APPENDIX I

———◆———

THE AFFAIR OF THE DEPORTATION OF THE FRENCH BY COUNT ROSTOPCHIN

IT was at the end of the month of August 1812 that the Governor of Moscow had arrested at random forty French Muscovites of various professions, and, after locking them up for forty-eight hours, had them sent to Kolomna, from where they were embarked on a vessel and taken to Nijni-Novgorod. They voyaged under extremely distressing conditions, but on arrival at their destination, their situation was that of people whose residence was under supervision rather than that of prisoners. What is interesting, and very damning for Rostopchin, is 'the address' he wrote and had read to them when they embarked. This disagreeable piece of prose was in 1851 inserted in the *Moscow Police Gazette*, No. 113, dated May 24th:

'Frenchmen!

'Your Emperor has said in a proclamation to his good town of Paris: "Frenchmen! You have told me so often that you loved me!" And to convince your sovereign of this truth, you have not ceased to serve him in these hyperborean climes, where winter and desolation dispute the sovereignty. The Russian people, so great and generous, is ready to go to extremes. I am removing you to spare it a task and to avoid soiling history with the story of a massacre, the feeble imitation of your infernal national furies. You will go to live on the banks of the Volga, in the midst of a peaceful people who are faithful to their vows and who despise you too much to harm you! For a certain period of time you will leave Europe and go to Asia. Cease to be bad subjects and become good ones. Transform yourselves into good Russian citizens from the French citizens you are; remain calm and submissive or fear severe punishment; board the bark, examine your consciences, and do not turn it into a bark of Charon.

'Greetings and *bon voyage*.' (Signed): COUNT ROSTOPCHIN
July 1812, Moscow.

The date of this document, which needs no comment, is also eloquent. The deportation did not take place until the end of August, but had been prepared in advance, in the same way as 'the address'.

APPENDIX II

LETTER FROM TSAR ALEXANDER I TO HIS SISTER
CATHERINE[1]

'I OWE you a detailed reply, my dear, and here it is.

'Nothing is more natural than for people to be unjust to the man who
has fallen into misfortune, for them to abuse and slander him. I have
never had any illusions on that score, I was certain that it would happen
to me as soon as fate was against me. Perhaps I am even destined to
lose the friends on whom I had counted most. All that is unfortunately
in the nature of things in this vile world.

'In spite of the repugnance I experience in tiring anybody with
details about myself, a repugnance that is infinitely increased when I find
fortune against me, the sincere attachment which I feel for you makes
me overcome it, and I am going to put matters to you as I see them.

'What more can a man do than follow his true conviction? It is that
alone which has guided me. It made me appoint Barclay to command the
1st army on the strength of the reputation he had made for himself
during the last wars against the French and the Swedes. It also made
me think that his attainments were superior to Bagration's. When this
conviction was further increased by the major errors which the latter
committed during this campaign and which partially contributed to our
defeats, I thought him less fitted than ever to command the two armies
united below Smolensk. Although dissatisfied with what I have been in
a position to see of Barclay, I believe him less inept than the other in the
field of strategy, of which Bagration has no idea. Lastly I did not have a
better man to nominate, according to this same conviction.

'It is completely untrue that my aide-de-camp Kutusov has brought
me, as you have been told, strong representations on the part of the
generals of the army. He simply came to give me an account of the
engagements that have taken place in the outskirts of Vitebsk. In reply
to a personal request from me, he told me that in the army they thought
both Barclay and Bagration equally incapable of commanding such a
large body and that it was Peter Pahlen the army wanted.[2] Apart from

[1] Reply to his sister's letter, dated from Yaroslav, September 6th/18th (cf. p. 98).

[2] Peter Alexeyvich Pahlen (1745–1826) was the leader of the conspiracy that led to
the assassination of Paul I on May 16, 1801. Alexander retired him in 1801. Obviously,
he could not retain him in his service. The sentence about 'the treacherous and immoral
character' and 'the crimes' of Pahlen is eloquent of Alexander's attitude to him. He
particularly detested him because this man knew perfectly well that Alexander had
given his tacit agreement to his father's assassination. Pahlen was, in a sense, the
incarnation of Alexander's remorse.

the treacherous and immoral character, and the crimes of this man, remember only that he has not seen the enemy for eighteen to twenty years and that the last time he fought he was only a Brigadier-general. So what reliance could I place on this man and where are the proofs of his military talent?

'At St Petersburg, I found everybody in favour of the nomination of old Kutusov as Commander-in-chief. The knowledge I have of this man made him repugnant to me at first, but when Rostopchin told me in his letter of August 15th that the whole of Moscow wanted Kutusov to command, finding both Barclay and Bagration incapable of it, and in the midst of all this, Barclay having done, as if on purpose, one foolish thing after another around Smolensk, I could not help yielding to the unanimous wishes and I appointed Kutusov. I still think at this moment that, in the circumstances in which we were, I could not have done otherwise than decide on the man who won the general vote, out of three generals equally unfitted to be Commander-in-chief.

'Now I come to a matter that is very close to my heart: it is about my personal honour. I confess, my dear, that it is even more distressing to me to touch on this subject, and that, in your eyes at least I believed it was intact. I cannot even believe that, in your letter, it is a question of the personal courage that every ordinary soldier has and to which I attach no merit. Besides, if I must have the humiliation of dwelling on this subject, I tell you that the grenadiers of the regiments of Lesser Russia and Kiev can certify that I know how to withstand gunfire as calmly as the next man. But once again, I cannot believe that this type of courage is the subject of your letter and I suppose that you meant to speak of moral courage: it is the only one that can be granted any merit in the most eminent vocations. Perhaps I would have succeeded in convincing you that I also have my share of it if I had stayed with the army. But what I cannot understand is that you who, in your letters to George[1] at Vilna, wanted me to leave the army, you who, in the letter of August 5th by Veliachef, said to me: 'For heavens' sake, do not adopt the course of wanting to take command yourself, for without delay we need a leader in whom the troops have confidence, and in this regard you cannot inspire any; besides, if failure happened to you in person, it would be an irreparable evil because of the feeling it would cause," after thus having posited as a fact that I cannot inspire any confidence, I cannot understand, I say, what you are trying to say to me in your last letter by: "Save your honour, which is attacked. Your presence may win people back to you." By that do you mean my presence

---

[1] Catherine's husband, Prince George of Oldenburg, who was to die suddenly two months later on December 15, 1812. (By her second marriage, the Tsar's sister became Queen of Würtemberg.)

with the army? And how can I reconcile these two opinions that are so opposed to each other?

'After having sacrificed my personal self-respect to necessity by leaving the army, because it was claimed that I was harmful there, that I was taking all responsibility from the generals, that I inspired no confidence in the troops, that defeats imputed to me were worse than those imputed to my generals, judge for yourself, my dear, how painful it must be for me to hear that my honour is attacked, when I have only done what people wanted in leaving the army, whereas I had no other desire but to stay there and was firmly determined to return to it before Kutusov's nomination, and when I only gave up the idea after this nomination partly owing to the memory of what the obsequious character of this man produced at Austerlitz and partly because of following your own advice and that of several others of the same opinion as you.

'If you ask me why I have not gone to Moscow,[1] I will tell you that I never made any engagements nor gave my promise to go there. Rostopchin often begged me to do so in his letters, but that was before the retreat from Smolensk, when, therefore, it was impossible for me to do so, owing to my journey in Finland; on the other hand, afterwards, in his letter of August 14th, he said: "Now, Sire, I come to the most important thing, that is to say, your journey here. There is no doubt that your presence here excites the people's enthusiasm even more, but if events are not to our advantage before your arrival, your person would further increase the general uneasiness, and, as it is not fitting for you to run risks by exposing yourself, it would be better that you took the decision to delay your departure from St Petersburg until the reception of some news that would change the present state of affairs for the better."

'At present, let us examine whether I could have gone to Moscow. Once it had been laid down as a principle that my presence with the army did more harm than good, with the army drawing closer to Moscow after its retreat from Smolensk, could I decently have been in Moscow? Although I could never have imagined that Moscow could be abandoned in such an unworthy manner, however I must have told myself that it could happen as the result of one or two lost battles. Then what role would I have played there and would I have gone to Moscow merely to pack up my kit with the others?

'But let us see by reckoning the time whether I could have arrived there in time or not? As soon as Bentinck returned, I left for Finland so as to be there at the time arranged for me. I only stayed three days in Åbo with the Prince Royal: you will agree that that was not long. From the 21st to the 22nd I was on my return journey to St Petersburg.

[1] Naturally, the Tsar's journey to Moscow on July 23rd is not referred to here. Catherine would have liked him to return there after the loss of Smolensk, so as to be closer to the military operations and reassure the Muscovites by his presence.

Suppose that I had left the next day, I would not have arrived in Moscow until the day of the battle, the 26th: consequently I would not even have been able to prevent the pernicious retreat that was carried out on the night of the battle and lost everything. Judge then of my position in Moscow! Would not all the responsibility for subsequent events have fallen on me, at the very instant when I was so near, on me alone, and, in truth, would I have been able to prevent what happened once they had neglected to take advantage of the victory and the favourable moment was lost? So I would only have gone there to assume the shame that others had brought with them.

'On the other hand, my intention was to seize the first moment of a real advantage gained by our army over the enemy and forcing it to withdraw, actually to come to Moscow. Even after the news of the battle of the 26th, I would have left at once, if, in the same report, Kutusov had not informed me that he had decided to withdraw six versts in order to recover. These fatal six versts, by poisoning all the satisfaction that the victory gave me, made me wait for the next report and that made me clearly foresee nothing but calamities.

'That is the exact account of the circumstances, my dear. I am going to add other notions which will strike you perhaps.

'This spring, before my departure for Vilna, I had been informed on good authority that the constant work of Napoleon's secret agents was to be directed to discrediting the government in every possible way, in order to put it at cross purposes with the nation; that, to succeed in this, it was determined, if I was with the army, to put all the reverses that might happen down to my account and to represent me as having sacrificed my personal pride by preventing more experienced generals than I from obtaining successes over the enemy; and, on the other hand, if I was not with the army, to impute it to a lack of courage on my part. But that is not enough; the infernal plan was also, in keeping with these same notions, supposed to sow disunion in our family.

'Won't you be astonished when I tell you that, eight or ten days before my departure, I was warned that the operation was to begin with you and that they would employ all their efforts to portray me in the most unfavourable colours in your eyes? Because your friendship for me has always made my heart and all my thoughts an open book to you, I have been perfectly calm and thought very little about it. In the same way they were to work on me by making me worry on your account, but they were very quickly convinced that they would be wasting their time. To carry out these infernal intrigues, beings completely innocent of all these conspiracies, frightened by every story the agents contrived to bring to their ears, were to become, unsuspectingly and out of their actual zeal, the echoes of the gossip originally spread by the tools of

Napoleon, so that by this means they ultimately reached us and so that the real authors remained well hidden. The epoch when all these methods were to be especially employed was when one of the two capitals should fall into the hands of the enemy.

'Here, at St Petersburg, I am daily in a better position to convince myself how accurate the warnings I was given this spring were and what you tell me in your last letter contributes not a little to proving it to me. Meanwhile, I am the first to agree that, in our present unfortunate circumstances, a machination of this kind meets every possible facility for success, and the propagators of remarks of this kind must naturally find large numbers of proselytes.

'As for me, my dear, all I can answer for is my heart, my intentions and my zeal for everything that can conduce to the well-being and needs of my fatherland, according to my true conviction. As for talent, I may lack it, but it is not there for the asking: it is a benefaction of nature and no one has ever procured it Seconded as badly as I am, lacking tools in all parties, leading such an enormous machine, in a terrible crisis and against an infernal antagonist, who combines the most horrible villainy with the most eminent talent and is supported both by all the forces of the whole of Europe and by a talented mass of men who have been trained during twenty years of war and revolution, one would be forced to agree, if one wishes to be just, that it is not astonishing that I am experiencing reverses. You will recall that we have often foreseen them when chatting between ourselves; even the loss of the two capitals was believed possible and perseverance alone was judged to be the remedy for the evils of this cruel epoch. Far from being discouraged, in spite of all the disappointments with which I am heaped, I am more determined than ever to persevere in the struggle, and all my efforts are employed to this end.

I confess to you frankly that being misunderstood by a public, or by a mass of beings who know me little or not at all, is a trial I feel less than being misunderstood by the small number of those to whom I have vowed all my affections and by whom I hoped to be known through and through. But even if this affliction had to be added to all those I am bearing, I protest to you before God that I would not accuse them and would only see in it the common lot of unfortunate beings, that of being abandoned.

'Forgive me, my dear, for having wearied your patience for so long both by the length of this epistle and by the time it has taken me to write to you, since I can only escape from my daily occupations for a short time.

'Now I must give you an account of minor matters. I have not succeeded in obtaining the ribbon of Saint Catherine for Princess Wolkonsky[1] from my Mother: she has written to you about it herself and I found her very up in arms against this proposal.

'As for Gagarin,[2] it is quite impossible for me to advance him for he would be passing over Saltikoff and a number of other senators, all senior to him. In general, at this moment when such major events are taking place, it seems to me we must suspend rewards for some time except for those who are going to shed their blood in defence of the fatherland.

'As for the two doctors, they are advanced. I must blame myself, my dear, for not having asked you in which regiment you want your little one[3] placed, as I did with the eldest.

Being accustomed to write to you both together, I will tell you, George, that at this moment you are more useful to me at the head of your three governments and the communications than at headquarters.[4] At a time when the enemy is employing every possible method to disorganize everything in the interior, we cannot use enough means to prevent it and maintain order. Never has the importance of your post of Governor-General of these three governments been greater. The only communications we have left with Europe now pass through Yaroslav; a part of Moscow is at Yaroslav, and there are many more considerations. If you keep order and calm for me in your three governments, you will certainly have rendered me and the state the greatest of services.

Lastly I close by exhorting you both to perseverance and firmness. You have so often advocated them to me yourselves, it is the moment to put them to work, and you may be sure that it takes more of them to fight against internal dissensions than against the enemy. To both of you from heart and soul for life.

'I enclose here the usual little presents for the baby.'

---

[1] *Princess Wolkonsky :* Grand Mistress of Catherine's Court. She was the mother of Decembrist Serge Wolkonsky.

[2] *Prince Gagarin :* Marshal of the Court.

[3] Catherine's second son, Frederick Constantine, born on August 14, 1812, at Yaroslav.

[4] Prince George of Oldenburg complained bitterly about not taking part in the military operations. His wife supported him in this.

APPENDIX III

ROSTOPCHIN'S DESTRUCTION OF HIS PROPERTY OF VORONOVO

ONLY one document still exists to relate to posterity how the Governor of Moscow destroyed his country house, which he had, as he wrote himself, 'been eight years beautifying, and where he had 'lived happily with his family'. The story of it has been told by an eye witness: General Sir Robert Wilson.[1] The Englishman, with his aide-de-camp, Lord Tyrconnel, General Ermolov and various officers accompanied Count Rostopchin in search of Kutusov's headquarters. They bivouacked in the main courtyard of Voronovo, around a fire. According to Wilson:

'The palace of Voronovo was magnificent, of genuine grandeur, with the colossal groups of horses of Monte Cavallo surmounting the entrance; the inside gallery contained copies of the principal Roman and Greek statues and monuments, while the furnishing exhibited the rarest luxury.

'We chatted around the fire. The Governor-general had banished any desire to sleep with his bitter complaints against Kutuzov, his evacuation of Moscow without having sent him the agreed warning, thus depriving the authorities and the inhabitants of the opportunity of proving a dignity, not Roman, but more than Roman—Russian . . . He declared that he would never forgive the Marshal for breaking his word and that he was going to set fire with his own hands to the palace that we were admiring so much, if the enemy approached, and he only regretted that it was not ten times more worthy of being sacrificed. His implacable resolution yielded to none of our exhortations.

'At dawn a deputation of peasants appeared: they had made their preparations to accompany the troops and asked their lord for permission to withdraw to a property he had [at Orel] . . . preferring exile to the domination of the French. When permission was granted, the whole population of 1,700 souls began to march . . . Rostopchin, hearing the gunfire in the distance and seeing the enemy on the move, went into the castle, asking his friends to accompany him. Lighted torches were distributed to them. Climbing the staircase and reaching his bedroom, Rostopchin stopped for a moment, then he said: "There is my marriage bed, I have not the courage to set fire to it: spare me that sorrow!"'

Passing from room to room and then to the stables, the little band lit

[1] *The Invasion of Russia by Napoleon Bonaparte and the Retreat of the French*, Oxford, 1860 (pp. 179–80).

the fire and 'a quarter of an hour later, everything was burning at once'. When the group of horses from Monte Cavallo collapsed into the main courtyard, the Count cried: 'Now I feel at peace!' Then he withdrew with the officers and stuck up the sign that was later taken to Napoleon in the Kremlin.

Sir Robert Wilson writes, and it seems difficult to contradict him on this point:

'I could not help feeling great distress at seeing this noble pile destroyed and ruined by the necessity of the times, nor restrain myself from paying homage to the superior public virtue, to the magnanimous philosophy of a man who contemplated this additional devastation of his property (after having lost in the burning of Moscow a palace worth more than one thousand pounds sterling, including the second largest library in the empire and a collection of precious objects)[1] without expressing regrets . . .'

[1] This was not true: the Rostopchin palace of the Lubianka had not burnt.

BRIEF BIOGRAPHICAL INDEX

BAGRATION (Prince Peter): Russian general, born in 1765. Sergeant in the army of Catherine II; General in 1794 under the orders of Suvorov. In disgrace under Paul I, was recalled by Alexander I. Austerlitz, Friedland, Smolensk. The troops, who adored him, made a pun on his name: *Bog-raty-on*: 'he is the god of the army'. Wounded at Borodino, he died shortly afterwards.

BARCLAY DE TOLLY (Prince Michael): born in 1761. Descendant of an old Scottish family, some members of which who supported the Stuarts took refuge in Russia. Field-Marshal and Minister of War at the beginning of the 1812 campaign, he was reviled by the whole country because of the Russians' retreat from the Niemen to Smolensk. Although a third generation Russian, he was called *niemetz*—a word which meant both *foreigner* and *German*. Posterity paid him homage by placing his statue in bronze next to Kutusov's in front of the Kazan Cathedral in St Petersburg. At the time of the erection of these statues (1837), a satirical quatrain circulated in the capital:

> *Barclay de Tolly and Kutusov*
> *Made the French freeze in the Year Twelve.*
> *For this noble deed, the ungrateful Russian people*
> *Exposed them bare-headed to the cold!*

BAUSSET (Louis-François-Joseph de Bausset-Roquefort): born in 1770. Prefect of the Imperial Palace. After the Russian Campaign, he was made Manager of the Comédie Française, whose statute Napoleon had drawn up at Moscow. After the abdication of the Emperor at Fontainebleau, he accompanied Marie Louise to Rambouillet, Orleans, Vienna, where he was Grand Master of her household, and lastly to Parma. Died in 1833.

BENNIGSEN (or *Benningsen*) (Count of Lev): born in 1743 in Hannover. Distinguished himself in the two wars against the Turks under Catherine II. Fell into disgrace under Paul I. Undoubtedly took part in the conspiracy which led to the assassination of that Tsar. General-in-chief at Eylau. Commanded the centre of the Russian army at Borodino. Left the service after his quarrel with Kutusov and did not return to the army until 1813. After the Peace of Paris, received the command of the Army of the South. Died after a long illness in 1826.

BERTHIER (Alexandre, Prince of Neuchâtel and Wagram): born at Versailles in 1753. American War with Lafayette. Chief of Staff during the Italian campaign. Minister of War after 18th Brumaire.

Left this post for that of Major-general in the army. He betrayed the deep affection the Emperor had for him by being one of the first to throw in his lot with Louis XVIII. During the Hundred Days he killed himself at Bamberg by jumping out of a window. He married the niece of the King of Bavaria.

BESSIÈRES (Jean-Baptiste-Barthélemy, Duke of Istria): born in 1766. Enlisted in 1791. Noticed by Bonaparte in 1796 and taken to Egypt. Marshal of the Empire in 1804. Commanded the cavalry of the Guard in 1805. Austerlitz, Friedland, Somo-Sierra, Essling, Wagram, etc. Created Duke in 1809. Killed on an audacious reconnaissance on the eve of the Battle of Lützen, May 1, 1813.

CAULAINCOURT (Armand-Augustin-Louis, Marquis of Caulaincourt, Duke of Vicenza): born in 1772. Mission to Russia in 1801. Aide-de-camp general of Napoleon in 1802. Master of the Horse in 1804. Ambassador to Russia from 1807 to 1811. Created Duke in 1808. Senator and Minister for Foreign Relations in 1813. Saved from condemnation under the Restoration thanks to the intervention of Alexander I, who had a high opinion of him. Died in 1827.

DARU (Count Pierre-Antoine-Noël-Bruno): born in 1767. Councillor of State, then Count of the Empire. Quartermaster-general of the *Maison militaire*, *Commissaire général* of the Grand Army, Minister of War. One of the first to rejoin Napoleon when he disembarked at Golfe Juan. Nevertheless was created Peer of France under the Restoration. Died in 1829.

DUROC (Gérard-Christophe-Michel, Duke of Frioul): born in 1772. Passed out of the School of Brienne with Napoleon, with whom he became intimate at the siege of Toulon. Aide-de-camp during the Italian and Egyptian campaigns. General and Grand Marshal of the Imperial Palace after 18th Brumaire. Mortally wounded during the Battle of Lützen on May 22, 1813, he wrote to the Emperor: 'All my life has been devoted to you. I only regret it for the usefulness it could still have for you.'

DUROSNEL (Count Antoine-Jean-Auguste): born in 1771. Brigadier-General in 1805. General of division in 1809. Aide-de-camp to the Emperor from June 30, 1810. Appointed Governor of Moscow on Napoleon's entry into that town. Remained on half-pay during the Restoration, but entered the service again under Louis-Philippe. Died in 1849.

ELIZABETH ALEXEYEVNA, Empress, wife of Alexander I, née Princess Maria Louisa Augusta of Baden. In spite of her love for Prince Adam Czartoryzky and the Tsar's infidelities, she was a help and a support to Alexander I. It was her failing health which drove the Tsar to leave for Taganrog with her, in 1825, where he died in mysterious circumstances. Elizabeth died at the age of forty-seven, in May 1826, during the voyage on which she was accompanying the body of her husband to St Petersburg.

GOURGAUD (Gaspard, Baron): born in 1783. Aide-de-camp to the Emperor. Served Louis XVIII at the time of the First Restoration, but returned to Napoleon during the Hundred Days. Aide-de-camp general. Followed the Emperor to Saint Helena, returning from it in 1818. Died in 1852.

KUTUSOV (Mikhail Larionovich) Prince of Smolensk: born in 1745 at St Petersburg and entered the Russian army in 1759 or 1760. Served in Poland 1764–69, and against the Turks 1770–74. Lost an eye in the latter year. Major-General 1784; Governor-General of the Crimea 1787; Lieut.-General in 1791 after distinguished service in the Turkish War of 1788–91. Subsequently Ambassador to Constantinople, Governor-General of Finland, Ambassador to Berlin, Governor-General of St Petersburg. In 1805 he commanded the Russian corps which opposed Napoleon's campaign against the Austrians and was wounded at Austerlitz. Governor-General of Lithuania and Kiev, 1806–11. Was made a prince in 1811 and Field-Marshal in 1812. Died in March 1813.

LARIBOISIÈRE (Jean-Ambroise de): born in 1759. Artillery officer in 1781. Distinguished himself before Mayence in 1793. Spanish campaign with Napoleon. Somo-Sierra. General of division. Essling, Wagram. Commanded the artillery of the Guard in 1812. Died of exhaustion on arriving in Prussia after the retreat from Russia (Jan. 1813).

LARREY (Jean-Dominique, Baron): born in 1766. Medical studies at Toulouse and Paris. Naval surgeon in 1787. Creator of the fast, so-called 'flying', ambulances. Italian and Egyptian campaigns. Doctor of surgery in 1803. Made Surgeon-in-Chief of the Grand Army. Camp of Boulogne, Austerlitz, Eylau. Baron of the Empire after Wagram. Russian campaign. Prisoner at Waterloo. Saved from execution by Blücher, whose son he had attended. Continued to practise his profession under the Restoration and became member of the Academy of Medicine. In 1842, Inspector of Military Hospitals in Algeria, in spite of his great age. Died the same year at Lyons. Napoleon said of him at Saint Helena: 'He is the most virtuous man I have ever known.'

LAURISTON (Jacques Alexandre Bernard Law, Count, then Marquis of): born in 1768. Son of the celebrated banker Law. Campaigns of the Revolution. Brigadier-general and aide-de-camp to Bonaparte. Ambassador in Russia in 1811, after the Duke of Vicenza. Left St Petersburg on July 30, 1812. Returned to France. Then joined Napoleon outside Smolensk. Prisoner at the Battle of the Nations (Leipzig) during the German campaign. Peer of France, Minister and Marshal of France under the Restoration. Died in 1828, in the dressing-room of a dancer at the Opéra.

LELORGNE (Elisée-Louis-Françis, Baron d'Ideville): born in 1780. *Auditeur* to the Council of State. Attached to the Office of External Relations. On July 31, 1812, appointed the Emperor's personal interpreter. Had stayed previously in Moscow, which he knew very well. Died in 1852.

LESSEPS (Jean-Baptiste-Barthélemy, Baron de): born in 1766. His father was Consul-General at St Petersburg. He himself was appointed Vice-Consul at Kronstadt at the age of twenty-one. Previously he had taken part in the voyage round the world of La Pérouse (1784–87) and was received by Louis XVI on that occasion. He succeeded his father as Consul-General in the Russian capital, in 1792, and stayed there until 1812. Died in 1834.

MARET (Hugues-Bernard, Duke of Bassano): born in 1763. Lawyer and politician, he was given missions in 1792 and 1793. Journalist in 1797, in 1799 he jointed Bonaparte, who showed boundless confidence in him, especially after 18th Brumaire. Secretary, then principal private secretary to the First Consul. All Napoleon's campaigns, without exception. Created Duke in 1809. Minister of Foreign Affairs in 1811. Remaining faithful to the Emperor, he was exiled by the Bourbons. Recalled by Louis-Philippe in 1831, he died in 1839.

MARIA FEDOROVNA, Dowager Empress, widow of Paul I, née Princess Sophia Dorothea Augusta Louisa of Würtemberg, in 1759. An unhappy wife, mother of a large family, she devoted herself to social work, developing the institutions set up by Catherine the Great and founding others. She was especially interested in abandoned children and the education of young ladies. Died in 1828.

MILORADOVICH (General Count Mikhail): born in 1770. Soldier at the age of ten. Took part in all the battles against the Turks, the Poles and the French in Italy. Austerlitz. Russian and German campaigns. Military governor of St Petersburg in 1820. Was the first and only victim of the *Decembrists* on December 14, 1825: he was killed by one of the conspirators, Kakhovski, in the Square of the Senate at St Petersburg, at the moment he had arrived on the scene as a truce-bearer.

MORTIER (Édouard-Adolphe-Casimir, Duke of Treviso): born in 1768. First campaigns at Quiévrain and Jemmapes. General of division in 1789. Commanded the artillery of the consular guard. Marshal of the Empire in 1811. Russian campaign. Appointed Governor of the province of Moscow in September 1812. Sided with the Bourbons, but returned to Napoleon during the Hundred Days. Returned to favour with Louis XVIII after Waterloo. Ambassador in Russia under Charles X. Minister of War and President of the Council under

Louis-Philippe. Died in 1835, victim of the attempt on his life by Fieschi.

SÉGUR (General Count Philippe-Paul de): born in 1780. Became a professional soldier in 1800. Bavarian campaign, under Moreau. Grand Master of Ceremonies in 1804. The Emperor gave him his confidence and the responsibility for diplomatic missions and the inspection of military works. After Austerlitz, attached to Joseph Bonaparte, made King of Naples. Battle of Gaete. Squadron leader. Taken prisoner at Jena. Freed after the Peace of Tilsit and sent to Spain in 1808. Brigadier-General and member of the Emperor's general staff. Russian and German campaigns. Faithful to Napoleon, he was put on half-pay by Louis XVIII in 1815, at the age of thirty-five. It was then he wrote his *Histoire de Napoléon et de la Grand Armée en 1812*, published in 1824. This work was attacked so virulently by General Gourgaud in *Napoléon et la Grande Armée en Russie, ou Examen critique de l'ouvrage de M. le comte Ph. de Ségur* (1825) that Ségur challenged Gourgaud to a duel and was wounded. Member of the French Academy in 1830 under Louis-Philippe. Died in 1875.

SURRUGUES (or Surugue, Abbé Adrien): born in 1752. Doctor of theology, former principal of the Royal College of Toulouse, then canon of the collegiate church of Pilten in the diocese of Vilna. Priest of the parish church of Saint-Louis-des-Français in Moscow. Died in that town, two months after the departure of the Grand Army, in December 1812.

WILSON (Sir Robert Thomas): born in 1777. Fought against Bonaparte in Egypt, against Napoleon during the campaigns of 1806–07. Attached to Russian Headquarters, as observer, in 1812. In 1815, participated in Paris in the plot which enabled Lavalette to escape. In 1818, fought in South America with Bolivar, with whom he quarrelled. Fought with the Spaniards against the French in 1823. Disgraced by his king, George IV, he was rehabilitated by William IV and appointed Governor of Gibraltar in 1824. Died in 1849.

ZAGRIASSKI (Nicholas Alexandrovich): born in 1763. Grand Cup-bearer and Chamberlain of Tsar Alexander I, remained in Moscow in September 1812 owing to negligence. Taken under the protection of the Duke of Vicenza, who lodged him in the mansion which he had requisitioned. He was discovered there by the Muscovite authorities on their return. Arrested on the spot, he was accused of having come to terms with the enemy and tried. Condemned to hard labour, he benefited by the amnesty of 1814. Certain Russian writings wrongly assert that Zagriasski had been made a French Duke and decorated with the Legion of Honour, on Caulaincourt's intervention! Died in 1821.

SELECTED BIBLIOGRAPHY

———◆———

(R) = *in Russian*

GENERAL WORKS ABOUT THE 1812 CAMPAIGN

C. Bertin: *La Campagne de 1812 d'après des Témoignages oculaires*, Paris, no date.

L. Beskrovny: *The Patriotic War of 1812*, Moscow, 1962 (R.).

F. de Chateaubriand: *Mémoires d'outre-tombe*, Paris, Garnier, 1947, Vol. III, Part III, Book II.

A. Chuquet: *Études d'Histoire* (4th and 5th series), Paris, no date. *La Guerre de Russie, 1812 (documents)*, Paris, 1912, 3 vols.

Clausewitz: *La Campagne de 1812 en Russie* (French trans.), Paris, 1900.

Denniée (Bon): *Itinéraire de l'empereur Napoléon pendant la Campagne de 1812*, Paris, 1842.

The Patriotic War and Russian Society, Moscow, 'Centenary Edition', 1912, 7 vols (R.).

L. Madelin: *Histoire du Consulat et de l'Empire : la Catastrophe de Russie*, Paris, Hachette, 1949, Vol. XII.

Méjan (Cte E. de): *Miscellanea Napoleonica*, Series II, Rome, 1896.

Mikhailovsky-Danilevsky (General A.): *Account of the Patriotic War of 1812*, St Petersburg, 1843 (R.).

A. Schuermans: *Itinéraire général de Napoléon Ier*, Paris, 1900.

E. Tarle: *The Russian Campaign, 1812*, Moscow, 1938 (R.), and Paris, Gallimard, 1950.

A. Thiers: *Histoire du Consulat et de l'Empire*, Paris, 1856, Vol. XIV.

B. R. F. van Vlijmen: *Vers la Bérézina*, Paris, 1908.

MOSCOW

(a) *The town*

History of Moscow, Academy of Science of the USSR, 1952, 6 vols.

N. Matveyev: *Moscow and Muscovite Life on the eve of the Invasion*, Moscow, no date (R.).

Pylayev: *Le Vieux Moscou*.

F. Tastevin: *History de la colonie française de Moscou*, Paris, 1908.

(b) *The fire*

A. de B.-Ch. (Beauchamp): *Histoire de la destruction de Moscou, en 1812*, *et des événements qui ont précédé, accompagné et suivi ce désastre* (trans. from German), Paris, 1822.

A. Gadaruel-Ladrague: *Relations du séjour des Français à Moscou et de l'Incendie de cette ville en 1812, par un habitant de Moscou*, Brussels, 1871.

Fusil (Mme Louise): *L'Incendie de Moscou et la Retraite de Napoléon*, Paris, 1817.

Souvenirs d'une actrice, Paris, 1841, 2 vols.

G. Lecointe de Laveau: *Moscou avant et aprés l'Incendie*, Paris, 1814.

Surrugues or Surugue (Abbé A.): *Lettres sur l'Incendie de Moscou, écrites de cette ville au R. P. Bouvet, de la Compagnie de Jésus, par l'abbé Surrugues, témoin oculaire et curé de l'église de Saint-Louis, à Moscou*, Paris, 1823, 2nd ed.

(All the French and Russian Memoirs of the period contain a more or less detailed account of the fire.)

MEMOIRS

Bausset (L.-F.-J. de): *Mémoires anecdotiques sur l'intérieur du Palais et de quelques événements de l'Empire, de 1805–1814*, Paris, 1827, Vol. II.

Bourgogne (Sergeant)*: Mémoires* (published from the original manuscript by Paul Cottin), 1st ed., 1896.

Buturlin (Colonel): *Histoire militaire de la Compagne de 1812*, Paris, 1824, 2 vols, 2nd *Russian* edition: St Petersburg, 1837.

Castellane (Mis de): *Journal*, Paris, Plon, 1895–97, Vol. I.

Caulaincourt (General de, Duke of Vicenza): *Mémoires*, Introd. and Notes by Jean Hanoteau, Paris, Plon, 1933, 3 vols.

Chambray (Mis de): *Histoire de l'Expédition de Russie*, Paris, 1823, Vol. II.

Coignet (Captain): *Cahiers*, published from the original manuscript by Loédan Larchay, Paris, 1883.

Ermolov (General A.): *Mémoirs (materials for the war of 1812)*, Moscow, 1863 (R.), Vol. I: *1801–1812*.

Fain (Bon): *Manuscrit de 1812*, Paris, 1827.

Fezensac (M. de): *Journal de la Campagne de Russie*, Tours, 1849; Paris, 1850.

Galitzin (Pce): *Souvenirs d'un officier russe pendant les campagnes de 1812, 1813, 1814*, St Petersburg, 1849.

Gervais (Captain): *A la conquête de l'Europe*, Paris, Calmann-Levy, 1939.

Gourgaud (General Gaspard): *Napoléon et la Grande Armée en Russie*, or *Examen critique de l'ouvrage de M. le comte Ph. de Ségur*, Paris, 1825.

Langeron (General L.-A.): *Mémoires*, Paris, ed. of 1902.

Larrey (Bon Dominique): *Mémoires de Chirurgie militaire et campagnes*, Paris, 1812–17, Vols I and II.

Laugier de Bellecœur (Cesare): *In Russia, nel 1812* (in Italian), no date.

Leher (M. J. A.): *Lettre d'un capitaine de cuirassiers sur la Campagne de Russie en 1812*, Paris, 1885.

Liprandi: *Neither Hunger nor Cold were the cause of the destruction of Napoleon's troops*, followed by: *Was it the Russians or the French who burnt Moscow?* St Petersburg, 1885 (R.).

Mameluk Ali (L.-E. Saint-Denis): *Souvenirs sur l'empereur Napoléon*, Paris, Payot, 1926.

Montesquiou (Cte. A. de): *Souvenirs sur la Révolution, l'Empire, la Restauration et le règne de Louis-Philippe*, Paris, ed. of 1961.

Ségur (Cte. Ph. de): *Histoire de Napoléon et de la Grande Armée pendant l'année 1812*, Paris, 1825, 3rd ed., 2 Vols.

D. N. Sverbeyev: *Memoirs* (1799–1826), Moscow, 1899 (R.).

Würtemberg (Pce Eugene of): Memoirs (Russian trans., in the *Military Journal*, 1848, No. 1).

CORRESPONDENCE

Alexander I: *Correspondance de l'empereur Alexandre Ier avec sa sœur, la grande-duchesse Catherine Pavlovna*, published by the Grand Duke Nicolas Mikhailovich, St Petersburg, 1910 (R. and Fr.).

Napoléon I: *Correspondance de Napoléon Ier*, published by order of Emperor Napoléon III, Paris, 1868, Vol. XXIV.

Lettres inédites à Marie-Louise (1810–14), Introd. and Notes by L. Madelin, Paris, 1935.

The War of 1812, according to Letters by contemporaries, published by D. Dubrovin, St Petersburg, 1882 (R.).

Lettres interceptées par les Russes durant la Campagne de 1812, communicated by M. Gorianov, Introd. by Frédéric Masson, Paris, La Sabretache, 1913.

L. V. D. Puibusque: *Lettres sur la guerre de Russie en 1812*, Paris, 1816.

MONOGRAPHS

C. de Grunwald: *Alexandre Ier, le Tsar mystique*, Paris, 1955.

La Fuye (M. de): *Rostoptchine : Européen ou Slave?* Paris, Plon, 1937.

Lydia Rostopchin (Css): *Œuvres inédites de Rostoptchine*, Preface by J. de Bonnefon, Paris, Dentu, 1894.

Les Rostoptchine, Paris, 1905.

N. Schilder: *Alexandre Ier, sa vie et son règne*, St Petersburg, 1897–98, Vols II and III.

Ségur (Cte A. de): *La vie du comte Rostoptchine*, Paris, 1871.

Irène de Vries: *Catherine Pavlovna, grande-duchesse russe* (1788–1819).

Thesis for doctorate (in French) published at Amsterdam, by Meulen-hoff, 1941.

K. Waliszewski: *Le Règne d'Alexandre Ier*, Paris, 1923–25, 3 vols.

IMPORTANT STUDIES, PUBLISHED IN PERIODICALS

In Russian

Review *Russkaya Starina* (Russian Antiquities):

1870, Vol. I: *The Manifesto of Alexander I.*
1872, Vol. II: *Moscow and Rostopchin.*
1875, Vol. I: *Moscow in 1812.*
1885 (Sept.): *Varvara Bakunina's Memories of 1812.*
1891, Vol. LXXI: *Notes on Kutusov.*

In French

J. Duhem: *Le Ballon incendiaire*, Revue de l'Institut Napoléon, 1938 (2nd quarter).

La Fuye (M. de): *Rostoptchine et Koutuzov*, Revue des Questions historiques, March 1936.

M. Lhéritier: *La Campagne de 1812*, Revue des Études historiques, Jan. 1948.

Lyautey (Lieutenant Hubert): *De Wagram à Moscou.* Letters published by Pierre Lyautey in the *Revue des Deux Mondes*, of December 15, 1962, and January 1 and 15, 1963.

COLLECTIONS OF DOCUMENTS

Documents of the State Archives of the U.S.S.R. : Kutusov, Vol. I (R.).

Recueil de la Societé impériale d'Histoire russe, Vol. VI.

P. I. Chtchukin: *Papiers relatifs à la Guerre patriotique de 1812*, Moscow, 1909–12, 8 vols.

INDEX